TERRORISM
Modern Law and Enforcing Agencies

TERRORISM
Modern Law and Enforcing Agencies

Naveen Mishra

MD PUBLICATIONS PVT LTD
NEW DELHI
www.mdppl.com

Published by :

MD Publications Pvt Ltd
"MD House", 11, Darya Ganj,
New Delhi - 110 002
Phone : +91-11-41563325 (Customer Service)
+91-11-41562846 (Editorial)
E-mail (orders): order@mdppl.com
Website: www.mdppl.com

ISBN: 978-81-7533-192-1

Published and Printed by Mr. Pranav Gupta on behalf of **MD Publications Pvt Ltd** at Times Press, New Delhi.

Preface

The need to provide the police and the counter-terrorism (CT) agencies with adequate powers, if necessary, through special legislation, for dealing effectively with terrorism was accepted before September 11, 2001, even in countries where the rule of the law is supreme such as the UK, the USA and France.

In the spheres of law and order and internal security, modern technology has been a doubled-edged sword. It has strengthened the capability of the agencies for intelligence collection and for the prevention of breaches of law and order and threats to internal security. At the same time, it has also placed at the disposal of criminal and anti-national elements better means of evading detection of their activities.

Criminal and anti-national elements succeed in their activities because they keep pace with the latest technologies. The agencies too try to keep pace with them in evolving appropriate counter-measures, but to be able to use them effectively; they need adequate powers under the law, which were denied to them. They were thus constrained to operate with inadequate powers of pre-World War vintage evolved at a time when such technologies were not available to these elements. Fears of possible misuse of enhanced powers are legitimate, but the answer is not to deny them to the agencies, but to make their use subject to strict external controls.

The agencies also need a capability for detecting and

identifying criminal and anti-national elements, which might have escaped detection through HUMINT. This might call for random, but not indiscriminate monitoring of communications, which could result in the interception of messages having a bearing on ordinary crime, terrorism, narcotics smuggling, espionage etc. However, public opinion and law-makers in democratic societies opposed random checks due to fears of their misuse for partisan political purposes.

The pre-September 11 laws in most democratic societies normally allowed the collection of communications intelligence (COMINT) only on persons already identified as threats to national security on the basis of specific intelligence recorded in writing. In some countries, the required authorisation was given by officials designated by law and in others by the Attorney-General or by a court. After the terrorist strikes of September 11, politicians and law-makers in the US have realised that their reluctance to grant to the CT agencies additional special powers needed by them to keep pace with the international networking of the terrorists and their misuse of modern communication and other technologies for committing acts of terrorism might have contributed to the horrendous acts. This has resulted in the US a flood of Congressional resolutions and laws to empower the CT agencies in their fight against terrorism and a collated list of them came on November 21, 2001.

One of these Acts on granting additional tools to the CT agencies and other law-enforcers is appropriately called "The USA Patriot Act", admitting that it is an act of patriotism to arm the agencies with the powers they need in their war against international terrorism.

India has been a victim of the proxy war being waged by Pakistan against its security forces and people for decades. Sponsorship of Pakistani or other foreign terrorist groups for achieving Pakistan's strategic objectives against India is a core component of this proxy war. Already 60,000 innocent civilians, many of them Muslims, and over 3,000 members of the Security Forces have been killed in this proxy war since 1989 in Jammu & Kashmir alone. The British and US political leaderships, whose love for democracy and the rule of law is no less than that of our political leadership, have had no qualms in ensuring that their CT and other law-enforcing agencies have the legal wherewithal to deal effectively with the cancer of terrorism.

I am very grateful to Mr. Pranav Gupta, Director of MD Publications Pvt Ltd, New Delhi, for his cooperation and support for this book.

Naveen Mishra

CONTENTS

1

Introduction

Law and Agency against Terror

Two things have simultaneously occurred after the aftermath of Mumbai terror attacks, one the entire nation has stood united behind the Government of India and supported all its action against terror attack, two, the entire world has appreciated India's commitment to peace in the direst of provocative act of heinous terror attack designed, contemplated and executed at the behest of the terrorist outfits operating on Pakistan soil and very much in the knowledge of the Pakistan ISI. The UN Security Council resolution proscribed Jamaat-ud-Dawa, the outfit behind the Mumbai blasts and previously known as Lashkar-E-Taiba.

The UPA Government after long persistence by the opposition and the compelling aftermath of the Mumbai terror situation has now taken stringent and some meaningful steps towards national security by introducing a bill in parliament. This bill has been passed by the cabinet which cleared the National Investigating Agency (NIA) and amendments in UAPA. The bill was passed by parliament with a thumping majority on 17/11/2008.

We have been watching that Democracy, Sovereignty, Integrity, Security and Secularism, the main pillars of modern India are under consistent attack from across the border since the last 30 years. We have tried to avoid a direct confrontation with Pakistan to save people of both countries from mass destruction and complete elimination in the face of a nuclear catastrophe. But Pakistan is continuously exploiting this situation and sending trained terrorist to create disturbance and mayhem in our country to destabilize us. We have been trying to make Pakistan understand the futility of terrorism because of its being counterproductive and destructive for the very country which generates it. It can achieve nothing except destruction.

Pakistan even after feeling the pinch of its folly does not hesitate to nourish terrorists on its soil. So we have to deal with Pakistan very cautiously and in the meanwhile raise the level of our defenses against any eventual terrorist attack. One big constraint in dealing with terrorism has been often pointed out regarding our laws and trial system being too loose to let any hard core terrorist walk free from the trial court for want of hard material evidence or sufficient material proof of being involved in the act. We do not have stringent laws and law enforcing agencies supported by a fast and fully equipped modern day investigating mechanism or a national agency which can act across the states and bring in its ambit and mandate of the authority to probe all cases that the defense of the nation internally as well as externally needs at present.

To compensate on this short fall the cabinet on Monday cleared NIA and amendment to UAPA and saw the provisions of admissibility of evidence being rejected along with putting onus of proof on the accused. Home Minister P. Chidambaram was keen to include the admissibility of confessions but this ran into political opposition from Ministers like Lalu Prasad and Ram Vilas Paswan. The option for a special law was also ruled out. A.R Antulay insisted that same law be applicable to communal riots also.

Still, minus admissibility of confession (which was there in the original draft of the new terror law and was dropped on opposition of the said three Ministers) many other aspects like use of wire tapes as evidence and stringent bail conditions are now set to be part of the Unlawful Activity (Prevention) Act.

Detention without bail up to 180 days instead of 90 days, police custody of accused up to 30 days instead of 15 days and imprisonment of those involved in terror acts are some of the provisions in the UAPA which were part of POTA also. The bill however excludes one of the most controversial provisions of POTA treating confession before police as evidence.

The bill makes using explosives, firearms, lethal weapons, and poisonous chemicals, biological or radiological weapons with intention of aiding and abetting or committing act of terror cognizable offence punishable with a term of 10 years or more. Any one raising funds in India or abroad, directly or indirectly to fund terrorist acts shall be punishable with at least for five years and may be extended up to life term. Similar punishments for running terror training camps are also there.

NIA which would be headed by a Director General rank at par with DGPS of states would deal with offences of terrorism, counterfeit currency, violation of SAARC conventions like human trafficking narcotics and organized crime, plane high-jacking and violation of atomic energy act and weapons of mass destruction act among others.

All said and done the most important factor which was missing in the entire exercise of parliament passing this law is that politicians did not refrain from indulging in cheap politicking of the serious national issue of India's security and integrity. They still seemed to be unfazed by the turn of events which should have brought upon them some degree of responsibility in containing their speech on such issue of concern as threat from terrorism and avoid blame game.

Human Rights and Accountability of Law Enforcing Agencies

The main reason why torture continued to be practised on such a wide scale through out India was that the police felt themselves to be immune - they were fully aware that they will not be held accountable, even if they kill the victim and even if the truth is revealed. It is a surgical tool for the policemen, para-military forces and even for other law enforcing agencies against the accused or the assailants. The incumbent has to undergo the physical and mental wrath beyond one's endurance.

Now with the enforcement of human rights hanging on the heads of the police and para - military forces like a Democles sword and even judiciary monitoring on its norms for compliance has changed the things for the better. Torture as such for an accused or assailant is now within limits of humanitarian sensibilities rather than an arbitrary assault in guise of punitive repulsions. This can be seen in the light of directives given by the Supreme Court in D.K. Bas V. St. of W.B.

Torture involves not only physical suffering but also mental agony It is naked violation of human dignity and destructive of human personality. Interrogation though essential must be on scientific principles. Third degree methods are totally impermissible. Balanced approach is needed so that criminals do not go scot free. Custodial death is one of the worst crimes in civilised society. State terrorism is no answer to terrorism. Transparency of action and accountability are two safeguards against abuse of police power.

The court further opined that the expression life or personal liberty in Article 21 cannot be denied to convict, under trials, detenus and other prisoners in custody except according to the procedure established by law, by placing such reasonable restrictions as are permitted by law. It cannot be said that a citizen "sheds off" his fundamental right to life the moment a policemen arrests him.

Nor can it be said that the right of life of a citizen can be put in "abeyance" on his arrest. Any form of torture or cruel, inhuman or degrading treatment would fall within the inhibition of Article 21, whether it occurs during investigation, interrogation or otherwise.

In numerous cases our Courts have dealt with the question of maltreatment of under trials, convicted prisoners and victims of police torture. All cases of police torture are decided on the" touch stone of right to life and personal liberty. In Neelabat Bahera V. State of Orissa the Court pointed out how torture is inflicted by the police on arrested person. The Court observed that: "the police have arrested a person without warrant in connection with the investigation of an offence, without recording the arrest, and the arrested person has been subjected to torture to extract information from him for the purpose of further investigation or for recovery of case property or for extracting confession, etc. The torture and injury caused on the body of the arrestee has sometimes resulted into his death. Death in custody is not generally shown in the records of the lock-up and every effort is made by the police to dispose off the body or to make out a case that the arrested person died after he was released from custody.

In this case the Court held the authorities accountable for the death in the custody and it also observed that it is the duty of care on the part of the state which is to be observed by it strictly without any exceptions.

In State of M.P. V. Shyamsunder Trivedi is an apt case illustrative of observations made above. In this case Ñathu Banjara was tortured in police station, and as a result he died. The police contended that he was released from custody and he died outside, which was proved to be false. In this case the Supreme Court has given a laudable observation that : " The courts are also required to have a change in their outlook and attitude, particularly in cases involving custodial crime and they should exhibit more sensitivity and adopt a realistic rather than a narrow technical approach while dealing with the cases of custodial crime, so that as far as possible within their powers, the guilty should not escape so that the victim of crime has the satisfaction that ultimately the Majesty of Law has prevailed." In this case respondents were convicted for torture and death of the concerned persons and were asked to pay a fine ranging from Rs. 20,000/- to 50,000/- along with imprisonment. The fine was directed to be paid to the heirs of Nathu Banjara by way of compensation.

In yet another case of Joginder Kumar V. State the Supreme Court emphasized about arrest as a means of torture. The Court specifically observed: ".... no arrest should be made without a reasonable satisfaction reached after some investigation about the genuineness and' bonafides of a complaint and a reasonable belief both as to the person's complicity and even so as to the need to effect arrest. Denying a person his liberty is a serious matter.

Thus it can be seen from all the above cases that our Supreme Court has issued directions to be followed in all cases of arrest or detention till legal provisions are made in that behalf by the State. Police and other law enforcing agencies are under a legal duty and has legitimate right to arrest a criminal and to interrogate him during the investigation of an offence but it must be remembered that the law does not permit use of the third degree methods or torture of accused in custody during interrogation or investigation with a view to solve the crime. The cure cannot be worst than the disease itself.

A Stigma

The allegation of death of two ultras in custody of the army in Kashmir valley and death of five AASV activists in army custody in Tinsukia District, Assam added a new dimension to the galling problem. The legacy of the police regrettably seems to have contaminated the army. Even the Scotland Yard and the police in the U.K. with all their sophisticated scientific aids in detecting crime have failed to overcome such a stigma. Informal interaction with a few officers of the Scotland Yard following the death of a person in the custody of the London police in 1993 disclosed that such deaths and the use of severe and protracted interrogation or the third degree are not remote in U.K. or in the continent.

Dispassionate analysis reveals that policemen, who wield considerable power and authority, tend to misuse their power. Anxiety to detect the crime and expose the offenders forces them to follow the short- cut i.e. the third degree method. The investigating officers are under constant pressure by the higher authority and the public who expect them to solve a case promptly. The police forces have been subjected to the media's reckless criticism and unfounded accusation and calumny have been heaped on the force for unsuccessful investigation. Inadequacy of scientific methods, recalcitrant witness, lenient judiciary and the distrustful public provoke the investigating officers to resort to rough and ready method. Overzealousness of callous officers to unfold the mystery goads them to indulge in boorish methods and abrasive tactics. In short this tendency to show spectacular result often invites criticism.

Ironically the attitude of the people goads an investigating officer to short-circuit the established norms of investigation and code of conduct of a policeman. The victims, their friends or relatives want quick and favourable result. In fact, any delay in producing quick results shakes their patience. They feel that the police are lukewarm in tackling the culprit. The police, who exercise judicious restraint in tackling the suspects or the offenders and respects their individual liberties, is thus accused of dragging its fee. The public pressurize the police to browbeat the suspect, and see nothing wrong in using force against the suspect which would lead to the recovery of incriminating materials and expose the culprits. Numerous complaints have also been made that the police is lenient and they allow the accused to go scot free.

There are numerous instances which have taken place in Nagpur and where several important politicians advise the police officers to use third degree methods to solve Gory murder cases. An educationist held in high esteem, suggested that the police beat the truth out of a servant, who was suspected of stealing his purse. In another case, a serving judicial officer was suspected of murdering his wife and alleging that she had committed suicide. He had reportedly pressed her parents for dowry. Tempers ran high, and the local women's forum demanded the immediate arrest of the suspect. However, the arrest was delayed, as efforts were being made to collect evidence to incriminate the suspect. At that juncture, several enlightened townsmen secretly advised the police officers to use force for securing a confession.

A deaf and dumb girl was raped by two constables. The culprits were arrested and placed under suspension. People's emotion in the area was highly surcharged and the government felt embarrassed. The Minister in charge lost his cool. He called the "police officer and in the presence of a few politicians, advised him to break the legs of the 'rogues'. Police officer simply acknowledged his advice and left it at that. Indeed, unrealistic public expectation is a grave provocation for the policemen to resort to unethical use of physical force in an investigation and unmask the culprits.

Custodial Deaths

In India, as per official statistics, 69 incidents of custodial deaths were reported in 1997. In 1996, 59 persons died in police custody. In 1998, this number shot up to 69 cases and in 1999, 68 cases were reported. Incidentally, in 1997 Maharashtra topped the list recording 26 cases, followed by Madhya Pradesh, where 10 cases were reported. In 1997, 1998 and 1999 Maharashtra maintained its dubious lead, recording 26, 20 and 30 cases respectively. In 1997, 12 cases were reported in Andhra Pradesh and 8 from West Bengal. No case was reported from Haryana, Himachal Pradesh and Tripura. Only two to three cases were reported in Delhi each year from 1997. In 1998, Karnataka and Tamil Nadu reported one case each. Kerala repotted no incident. In 1999 till August, Kerala, Haryana and Madhya Pradesh were free from any such incident. Bihar in earliest years registered highest custodial deaths.

Now the incumbency has fallen on Maharashtra. The police investigate 80.0 lakh cases annually under IPC and other Acts. Nearly 400 lakh persons are taken into custody. Hence, it may be argued that in spite of such a large number of arrests the number of deaths in custody is relatively on the low side. Many deaths in custody also include bonafide natural deaths or suicides. Thirdly, there are significant checks to prevent custodial deaths and to penalise the erring policeman who prefer the third degree to straight forward investigation. Fourthly, training curriculum in police has been purposefully galvanised to discard archaic ideas in controlling crime and neutralising the criminals. The *darogas* have been replaced by the progressive policemen whose attainments and educational background are quite high. Broadly speaking, all conscious efforts are afoot to banish the brutal methods of dealing with a suspects and the accused.

Article 5 of the Universal Declaration of Human Rights (UDHE) (1948) States; "No one shall be subjected to torture or to cruel, inhuman or degrading treatment or punishment." In pursuance of this, on December 10th 1984 the UN adopted and opened for signature, ratification and accession, the Convention Against Torture and Other Cruel, Inhuman or Degrading Treatment or Punishment, which came into Force, from June 26, 1987. Article 2 of the Convention prescribes: "Each State Party shall take effective legislative, administrative, judicial or other measures to prevent acts of torture in any territory under its jurisdiction." Another significant step was taken in the U.N. World Congress on Human Rights (Vienna, 1993) where special attention was drawn to freedom from torture. In spite of the UDHR and the Convention provisions, torture, especially custodial torture, has not declined; in fact, incidents of custodial torture have been on the increase worldwide. Although India signed the Convention in 1997 it has yet to ratify it.

One need hardly emphasize the point that in the category of the extreme form of all organised violence the custodial violence is included and it is a torture, and that it is one of the most cruel and obnoxious forms of human rights violation. The civil society has a special and inescapable responsibility to not only protect tortured victims but also to create a climate of freedom from torture; and without this freedom the foundation to democracy will always remain weak. The civil society, specially the members of the medical profession, has also the responsibility of treating, counselling, and rehabilitating tortured victims.

We have inherited a culture of violence and intolerance. This finds reflection in the behaviour of our law-enforcing agencies, specially their behaviour with, and treatment of the deprived and depressed section of our population. Let us not forget that for centuries we have not recognised the depressed section of our people even as persons, not to speak of treating them with dignity and respect. Let us not, therefore, romanticize our past. Our first task is to acknowledge the fact that there are horrendous comers which exists in our society; once we accept this fact we will be able to close the doors on that ugly past. We must revive that past which is characterised by humanism, tolerance, and non- violence. Then only we can create new men and new women and a new society, a kind of, society of Buddha's ideal. Buddha's concept of non-violence must not be summarily dismissed as utopia it is eminently relevant today, and can be implemented provided we shed a bit of our unnecessary arrogance. Gandhi tried but failed. But this concept which is our heritage remains relevant even today.

It is in the above context that this writer presents an account of torture in custody specially the kind of torture inflicted on people by Special Task Force (STF) of Karnataka and Tamil Nadu. A brief summary that follows is based on a fact-finding report conducted by a number of NGO's including the PUCL unit of Karnataka. The governments of Karnataka and Tamil Nadu set up STF in 1992 to nab the forest brigand and sandalwood smuggler Veerappan. They have not yet succeeded in catching him. In the process they have, however, inflicted indescribable torture on a large number of people. On mere suspicion that these people are in league with Veerappan or would not disclose his whereabouts.

The S.T.K detains people illegally for months, and then arrests them (in the past most of them were arrested under IAUA). The ostensible charge against them is then added. These tribal people are kept in torture camps for months before they are sent to Mysore Jail. It is sad to note that the Bar Association of Mysore had once decided that no lawyer from outside Karnataka be allowed to represent détenues in courts! And, mind you, they are "Officers" of the court! The fact-finding team, members of which are distinguished people from Karnataka and Tamil Nadu, met victims who had been released on bail and video-recorded their versions. They have given an account of the horrendous tortures inflicted on them. I give below a few by way of illustration.

A woman in the STF's custody gave birth to a child fathered through rape by the STF personnel. When the woman was having labor pain and was in the process of giving birth to the child, the STF men rejoiced at her discomfiture and added to her pain-they squeezed her breast. And, we say we Indians worship women as goddesses! Large number of these tribal women were raped by the STF personnel and made pregnant.

There is one torture camp which is known as "workshop", a place of no return for the victims. They are made to put on clothes like those of the Veerappan gang and shot dead. Electric shock treatment is very common. Men are forced to place the clips with the electric wires on the genitals and nipples of breasts of women, while women are made to do the same on the male organ. Horse shoe method (beating the soles of feet until the *lathi* breaks); pulling apart the legs; torture with irritants such as chilly powder salt, etc. applied on delicate parts of the body and on open wounds are routine methods of torture. Men and women are compelled to undress and stand naked facing each other for hours; if anyone tries to cover herself/himself with their hands they are kicked and beaten. The STF personnel force children to have sexual intercourse in their presence.

Reference can also be to one case study - Manjula's cry of agony. Manjula, a young wife, and her husband, Abhay, were detained by the STF personnel. There were tortured, and then handed over to the Superintendent of Police (SP). The SP raped Manjula in her husband's presence and they are then released. Manjula's cry of agony does not end there. Abhay, her husband tells his parents about rape. Manjula is thrown out of the house. Can there be shriller cry of agony than Manjula's? Let us be honest with ourselves. We are what the great humanist and rationalist, Ishwar Chandra Vidyasagar, exclaimed long ago, in sheer disgust, in the context of widow-remarriage: "Oh, unfortunate women, what sin have you committed that you should have been born in this blessed country where men are so insensitive."

Custodial violation is now considered to be the vital armory for the policemen and even for the military personnel to outstrip and weaken the physical resistance and mental barrier of the detenu. Such atrocities by the enforcement authorities have been ubiquitous in police and military fraternity. Recorded evidences are being manipulated or turned in disguise to prefect the rights of enforcement authorities caused for custodial violation against the convict or accused. Militants, insurgents, mafias, drug traffickers and even arms dealers whose clandestine nefarious operations are under covers and their collusion with enforcement authorities enables them to go scot free and devoid of torture or custodial infringement. Unlikely the reasons are! The police, para- military forces and several other government authorities like Directions of Revenue Intelligence, Directorate of Enforcement, Coastal Guard, and Central Reserve Police Force (CRPF). Border Security Force (BSF), the Central Industrial Security Force (CISF), the State Armed Police, Intelligence Agencies like the Intelligence Bureau, R.A.W., Central Bureau of Investigation (CBI), CID, Traffic Police, and even the Military, are certainly a part of a resourceful recourse to help these mercenary's or covens in exchange of heavy pelf. Inconsequence, some of the oysters gets entangled as a victim of custodial violations at the hands of these law enforcing authorities.

This aspect needs a serious and thought provoking intelligence review and reprimand to do away with such criminal practices by the enforcing authorities in collusion with the white collar criminals in the form of Mafia don and mercenaries. It was during the epic days of Ramayana and Mahabharata, the Greek fables of physical torture, Nazi's torture camps, and the anecdotes of maltreatment meted out by Roman Army, horrifying tales of Hitler-as inimical sentinel of extinctions, CABAL'S brutal gender violations under reign of King Charles, Moghul reign of terror. British onslaught over the Indians during pre-independent period and many other instances of horrendous events of torture and physical brutalities are indelible in the records of tortures. Violation of personal freedoms, mainly subjugated due to physical and mental suppressions have prevailed upon in alarming proportions since time immemorial. The modern mentors of enforcement authorities still act as a compare to bench mark these traditional and conventional practices of torture, mental strife, physical conspiracy and other blatant resisting modes to cut and nip to bud the incumbents who are deliberate victims of such atrocities and violations at the hands of law enforcing personnel.

2

Federal Bureau of Investigation and SLATT

The Federal Bureau of Investigation (FBI) is the primary law enforcement agency in the United States Department of Justice. The formation of the FBI dates back to the late 19th century when special investigators in the Justice Department were assigned to enforce federal criminal statutes. In 1907, President Theodore Roosevelt requested U.S. Congress to create a new law enforcement agency in the Justice Department. When Congress opposed, Roosevelt in 1908 created the Bureau of Investigation by executive order (the word Federal was added in 1935). Initially, the Bureau's jurisdiction included only a limited number of federal offenses that related to interstate commerce. Yet, the Bureau would rapidly rise to become the most important federal law enforcement organization in the United States, especially as the Bureau was assigned to enforce new federal criminal statutes, such as the 1912 Mann Act, prohibiting the interstate transportation of women for prostitution or other immoral purposes, and the National Motor Vehicle Theft Act of 1919.

By the early 1920s, the Bureau was still riddled with scandal and incompetence due to a lack of professionalism. In order to turn the Bureau into a more accountable and professional organization, J. Edgar Hoover was in 1924 appointed as the Bureau's new Director, a position he would hold until his death in 1972. During his nearly five decades as FBI Director, Hoover was one of the most powerful public officials in the United States. Under his direction, the FBI became a modern law enforcement agency that acquired world fame. However, it was also rumored that politicians and other leaders feared Hoover because of the information that the FBI collected about them. Not until several years after Hoover's death, it was uncovered that the FBI under Hoover's direction had collected vast amounts of personal information about political leaders and community activists, among them Dr. Martin Luther King, Jr., whom Hoover accused of having ties with the Communist Party.

The gangster era of the 1930s provided an important impetus for the Bureau's public image as a top law enforcement organization. The Bureau's involvement in some heavily publicized criminal cases captured the public's imagination and garnered political support as well. The Bureau also became increasingly responsible for cross-border and international crimes, such as violations of immigration laws and the prostitution trade. In order to successfully accomplish its broadened functions, the FBI acquired additional personnel, an ever-growing budget, and advanced technological means, such as the Uniform Crime Reports, the Scientific Crime Detection Laboratory, and an elaborate fingerprint system.

The events surrounding World War II were a critical moment in the development of the FBI. In 1934, President Roosevelt had given a secret order for the Bureau to investigate the American Nazi movement, and shortly after the outbreak of war in Europe in 1939, the FBI was formally charged to investigate violations of neutrality laws as well as espionage, sabotage, and subversive activities. During the Second World War, the FBI would drastically expand its powers, as the Bureau's budget and personnel increased more than fivefold.

After World War II, the FBI further solidified its position. The FBI became responsible for the enforcement of hundreds of federal criminal statutes, pertaining to such issues as gambling, racketeering, and civil rights violations. The Bureau was also very actively involved in government actions against the Communist threat in the United States during the 1950s and the violent excesses of the anti-Vietnam War movement in the 1960s and 1970s. With its ever-broadening powers, FBI activities would occasionally also touch on legitimate forms of dissent, but the abuses of the FBI would not be exposed until several years after Hoover's death. From then on and until today, the FBI's activities in matters of domestic security and counterintelligence are often debated in terms of their potential to harm Constitutional rights.

The FBI is traditionally also heavily involved in international police work. In 1938, the FBI became the official U.S. representative in the International Criminal Police Commission, the organization today known as Interpol. In the late 1950s, the FBI left Interpol and from then on pursued a more independent international course. The Bureau became responsible for the enforcement of federal violations with international dimensions, such as extradition, terrorism, and drug trafficking. The FBI also maintains an extensive system of agents abroad, the so-called legal attachés, and oversees training programs of foreign police.

Besides its usual federal duties, the FBI was from the late 1980s onwards turning to the rising crime problems in the former Communist countries in Eastern Europe, when suddenly new domestic issues emerged. In 1992, the FBI was involved in a stand-off with a criminal suspect in Ruby Ridge, Idaho, that left a woman, child, and law enforcement agent dead. Less than a year later, the FBI could not prevent the deaths of some 80 members of the Branch Davidians, a religious sect in Waco, Texas, whose compound burned down after a 51-day standoff. These events led to congressional inquiries about the FBI's ability to respond to emergencies. During the 1990s, the FBI was further exposed to public criticisms because of mistakes that had been made in investigations involving the Bureau's crime laboratory.

Although terrorism had gradually developed as a priority in the FBI throughout the 1990s, the tragic events of September 11, 2001 have launched in a new phase in the Bureau's development. In the months following 9/11, the FBI assigned some 4,000 of its 11,500 special agents to counter-terrorist activities, and since June 2002, the FBI has been reformed as the leading counter-terrorism agency in the United States. Dating back to a system developed in the 1980s, the FBI oversees various Joint Terrorism Task Forces across the United States in collaboration with agents from local and state agencies.

Independent from the Department of Homeland Security, the FBI has also been given increased intelligence and investigative powers by the USA PATRIOT Act. The FBI budget request for fiscal year 2006 amounts to $5.7 billion to support 31,475 positions, of which 12,140 are special agents and 2,745 are intelligence analysts. Thus, as was the case during other momentous social disturbances, such as World War II and the Cold War, the events of 9/11 have brought about important changes for the FBI, the impact of which may last for a considerable time to come.

State and Local Anti-Terrorism Training Programme

American law enforcement and intelligence agencies face threats of unprecedented terrorism and criminal extremism that present unique challenges to conventional investigative strategies and intelligence operations. Tragically, these challenges were made clear by the terrorist attacks of September 11, 2001. To help our nation's law enforcement and intelligence agencies confront these threats, the State and Local Anti-Terrorism Training (SLATT) Program provides training in detecting, investigating, and prosecuting extremist criminal activity, including activity that is inspired by international events. This focus distinguishes SLATT training from first responder and related weapons of mass destruction/nuclear, biological, and chemical response training provided to emergency service personnel. In response to the September 11 attacks, SLATT expanded its training and research on foreign-inspired terrorism to include specific organizations believed to be involved in the attacks. SLATT is a joint effort of the Institute for Intergovernmental Research (IIR) and the Federal Bureau of Investigation (FBI). It is funded by the Bureau of Justice Assistance (BJA) of the U.S. Department of Justice.

About BJA

The Bureau of Justice Assistance was established in 1984 as a component of the Office of Justice Programs, U.S. Department of Justice. BJA provides leadership and resources to state, local, and tribal governments and communities to reduce crime, violence, and drug abuse and to strengthen the nation's criminal justice system. BJA provides this assistance through formula and discretionary grants, training and technical assistance, publications, and the BJA Website.

SLATT Training

SLATT specialized courses are designed for state and local law enforcement executives, command personnel, intelligence officers, investigators, training directors, and prosecutors. Courses cover the gamut from street-level officer safety to executive policymaking issues. SLATT's service includes the coordination of training logistics, the selection and development of instructors, the preparation of training and resource materials, the selection of training sites, liaison with potential trainees and cosponsors, and close coordination with the FBI's National Security Division Training Unit. Since its inception, SLATT has trained more than 15,600 law enforcement personnel.

SLATT Training Topics Terrorism

Overview and Identification of Terrorist and Extremist Crimes—Offers a global perspective of terrorism and criminal extremism by addressing international, domestic, and special-interest groups, organizations, and ideologies. Law Enforcement and Its Role in National Defense—Identifies the roles and responsibilities of state and local law enforcement in the protection of American communities against attacks by foreign-inspired terrorist groups and organizations. Antigovernment Extremism: Origins, Ideology, and Tactics—Contrasts the realities of the historical militia with the modern-day militia philosophy. Political Violence—provides a briefing on the ideologies, tactics, and goals of foreign-inspired terrorist and extremist groups and organizations. Explores the theological divisions of mainstream and fundamentalist Islam and how extremist groups misrepresent the teachings of Islam. Legal Issues in Extremist Investigations— Explains the federal legal issues associated with the investigation of domestic terrorism.

Domestic Terrorism Investigations—explores the process, complexity, and differences in conducting a domestic terrorism investigation versus a typical criminal investigation. Who Are They, How Are They Different, and How to Assess Your Community—delineates the characteristics of criminal extremists and how those characteristics differ from typical criminal behavior. Behavioral Considerations and Threat Assessment for Group-Related Targeted Violence—Identifies the behavioral characteristics of domestic terrorist and criminal extremist personalities. The Intelligence Process and Preparation of Threat Assessments—Demonstrates the need to effectively gather and analyze intelligence information to produce a specific threat assessment. Investigative Techniques—describes the surveillance process and provides recommendations for assessing when to conduct a surveillance operation, the benefits of employing surveillance, and the drawbacks of surveillance operations.

Explains the use and management of informants and Interview Techniques with Extremists—introduces the unique challenges of conducting investigative interviews with criminal extremists. Explosives and Explosive Devices—Explores the dangers of investigating individuals who use explosives as part of their crimes, and how to recognize explosive devices. The Internet: An Investigative Tool—Provides insight into how terrorists and criminal extremists use the Internet for communication and offers instruction on using the Internet to find information. The Future: What to Expect—Addresses general ideas concerning the future of terrorist and criminal extremist activity, and summarizes a number of national assessments and possible future trends and scenarios.

SLATT Research SLATT

Program staff collects information on terrorist acts committed on U.S. soil; international terrorist groups and ideologies; U.S. extremist groups and criminal activities; pre-incident awareness, preparation, prevention, and interdiction; and other related areas. SLATT provides a public source research database and research products such as publications, videos, and multimedia applications that are disseminated "Providing SLATT's unique training to state and local law enforcement personnel is one of the best investments we can make to improve community security." —Richard R. Nedelkoff, Director, Bureau of Justice Assistance through training classes, the Regional

Information Sharing Systems secure intranet, and other means as appropriate.

Issues and Curriculum Development

SLATT convenes focus groups to evaluate law enforcement and prosecution issues to ensure that training and related activities are timely, relevant, and responsive to the needs and requirements of the law enforcement community. The focus groups comprise select law enforcement and prosecution practitioners and other experts. They identify issues emerging from terrorist and extremist movements and review and refine SLATT's training curricula, products, and research agenda.

Technical Assistance

An important part of SLATT assistance is meeting the technical assistance needs of state and local law enforcement in terrorism detection, investigation, and prosecution. The SLATT Program has established a pool of anti-terrorism experts who deliver specialized training and research products in response to requests from law enforcement agencies and referrals from the FBI and BJA.

3

Meeting the Challenges of Terrorism

Indian Model

Terrorism is not a new phenomenon. It is known to have existed, in one form or the other, at several stages in the recorded history. It is only that in recent times it has turned into a critical issue of utmost importance; the issue of very survival of human civilization. In various fora at different points of time, the issues of terrorism, the need for civil societies world over to adopt counter-terrorism measures, the extent to which such measures can go or the extent of departure from ordinary laws – substantive or procedural, the effect they have on basic human rights have been discussed endlessly.

Much has been said as to what are the possible causes of this dark facet that refuses to go away. We need not dwell much on the issue as to what exactly is the roof cause of terrorism in our respective parts of the world since that concerns State policy and would rather be left to the domain of the Executive or Legislative wing of our respective Governments. As members of the legal fraternity the questions that beg to be addressed by us revolve around the conflict, consequential to counter-terrorism efforts, between human rights and the concerns for defence of the

State of which we are part. The conflict stems from the necessity felt for entrusting the law-enforcement agencies with extraordinary powers to meet what is genuinely perceived as an extraordinary situation. The irony is that the first and foremost impact of such measures is felt by law-abiding citizens on account of inroads they make into individual liberties.

Civilized people do not expect their governments to enact laws that turn into mere "scarecrow" for the "birds of prey" to use as their "perch", as Shakespeare would put it. In this scenario, the role and attitude of the judicial apparatus assumes great importance, in which context we have certain responsibilities. India is wedded to the concept of rule of law. State power is divided amongst the three chief organs, the Legislature, the Executive and the Judiciary. The role and responsibility of each has been properly defined and circumscribed, the Judiciary being given the prime place, and planted as the instrumentality of the Constitution to test the validity of acts of each organ through the concept of judicial review; the foremost reason for this scheme of things being the view that rule of law is the sole *raison d'etre* for the survival of human rights which India is determined to conserve and preserve.

Fortunately when founding fathers of the Constitution of India were deliberating upon the contours of our system of governance, available to them were several models of the rights-based regime including the principles enshrined in Magna Carta, the corner-stone of liberty and the principles against arbitrary and unjust rule; the UK Bill of Rights, 1689; US Bill of Rights, 1791; the Declaration of the Rights of Man and of the Citizen, adopted in 1789, by the National Constituent Assembly of France; Universal Declaration of Human Rights, 1948 etc. India borrowed wisdom from these various instruments, but charted its own course developing a full-fledged elaborate chapter on 'Fundamental Rights'.

The Constitution of India guarantees, to all persons, citizens and aliens alike, amongst others, equality before law; equal protection of the laws; guarantee against discrimination; freedom of speech & expression; freedom of peaceable assembly; freedom to form association; freedom of movement; freedom of fair procedure; protection of life & personal liberty; freedom against exploitation; freedom of conscience; freedom to profess practice & propagate religion and so on & so forth. The Constitution facilitates a State action to be invalided should it be found to be inconsistent with or imbued with the trait of abridging the fundamental rights. The Supreme Court of India is the guarantor and vested with the responsibility of securing enforcement of fundamental rights through wide-ranging powers.

Through the Constitution, India resolved to strive for good governance and with this object set out certain Directive Principles of State policy, the prime object of which was to secure the welfare of its people. They embody the concept of a welfare State.

India has throughout been conscious and alive to its obligations under the International multi-lateral treaty regime. These International Treaties and Conventions have established a very substantial jurisprudence on the subject of basic human rights for the preservation of which India stands committed, particularly in view of the declaration in the Constitution itself that the State "shall endeavour", amongst others, to "promote International peace and security" and "foster respect for International law and treaty obligations in the dealings of organized people with one another". Indian Parliament has converted a number of International Conventions on the subject of Human Rights into legislative measures. Indian Judiciary has been proactive and has scrupulously and over-zealously guarded the rights fundamental for human existence.

This has been done on the premise that the international instruments cast an obligation on the Indian States to see that the message is not drowned, that the core principle is never forgotten and as far as possible effect is given to the commitment made to the global community and for such purposes regard is had of the international norms for construing domestic laws, more so when there is a void in the latter and there is no inconsistency between the international law and the local law. The human rights regime that we follow in India is similar, if not almost identical, to the one that is in vogue in European Union in the form of European Convention on Human Rights ('ECHR'). After all, the concept of human rights is universal, resting on the principle that they are sacrosanct bundle of rights vested in human beings so that they can live a dignified life "not by chance or choice but by being human".

As put succinctly in the US Declaration of Independence, these spring forth from self-evident truths "that all men are created equal; that they are endowed by their Creator with certain inalienable rights; that among these are life, liberty, and the pursuit of happiness". India has had its own periods of tests, even after independence. These tests have been coming up in the form mainly of complaints of human rights abuses by State functionaries against under-privileged sections of the society or hydra of communalism, each such episode adding to the lurking dangers to the rule of law since it would involve abridgement of civil, cultural, economic, political or social rights of those at the receiving end. But, terrorism perhaps posed the biggest challenge. India has been grappling with the "brute" of terrorism that broke loose more than two decades ago.

Terrorism, now it is universally accepted, has cross-border fingerprints. India's answers to the bane were initially an endeavour to control through general law. But since the menace reached alarming levels, it escalated into the need for special measures in the shape of enactment called 'Terrorists and Disruptive Activities (Prevention) Act, 1985' (commonly known as 'TADA, 1985'). The enactment was justified by the Legislature inter alia in the wake of state of "fear of panic" sought to be created and the object of disruption of "communal peace and harmony" sought to be achieved by the perpetrators in certain parts of India.

TADA, 1985 created two new offences, namely, "terrorist act" and "disruptive activities". Noticeably, in the offence of "terrorist act" the offender would have to be imputed with "intent to overawe the government" or "to strike terror in the people" or "to alienate any section of the people" or "to adversely affect the harmony amongst different sections o the people". The "disruptive activities", in order to attract the penal clause, were required to be such as to be intended to disrupt "the sovereignty and territorial integrity of India" or to bring about, amongst others the "secession of any part of India from the Union".

TADA 1985 established a system of special courts ("Designated Courts") and placed restriction on the grant of bail unless the Court recorded the existence of "reasonable grounds for believing" that the accused was "not guilty". The police were given enhanced powers of detention of suspects; provision was made for protection of witnesses and at the same time it was provided that trials under the law shall be speedy by being accorded "precedence" over other cases.

TADA 1985 had been enacted with intended life span only of two years in the fond hope that the hazard would fade out. But it was not to be. The Legislature thus renewed the law in the form of 'Terrorist and Disruptive Activities (Prevention) Act, 1987' (commonly known as 'TADA 1987'). Since the activities of terrorist violence, in the meantime, had continued unabated and rather had spread its tentacles to other parts of the country, and with addition of new and disturbing dimensions in the form of

International involvement and use by terrorist groups ("inspired from abroad") of sophisticated weaponry and professional training, TADA 1987 sought to strengthen the mechanism that had been provided in TADA 1985. TADA 1987 was initially enacted for limited period. But its life was extended from time to time, finally in 1993 so as to make it valid till 1995. India, by then, had entered into an agreement with the UK for mutual assistance in the investigation of the proceeds and instruments of crime and terrorist funds and in order to "concretize the said agreement" for mutual assistance in investigation and prosecution of terrorists crimes and the "tracing, restraint and confiscation of the proceeds and instruments for crime" the existing anti-terrorism law was further amplified in 1993.

The main features of TADA 1987, thus amended from time to time, included certain other related offences being properly defined (e.g. harboring or concealing terrorists; for being a member of terrorist gang or terrorist organization; for holding of property derived as a result of terrorist acts etc.). TADA 1987 provided for a new offence of "possession" in "notified area" of unauthorized arms (mainly "prohibited arms and ammunition") or bombs etc. It also provided for enhanced penalty for certain specified offences with arms, ammunition etc., if committed "with intent to aid any terrorist or disruptionist".

TADA 1987 also relied upon the system of 'Designated Courts' specially constituted to deal with such crimes. It gave enhanced powers to the investigating police officers in the matter of seizure of property regarding which there was "reason to believe" to have been derived as a result of terrorist acts, besides provision for attachment and forfeiture of such property. It extended the possible period of detention of a suspect in police custody pending investigation. It made a significant departure from the general law by rendering admissible confession made before a police officer not below the rank of Superintendent of

Police. The legislature introduced a safeguard against abuse of powers given by TADA 1987 to the executive by creating a bar against registration of "First Information Report" (FIR), the starting point of criminal justice apparatus, except after "prior approval of the District Superintendent of Police".

TADA 1987 gave rise to protests by human rights groups questioning the validity of the law on various grounds, mainly that it encroached on certain fundamental rights of the persons arrested and it being an unnecessary departure from the general law arming the executive (police) with unbridled and oppressive powers, without sufficient accountability.

On the constitutionality of TADA 1987 being challenged, its provisions were subjected to judicial review by the Constitution Bench of Supreme Court of India. The Court found, in the case of Kartar Singh v. State of Punjab, the law to be generally valid passing the muster of the Constitution. The Court struck down as unconstitutional one of its provisions, that had provided for "identification of accused" on the basis of his "photograph", during proceedings *in absentia* upon he being declared an absconder.

Supreme Court of India, in Kartar Singh, proceeded to temper certain provisions of TADA 1987 so as to bring them within reasonable bounds or to introduce requisite safeguards against abuse. The offence of "abetment" of a terrorist act, under the law laid down, would require the ingredient of "intention or knowledge". The offence of "possession of specified arms and ammunition" was found to be harsh and, in order to save it from arbitrariness, the Court held that it shall be invocable only where possession was "connected with use thereof".

In the context of provision rendering confession before a police officer admissible, Supreme Court laid down certain guidelines including by insistence on "free atmosphere", use of "language" of the person examined and, most important, production of maker of the confession "without reasonable delay" before Chief Judicial Magistrate who would be expected to record the statement, if any, made by the confessor and who would also order his medical examination in case there was a complaint of torture. Supreme Court insisted, in the guidelines, that the investigation of offences under the special law would be handled by senior police officers (not below the rank of Deputy Superintendent of Police), who would be accountable for reasons of taking the accused in police custody or for delay in investigation, after arrest of the suspect, by being obliged to state the facts on affidavit.

The most significant contribution to the jurisprudence governing counter-terrorism measures in India came in the form of a direction from the Supreme Court, in the case of Kartar Singh, for constitution of Screening or Review Committees for periodical "scrutiny" of the cases registered and also of the prevailing situation in the areas notified as ones affected by terrorist activities.

TADA 1987 was found to be a valid legislative response to the menace of terrorism because the "defence of India" was under threat. The Court upheld the constitutional validity of the law but introduced certain changes in the way the law would be worked so as to ensure that the vice of arbitrary use of powers did not creep in. It would be interesting to note as to how the system of review evolved in the period that followed.

In compliance of aforesaid directions, Screening Committee or a Review Committee was constituted by the Governments in various States. A High Power Committee under the Chairmanship of the Chief Secretary of one particular unit of the Union of India (Union Territory of Delhi) reviewed the prosecutions made under TADA and the Government conveyed its approval to the Director of Prosecution for deletion of the charges under TADA in the specified criminal cases pending before the Designated Court. The Special Prosecutor filed applications in the Designated Court for withdrawal of charges under TADA in all those cases pending in the Designated Court, mainly referring to the recommendation of the High Power Committee. The Designated Court dismissed those applications taking the view those administrative decisions cannot interfere with the working of the judicial system. Apparently, the view taken was that a mere administrative decision taken on the basis of the recommendation of the Review Committee was not sufficient to permit withdrawal of a criminal prosecution pending in a Court of law. Appeals by special leave and writ petition were preferred to challenge the orders of the Designated Court *inter alia* for a direction to the Designated Court to permit withdrawal of all prosecutions recommended by the Review Committee.

Supreme Court of India in the said matter, reported as R. M. Tewari V. State (NCT Of Delhi), found that the Designated Court was right in taking the view that withdrawal from prosecution is not to be permitted mechanically by the Court on an application for that purpose made by the Public Prosecutor and that the latter also had not to act mechanically in the discharge of his statutory function in such regard on such a recommendation being made by the Review Committee; and further that it was the duty of the public prosecutor to satisfy himself that it was a fit case for withdrawal from prosecution before he sought the consent of the Court for that purpose.

It was, however, clarified that the review ordered in Kartar Singh was intended "to ensure that there was no misuse of the stringent provisions of TADA and any case in which resort to TADA was found to be unwarranted, the necessary remedial measures should be taken" and that the Designated Court was expected to give "due weight to the opinion formed by the Public Prosecutor on the basis of the recommendation of the High Power Committee", if it was "based on the material present" indicating that "resort to provisions of TADA is unwarranted". The Supreme Court took this view in several cases relating to application of TADA.

In spite of the close monitoring of the use of TADA 1987 by the Court, *inter alia* through review committees, complaints of its gross abuse continued being raised. The executive felt constrained to draw curtain on the law and thus withdrew TADA 1987 from operation.

The scourge of terrorism, however, would not end. It only went on to rise in a more and more sinister manner in course of time with such events coming to a head in the form of attack on Indian Parliament on 13th December 2001. The legislature recognized the fact that terrorist groups and organizations, having a close inter-linkage with organized crime and having acquired global dimensions, taking advantage of modern means of communication and technology and using high-tech facilities, were able to strike and create terror among people "at will" even while the "existing criminal justice system" was not designed to deal with such types of heinous crimes. The Prevention of Terrorism Act, 2002 (commonly called as 'POTA') was enacted to make provisions "for the prevention of" and "for dealing with" terrorist activities, in the face of multifarious challenges in the management of internal security of the country and an upsurge or intensification of "cross-border terrorist activities and insurgent groups".

POTA was a measure introduced by the State to adopt twin-legged strategy, one dealing with the terrorism as a crime, and the other for steps that could be termed as preventive in nature. Learning from past experience in the enforcement of special anti-terrorism legislation adopted earlier in the country, and conscious of the fact that the extra-ordinary nature of the powers and procedure provided by this new special law were prone to abuse for ulterior purposes by law enforcing agencies and pressure groups, the Legislature declared its intent to prevent such misuse by referring to the fact that "sufficient safeguards" were being engrafted in the law.

POTA would confer special powers of arrest or detention of suspected terrorists, of seizure and forfeiture of terrorist property, for prohibiting and penalizing terrorist funding, the interception of communication amongst suspects and for dealing with terrorist organizations by, *inter alia*, making their membership an offence. POFA contained revised form of definition of the offence of "terrorist act" requiring, as the first and foremost ingredient, the "intent to threaten the unity, integrity, security or sovereignty of India or to strike terror in the people".

While reintroducing the related offences of conspiracy, abetment, harboring etc., POTA also provided for the offence of "possession" in "notified areas" of unauthorized arms (mainly "prohibited arms and ammunition") or bombs etc and retained enhanced penalty for certain offences under Arms Act, Explosives Act etc., if committed "with intent to aid any terrorist". POTA also gave enhanced powers to investigating police officers in the matter of seizure & attachment of property regarding which there was "reason to believe" to be "proceeds of terrorism", giving the power to order "forfeiture". It permitted police custody for a period double than that permissible under the general law and would also moot setting up of Special Courts for trial of offences under the Act. The stringent bail provisions were reintroduced.

The law under POTA would also permit use of confession made before the police officer rather than a judicial authority. It is significant to note that the safeguards in such regard, which had been introduced by the Supreme Court through the judgment in Kartar Singh, now found adoption by the legislature as statutory requirements.

POTA also provided for measures to deal with organization declared by the executive to be "terrorist organization" making membership of, support to, or activities connected therewith penal offences. It also made elaborate provisions for interception of communication, authorisation for and control/use of intercepted communication.

Besides introduction of statutory safeguards for abuse of power relatable to confession before the police, POTA also provided for speedy trials, and introduced the concept of quasi judicial review of the State action vis-à-vis organizations declared to be terrorist organizations besides review of arrest or prosecution of a person for offences under POTA, thus again respecting the view of the judiciary for need for adequate safeguards against abuse of powers by the executive, as declared in Kartar Singh. It bears special mention here that the Central Government put the mechanism to use by constituting a Review Committee, under the chairmanship of a former Chief Justice of High Court, and thereby giving to it a High-power status, calling it upon not only to "entertain complaints or grievances" with regard to the "enforcement of" POTA and accordingly "give its findings" but also for making suggestions "for removing the shortcomings, if any, in (its) implementation" and measures "to ensure" that provisions of POTA were "invoked for combating terrorism only".

It may be added that POTA also came with a 'sunset clause' for expiry at the end of three years but came to be repealed ahead of its time with effect from 21st September 2004. The constitutionality of POTA was also challenged before the Supreme Court of India, but found without merit. The judgment on the point is known as People's Union for Civil Liberties V. UOI. The challenge was on the ground the basic human rights were being violated. The view of the Court in this regard is now well known, namely, that the "protection and promotion of human rights under the rule of law is essential in the prevention of terrorism", involving "court's responsibility" and that if human rights are violated in the process, it will be "self-defeating". It would also voice concern that "lack of hope for justice provides breeding grounds for terrorism" and, therefore, in the fight against terrorism "human rights" will have to be respected.

The Court upheld the constitutional validity of POTA in People's Union for Civil Liberties, but again proceeded to temper the law so as to obviate the vice of arbitrary use by giving certain directions. It insisted on the element of *mens rea* for the offence of 'abetment' and on the element of "knowledge of the terrorist act" for the offence of "possession of unauthorized arms". It further added the ingredient of "intent" in the offences relating to membership of, support to, or raising of funds for a terrorists organization.

India does not subscribe to the radical view in certain quarters that "torture" should be available in extreme situation of terrorist acts. I would agree that no civil society would concede such powers of torture (even limited one) unto the police forces. This would be in total derogation of basic human rights guaranteed not only by the municipal laws but also under international treaty obligations. It would be highly inadvisable for the simple reason that concessions of this nature once made will be difficult to be controlled once the purposes for which they are demanded cease to subsist. The view of the Supreme Court of Israel in the case of Public Committee against Torture in Israel & Ors V. The State of Israel, provide the model judicial response. When President Barak spoke of preservation of "Rule of Law" strengthening the "security", he probably implied that terror created by law might breed more terrorists. In the words of Ausonius "if you are terrors to many, then beware of many".

The views of the Supreme Court of Israel that preserving the rule of law and recognition of individual's liberty constitutes an important component in a democracy echo what was said by Supreme Court of India in the judgment rendered by the Supreme Court of India in the case of D.K. Basu V. State of West Bengal, wherein it was held that a suspect cannot be tortured even if there is a prospect of the crime going unpunished.

The out-rage felt by the public every time a terrorist crime is perpetrated, evoking a strong desire to seek revenge, on first blush, might sound genuine. But then, the urge has to be curbed lest government should become "a source of terror to all its citizens" and "creates a country where everyone lives in fear".

At the same time it has to be granted, for the sake of future of humanity, that the States have an obligation and, therefore, are legitimately concerned about their citizens and thus must do everything that needs to be done for general protection of the society and of the national security. This gives rise to a dilemma as to how the issues arising out of terrorism - political, legal, ethical, sociological or those concerning human rights - are to be handled so as to restore the general feeling of security all round without abandoning the very values which a democratic society is avowed to protect. Oscar Wilde was of the view that "the basis of optimism is sheer terror". The ethos followed by India takes its cue perhaps from the following words of Seneca: -

> "To be feared is to fear: no one has been able to strike terror into others and at the same time enjoy peace of mind."

India has tried to follow a path wherein "rule of Law" continues to be the fundamental benchmark and the basic rights are ensured even to those who are suspected of involvement in terrorist crimes. Such rights consistently insisted upon by Indian jurisprudence include right to life & liberty; right against torture or inhuman degrading treatment; right against outrages upon personal dignity;

right to due process & fair treatment before law; right against retrospect city of penal law; right to all judicial guarantees as are indispensable to civilized people; right to effective means of defence when charged with a crime; right against self-incrimination; right against double jeopardy; right of presumption of innocence until proved guilty according to law; right to be tried speedily in presence by an impartial & regularly constituted Court; right of legal aid & advice; right of freedom of speech besides right to freedom of thought, conscience & religion.

The scale of terrorist crimes directed against India and her citizens has been alarmingly high. The declared objects of terrorist groups brazenly pose a grave challenge to the security of the State. Since these terrorist acts tend to create a state of public emergency threatening the defence of India, no one would be able to fault India if it were to invoke the discretion for derogation from international treaty obligations to take tougher measures. Yet, India has refrained from doing so and its responses have been tempered by the principles of "necessity" and "proportionality" and "non-discriminatory", which were recently used in UK as guidelines by the House of Lords. Our response has throughout abided by the principle of "universal respect for and observance of human rights and fundamental freedoms", as commended by various UN resolutions.

The approach of judiciary in India to the issues that arise has consistently been that while it may be appropriate that the courts show respect for the opinion formed by the executive as to the existence, or extent of, challenge to the national security, whether one calls it "deference" or "margin of appreciation", the State action making inroad into the personal liberties or basic human rights of an individual must always be scrutinized by the judiciary on the basis of objective proof, relevant material in accordance with law and through a procedure which passes the muster of fairness and impartiality. Mere *ipse dixit* of the executive as to the complicity, or suspicion of complicity, in such crimes on the part of an individual cannot result in judiciary upholding the State action so as to smack of blind abdication of its responsibility to ensure that all organs of the State are governed by the principle of "rule of law".

It was with the above in view that the Supreme Court of India introduced additional checks and safeguards in the provisions of TADA 1987 in the form of guidelines in the matter of recording of confession by a police officer, reading the element of *mens rea* in certain offences the definition of which was found to be wanting and the insistence upon review by independent agencies.

It is a matter of satisfaction that the other organs of the State in India respected the judicial review in this regard and took the requisite follow up action which facilitated scrutiny of all such cases within reasonable time and relief to those who were found to have been wrongfully roped in. When the anti-terrorism legislation was resurrected in the form of POTA in 2002, the executive and the legislature abided by the judicial view once again by giving the guidelines, laid down earlier, a place in the statute itself. The concept of "review" has thus been successfully followed in India as a major check on abuse of power by the executive, thereby minimizing the complaints of wrongful detention.

Credit is due to the Indian legislature which was concerned about the possibility of abuse of powers to such an extent that, in POTA, it included a new offence providing for punishment to such police officers who were found to have engaged themselves in exercise of powers under the law corruptly or maliciously, also equipping the Special Court with the jurisdiction to award compensation to the person who had been corruptly or maliciously proceeded against. India, fortunately, has not felt the need to adopt such anti-terrorism measures as would permit indefinite detention of suspects without trial or without legal remedies. The provisions of Prevention of Terrorism Act, 2005 enacted by UK introducing the mechanism of "control orders" are an interesting development on account of its promised utility in preventive measures without compromising, beyond a point or unreasonably, the individual liberties. We would like to study the manner in which the system of "control orders" is used or worked.

4

Eco-Terrorism and International Environmental Security

Among the evidence to emerge after September 11 concerning international terrorist's intent to commit acts of Eco-Terrorism, is that of a car dealer in Tennessee. According to him, a man calling himself "Mo" landed his small plane at an airport in March 2001 and began asking questions about a nearby chemical plant. As recounted to the FBI and the press, the stranger wanted to know "What kind of chemicals are in those massive storage tanks?" He informed the pilot he thought the tanks were empty but he was in fact wrong. The tanks actually contained as much as 250 tons of sulfur dioxide, an amount that if released would be sufficient to harm as many as 60,000 people, according to worst-case estimates developed by the plant. Two other witnesses identified the stranger as Mohamed Atta, a key suspect in the strike that felled the World Trade Center.

Recent terrorist attacks and the plans of terrorist groups to use chemical, biological, and nuclear weapons has altered the calculus of risk that underpins much of environmental law and brought international mandates for greater security. Risks that seemed too remote to be addressed in serious and comprehensive ways by many governments, corporations, or individuals are being focused upon with new urgency. The priorities of environmental security efforts have shifted accordingly to reflect this on national, international, and local levels. National and State anti-terrorism legislation was introduced placing new restrictions on hazardous materials transportation. Facilities with large amounts of hazardous chemicals stepped up security efforts and minimized the amounts of the most hazardous substances kept on site. For example, a Waste Water Treatment Plant, just a few miles from the Capitol removed 900 tons of liquid chlorine and sulfur dioxide. Within days they accelerated a program to use less toxic chemicals like bleach instead of chlorine gas for wastewater treatment.

International efforts at environmental security have sharpened to include a focus on immediate risks from biological, chemical, and nuclear materials, and those individuals and groups who would use them as weapons of mass destruction and terror. Addressing these risks in an era of global commerce and freer and faster trade, requires better international frameworks for systematic integration of information among law enforcement agencies, customs services, environmental regulatory agencies, trade agencies, and intelligence sources. Nations must improve their capabilities to share and analyze such data across borders, using new information technologies, to detect shipments of chemical, biological, or nuclear agents that may be precursor to acts of terrorism or environmental crime.

Around the world, the environmental laws themselves were designed to address risks to human health and the environment posed by complex industrial societies. Many environmental laws, and the capacity to enforce them, were developed in response to industrial risks that became tragically manifest with the death of thousands in Bhopal, India and other serious incidents around the world. Environmental laws reflect a calculus of risk and construct compliance requirements designed to reduce those risks. Recent events have changed those terms, imposing security as a paramount value in environmental law, regulation, and environmental management. New legislation has superimposed new security measures on existing environmental laws.

The imperative to implement environmental security measures for critical infrastructure will provide a new lens in considering implementation of international agreements with greater emphasis on facilitating the deployment of more strategic and efficient approaches to minimizing environmental risks. Even with advances in environmental management over the last decade, few facilities have integrated security monitoring and defenses, or adequately addressed risks of sabotage from outside or inside the facility. Conversely, despite advances in technologies for security systems, often a very separate operation from environmental management at facilities, very few adequately address threats from chemical or biological agents. In recent years, certain sensitive facilities have begun to deploy environmental management systems with integrated approaches to information management and security monitoring, using new technologies. The search for safety from a newly apparent array of threats has created new incentives for sustainable and secure environmental management practices, as well as a new urgency in defining and implementing environmental security.

An Integrated Law Enforcement Response

Over the last decade, as the concept of environmental security evolved from a minor point to a significant element of national security policy in many nations, the capacity of the various agencies required to work together to implement these policies lagged behind. It was widely recognized that environmental threats do not heed national borders and pose long-term dangers to security. Natural resource scarcities can trigger and exacerbate conflict. Environmental threats such as climate change, ozone depletion, and the transnational movement of hazardous chemicals and waste directly threaten the health of citizens.

Internationally, while the late 1990s witnessed a proliferation of environmental policy initiatives, rarely was there a mechanism for implementing these policies across the different agencies with overlapping jurisdiction for international traffic in hazardous substances, much less resources to follow through in a serious way. Many of the environmental initiatives themselves consisted largely of urging ratification of the various conventions and calling for increased cooperation in fighting trans-boundary environmental crime. This latter point reflected a growing recognition that the treaties themselves had little or no impact on actual environmental security unless the Multilateral Environmental Agreements (MEAs) were adequately implemented in law, and unless there was a capacity to enforce these laws across national borders. As the United Kingdom's Secretary of State for the Environment John Gummer put it: "These Conventions are worthless words on paper, unless their provisions are enforced in practice."

At about the same time, several multi-agency, multinational enforcement initiatives emerged to bring together the data from environmental agencies with law enforcement agencies charged with international investigations in order to detect violations of international environmental agreements. These operations provide a model for the broader and more systematic approaches of information and law enforcement integration required for security from chemical, biological and other threats that cross national borders. These multi-agency initiatives involved bringing together Customs agents with their automated customs and trade data, environmental and regulatory data regarding the notification and controls of lawful shipments of chemicals, tax authorities and their tax information on such shipments and receiving facilities law enforcement agencies and prosecutors. Some involved foreign international organizations such as the World Bank, and private companies around the world with their data on the lawful production of controlled chemicals by facilities around the world.

These initiatives illustrated the type of compliance information, trade data, and various law enforcement information that needs to be brought together in a systematic way to detect illegal shipments of chemical, explosives, hazardous and nuclear wastes and other goods in international commerce that may be precursor to acts of terrorism, or forms of international environmental crimes that threaten environmental and national security. It also demonstrated the type of public and private partnerships necessary to detect illegal traffic that can be easily disguised as lawful commerce in chemicals or biological substances.

By the late 1990s, senior policy makers around the world recognized the need for better mechanisms for sharing data within and among nations as a prerequisite for meaningful enforcement of laws governing international commerce in regulated substances. For example, at the G8 Summit Meetings, those nations committed to greater cooperation among them and the developing world to address threats to national security posed by international environmental crime, estimated at that time to exceed 20 billion dollars a year in illegal trafficking in chemicals, hazardous wastes, and other regulated substances.

The G8 Nations' Lyon Group of Senior Experts in Transnational Organized Crime initiated a law enforcement project on international environmental crime, including acts that constituted ecological terrorism. This project was launched to improve information exchange, data analysis, and cooperation among law enforcement agencies, international organizations such as INTERPOL, the World Customs Organization, and the Secretariats of the MEAs, as well as environmental and trade regulators. The G8 Project was asked to develop collaborative mechanisms to detect violations of international environmental laws, and the organized crime and terrorist groups associated with them.

The challenges of coordinating different law enforcement agencies and integrating information among them have long been recognized, but difficult to surmount absent a task force approach in a high priority case or initiative, or a galvanizing event such as September 11. In May 2000, the United States President's Interagency Commission on Crime and Security in U.S. Seaports published its report, urging throughout greater coordination of all federal, state, and local law enforcement agencies with significant regulatory and enforcement missions. Just on the federal level, for detecting illegal imports that threaten security, these agencies include Customs, Immigration, the Food and Drug Administration, the Environmental Protection Agency, the Bureau of Alcohol, Tobacco, and Firearms, the Drug Enforcement Administration, the FBI, the Coast Guard, and the Departments of Agriculture, Commerce, and Labor, and aspects of the intelligence community.

The report's first recommendation was to strengthen interagency, intergovernmental, and public/private sector efforts to address the threats of seaport crime (including terrorism), and to enhance control of imports and exports. While this report focused on crime and security at the 361 public seaports themselves, these ports are among the most vulnerable components of the international and inter-modal trade system. With the billions of tons of cargo coming through these ports every year, and the smuggling of contraband and illegal aliens that may be connected to terrorism, the report's finding that the state of security in U.S. seaports generally ranges from poor to fair is not comforting.

Among the reasons for vulnerabilities at ports is the exponential growth of trade over the last twenty years, the nature of modern container shipments, and the failure of inspection and control resources and technologies to keep pace. Economic globalization has compressed reaction time for law enforcement and has blurred national borders. Most import crimes go undetected at ports because less than two percent of cargo is inspected. This includes illegal transport of pre-cursor chemicals, hazardous materials, drugs, munitions, and potential weapons of mass destruction. Less than one per cent of export cargo is inspected.

Complicating efforts at homeland security from illegal imports further, the 'stove-piping' of traditional law enforcement agencies presents obstacles to working together and sharing data to combat newer crimes that cut across law enforcement jurisdictions and involve regulatory agencies. With different law enforcement agencies, regulatory agencies, all with their disparate data collection and dissemination systems designed for their administrative functions, there is too little integration across these functions to allow for a central assessment of illegal imports that may pose threats to national security. Meanwhile, international criminal and terrorist threats change constantly and adapt to law enforcement capabilities. In an era when organized crime and terrorists use advanced communications around the world, national law enforcement agencies can no longer afford "not to know what we know".

While reports like the Seaport Crime and Security study have identified these issues in recent years, little has been done to implement recommendations from these reports in a serious and comprehensive way across the government agencies. Indeed, agencies spread thin to cover their core functions are often reluctant to devote their resources to an inter-agency process. They are particularly reluctant where other agencies have overlapping jurisdiction and when an investment in new information technologies may be required. Even with the current mandate, resources that are likely to be appropriated, and a new focus on asymmetrical threats to national security from terrorists, it presents many challenges to existing institutional structures to bring the right information together in the right way and in time to detect threats before it is too late.

It is clear, however, that technology that is widely used in the private sector and for military purposes is available to bring together relevant information across agencies and nations through link analysis and other measures to enable law enforcement authorities to better determine threats as they cross national borders. It is imperative that agencies and international organizations that have designed and are administering regulatory processes, or are developing new ones, structure them in such a way to take full advantage of these technologies, particularly electronic reporting, and design them to be compatible with other agencies information systems, particularly Customs automated data systems.

Government agencies should move forward aggressively with electronic reporting and record keeping, which is the only way to facilitate comparison with Customs data, and other agencies law enforcement information in a timeframe consistent with detecting illegal imports before it is too late. Efforts to move forward with bar coded electronic manifests and with rendering as much compliance data in secure and harmonized electronic form as soon as possible can only improve the ability of law enforcement to detect and track illegal shipments and other violation of international agreements. If trucking and shipping lines can track their cargo using Global Information Systems, and grocery stores can track their inventory using bar codes and electronic systems, shouldn't governments be in a position to use these same technologies to detect and track shipments that pose threats to national security?

Structuring International Environmental and Trade Agreements to Take Advantage of Integrated

Communications and Deliver More of the Security They Promise. Unless law enforcement agencies at the border have systematic real time access to regulatory information to determine whether a shipment complies with regulatory requirements, nations cannot realistically expect to achieve widespread compliance with international agreements designed to control the trade in hazardous substances, including those that may be used as weapon ns of mass destruction. Yet, many international agreements, such as the Basel Convention on the Control of Trans-boundary Movement of Hazardous Wastes and their Disposal, still rely on the environmental agency from the exporting nation faxing notification and consent forms to the environmental agency of the importing nation, with no direct connection to customs agencies and their largely automated data systems for tracking trade.

Moreover, the regulatory classification systems for hazardous wastes bore little resemblance to the tariff codes and other nomenclature used by customs services to track goods in international commerce. These are among the obstacles that have made certain international agreements notoriously difficult to enforce. New environmental agreements, and revisions to existing ones, must facilitate the exchange of compatible data between regulatory agencies and customs services, using electronic reporting harmonized with the automated data processes governing international trade and customs' clearance processes. Negotiators of recent agreements have considered the problems of detecting illegal traffic, but whether nations implement measures enabling them to detect violations in the real world of international trade remains to be seen.

For example, leading up to the agreements last year on Persistent Organic Pollutants (POPs) and Prior Informed Consent (PIC), parties at preparatory meetings considered recommendations for detecting and preventing illegal traffic in these chemicals, based upon the experience of those with experience in enforcing the import and export laws governing hazardous wastes and ozone depleting substances. While these agreements adopted language on compliance and enforcement, unless nations implement administrative notification and consent regimes using electronic reporting with real time connection to customs trade data and inspection and control functions, an opportunity will be lost to use the best available technologies to provide a greater measure of international environmental security.

Other avenues for pursuing the type of data integration required to better assure compliance with international environmental agreements include the trade agreements, and the Customs agreements that implement technical exchange of information between nations. While trade agreements have become increasingly sophisticated in their use of technologies, and Customs electronic data systems have facilitated faster trade with expedited clearance processes, they do not have adequate interface with environmental regulatory information under the statutes that implement most environmental agreements. With increased international trade and relatively fewer opportunities for meaningful inspection, it is all the more important that the framework for data exchange imbedded in trade agreements, such as free trade agreements, facilitate a link with the environmental compliance data necessary to determine whether a shipment is legal, or may pose a threat.

The World Customs Organization and governments have supported such measures as a matter of policy. When it comes time to negotiate the actual trade and technical agreements themselves, however, integration with environmental agencies' compliance data has not been a priority or received much in the way of resources from Customs or from the environmental agencies themselves. While harmonizing waste, chemical, and pesticide definitions and codes under environmental laws with corresponding Customs' nomenclature for categories of goods in commerce may require additional attention and resources, without such harmonization, there is no effective way to detect suspect shipments on a broad enough scale to minimize the risks illegal shipments currently pose, with trade predicted to triple by 2020.

Secure Management Practices

Just as better integration and management of data from different sources is a key to improving national and international efforts to enhance security, these same fundamentals apply to achieving greater environmental security for industry, critical infrastructure, and specific facilities. The potential infiltration or sabotage of a large chemical facility or a petroleum refinery raises a host of other scenarios. According to the U.S. Environmental Protection Agency, more than 123 plants each maintain amounts of toxic chemicals that if, if released, could endanger more than 1 million people. The submittals of firms under the Clean Air Act Risk Management Program Rule describe a host of evils that could occur in the event of an explosion or significant toxic chemical release.

Since September 11, many facilities have reviewed both their security and environmental management practices to create greater defenses. Measures to enhance security have included the following: centralizing receiving operations; increasing surveillance and the number of security guards; enhancing access control measures; moving rail tank cars within the fence-line; permitting employee vehicles only on facility premises.

While many facilities are just now reassessing crisis management, response, and evacuation plans and reviewing their environmental management approaches, other companies have been minimizing the risks and liabilities of their operations by implementing strategic approaches to environmental management over the last decade. The elements of these environmental management systems designed to assure compliance with law, minimize or eliminate the use of the most hazardous substances and wastes, reduce emissions and releases, and improve process efficiencies are important from a security perspective as well.

In recent years, as part of their environmental and information management systems, some facilities have deployed innovative technologies, electronic commerce techniques, remote sensing, and integrated monitoring for compliance and security over secure internet based systems. In addition to achieving new levels of environmental security, such facilities in the public and private sectors have realized efficiencies that have saved costs and natural resources. These facilities have come to rely on Environmental Management Information Systems that allow for real-time monitoring and integration of many different systems over the internet.

Certain NATO Nations' military bases have also moved to sophisticated environmental management information systems. In addition to monitoring for environmental compliance, these systems also monitor for minute amounts of biological and chemical agents upstream of the facility, monitor for meteorological conditions, releases from off the site, and other parameters that are important from a security perspective, using remote and wireless devices, accessible from the secure web based control center. In the last year, one of these facilities saved 400,000 gallons of water a day due to the efficiencies realized by moving to this system. Another facility, by moving to electronic commerce and just in time delivery of the most toxic chemicals, was able to eliminate an on-site warehouse where these chemicals were stored, and avoid having to submit a hazardous waste permit at all because they remained under the regulatory threshold.

Some of the same techniques that leading companies have come to deploy for sound environmental management purposes may be brought to bear at facilities to achieve new levels of security and efficiency. Accordingly, facilities looking to minimize their risks from acts of terrorism and other threats need to evaluate both their traditional security operations and their environmental management practices. A security audit, terrorism threat assessment, and environmental management gap analysis may reveal vulnerabilities that may be addressed through various commonsense measures. Advances in communication technologies and remote sensing over the last decade offer new ways to monitor and integrate information relevant to detecting a greater array of risks than ever before. These tools put managers in position to know what is happening, respond quicker, and minimize consequences from risks that materialize.

5

Economic Cost of Terrorism in South Asia

Terrorism has been a major concern in the politico-economic arena of the recent world, particularly after the massacre of 11th September 2001. However, the act of terrorism is not a recent phenomenon. While it is very difficult to define terrorism, there is no doubt about the severity of social and economic cost of terrorism. Terrorism has rendered a threat to the humanity. While the act of terrorism is very unevenly distributed over the world in terms its nature, intensity, and coverage; its negative impact is spread over both in the developed and the developing countries, directly and indirectly. Terrorist activities not only discourage economic activity by threatening the safety of life and property, it also damages the overall investment environment of a country by creating turmoil and anarchy. LDCs and developing countries, which are striving for development with poor resource base, can hardly afford such a cost of terrorism.

South Asia is a region of LDCs and developing countries. South Asian countries (except Afghanistan) have been performing much better in terms of economic growth compared to the average performance of the low-income countries. Some of the countries have already graduated from the status of LDC to the status of developing countries.

However, these countries had even better potential; some of these economies could have stood at the same level as the newly industrialized countries (NICs). During the early 1960s, economic conditions of the South Asian countries were similar to that of many NICs. The potential of the South Asian countries could not be fully realized for many reasons including terrorism. Terrorism is a common phenomenon in this region, although the nature of terrorism is not identical across the South Asian countries. This paper will make a brief attempt to analyze the economic cost of terrorism in Bangladesh, particularly in the recent years.

In the literature, attempt has been made to arrive at some numerical estimate of direct and indirect cost of terrorism. This requires counterfactual estimates of the economic scenario with and without terrorism. It is very difficult, if not impossible, to apply such a rigorous methodology in Bangladesh because of the very nature of terrorism existent here. Instead of exact quantification, the paper will limit its endeavor to make an analytical exposition of the economic cost of terrorism. However, this will be fair enough to provide a gesture about the damage of the economy of Bangladesh due to terrorism. Structure of the paper is as follows. Section II defines the nature of terrorism. Section III briefly discusses the nature of terrorism that exists in Bangladesh.

Nature of Terrorism

Terrorism, by nature, is very difficult to define. The old adage, "One man's terrorist is other man's freedom fighter" is still alive and well. For the purpose of our analysis of cost of terrorism, we take the FBI definition, "Terrorism is the unlawful use of force or violence against persons or property to intimidate or coerce a government, the civilian population, or any segment thereof, in furtherance of political and social objectives". James M. Poland views that "terrorism is the premeditated, deliberate, systematic murder, mayhem, and threading of the innocent to create fear and intimidation in order to gain a political or tactical advantage, usually to influence a audience." While terrorism is usually meant to be an act of an organized group of people, or small groups of miscreant, it may also be government controlled or directed.

Similarly, while terrorist activity sometimes confined within some locality, scope of terrorist activity may also be extended beyond the national boundary. There are several types of motivation behind the terrorist activities. For example, ideological terrorism aims at the revolutionary change of social structures. Ethno-national terrorism strives for the liberation of certain territory. Very lately, there is an increasing dominance of religiously motivated terrorism.

Terrorism in Bangladesh

Bangladesh is a country virtually with a homogenous society. There is some ethnic diversity, basically due to very small numbers of tribal habitant in the Chittagong Hill Tracts and some other part of the country. Bangladeshis are, by nature, peace-loving people. Bangladesh has set up an unique example of communal harmony, although some scattered incidence took place after the general election of 2001, mostly due to political motivation. In general, terrorism in Bangladesh is not as severe as that in some of the other countries in South Asia. This does not, however, mean that Bangladesh is quite free from terrorism. Bangladesh also has to bear a large cost out of terrorism. However, nature and severity of terrorism in Bangladesh is somewhat different from that in other countries in this region. Several types of terrorist activities have been observed in Bangladesh. The most severe type of terrorism is associated with activities of the groups who are ideologically and politically motivated.

This includes:

a. Activities of outlawed political parties,

b. Threat from the terrorist group of fundamentalists and

c. The terrorism in the Chittagong Hill Tracts.

Right after the independence, an activist group became involved in terrorism that was politically motivated to establish communism in this country. They targeted the rich people who have accumulated wealth within the capitalist system. Direct action against those people, they believed, would ease the path towards establishing communism. Initially they were organized in a political party. The government of Bangladesh outlawed this party at some point. Since then, this group started to be involved in terrorist activities. Although, their terrorist activities were scattered around many parts of the country, they were more organized in the southwestern part of the country. Thanks God, activities of this terrorist group have been declining in the recent years. However, still they are very active in the southwestern part of the country.

Many of the killings and bomb attack in the past few years were believed to conduct by this terrorist group. Majority of the people in Bangladesh is believes in the religion of Islam. They are basically peace-loving Muslims who do not support any terrorist activity. Despite this, a very small group of Islamic fundamentalist who had been alleged to be involved in many terrorist activities in the past few years also exists. This group is called Harkat-ul-Jehadi-e-Islami, who is committed to establish Islamic *hukumat* in Bangladesh. This extremist group is believed to have close links with Pakistan. They were also believed to have a close tie with Talibans. However, the activities of this group were very minimum and were very scattered in Bangladesh. It seems that the presence of Islamic fundamentalist group of more propaganda than its real existence and activities.

Lately, terrorist activities of this group have virtually been ceased, although some scattered incidence of bomb blast is alleged to be done by some fundamentalist group.

Natives of the Chittagong hill tracts had been fighting to establish their rights and 'independence' since the early 1970s. They were organized in political parties and militant groups to fight against Bangladesh. Since then they have carried on many terrorist activities in the Hill Tract area. Government signed a peace treaty with them (the Chaittagong Hill Tract (CHT) Accord) in 1997, which brought a hope to establish peace in that region. However, a sub-group of the remained discontented with the treaty.

The accord promised the tribal restitution of their land, greater participation in the government and a reduction of the presence of Bangladesh military force in the CHT. However, the accord did not solve many of the outstanding questions and the implementation of the treaty ran into snags so that its full potential for peace, development and coexistence between the tribal and the settler segments of the region's inhabitants remained practically unrealized. Within the tribal community there is a persistent tension between pro and anti peace accord groups. On February 2001, three foreign nationals were abducted in the forest of Rangamati districts and they were kept hostage for a month until they were rescued by a commando action. According to Indian government sources, terrorist groups such as the United Liberation front of Assam (ULFA) and All Tripura Tiger force (ATTF) and National Liberation Front of Tripura (NLFT) run several base camps in the jungles of CHT areas and Sylhet, which actually appears as a piece of discontent in the bilateral relationship between India and Bangladesh.

The most common terrorism in Bangladesh is the terrorist activities of the miscreant that is associated with deterioration in the law and order situation. The miscreants become violent to the civilian population to have unlawful possession over their money and property. The 'mastans' exerts threat, physical torture, and force on the innocent people to compel them to surrender to their unlawful will. Severe unemployment problem, influx of illegal weapon, patronage from the political parties, along with the inadequate, inefficient and corrupt role of the law enforcing agencies are responsible for the rise of General mastanism in the country. Common people of Bangladesh have become captives by the miscreants. In addition to these two major types of terrorism, political confrontation also gives rise to terrorist activities.

Even though Bangladesh has started its journey on the path of democracy, there is a higher degree of political instability as the democratic values and institutions are severely undernourished. Two major political parties seem to be very stubborn and intolerant to each other. There are frequent calls for *hartal* and other destructive programs due to political fragmentation and conflicts. Sometimes political programs give rise to terrorist activities like bomb attack or setting fire on properties. Even the members of the law enforcing agencies sometimes become so brutal with the suspects who may be even innocent people that it could be also categorized as a type of terrorism. Bangladesh is also affected by the regional and international terrorist activities.

On the Economy of Bangladesh

General mastanism and the associated terrorist activities of the miscreants have the most negative impact on the economy of Bangladesh. The business people are oppressed by the higher incidence of toll extraction by the political and local miscreants. The businessmen are alleged to pay involuntary tolls at every stage of business operations. It increases cost of doing business directly or indirectly and lowers business competitiveness. New investment in productive activities is heavily discouraged, because of the up front involuntary tolls that have to be paid to the miscreants while anyone goes for a new construction or new establishment. Sometimes, peoples' lives are jeopardized if they hesitate to pay tolls to miscreants. Overall law and order situation in Bangladesh is far from satisfactory. Recently, government had to involve military and paramilitary force along with the law enforcing agencies to arrest the miscreants and recover illegal weapons so as to improve overall law and order situation of the country. As we have explained in the earlier section that political confrontation may give rise to destructive programs that may lead to terrorist activities like bomb attack or setting fire on properties.

This destructive activity not only hampers profitability of existing production activities, it also reduces incentive to invest in this country. More importantly, terrorist activities by the miscreant along with political violence created a negative image about the investment potential in the country to both the local and foreign investors. Although private investment in this country started to increase since the early 1990s due to economic liberalization, investment GDP ratio became stagnant in the recent years. Similarly there was a massive inflow of FDI in the mid 1990s. However, FDI is showing an alarmingly declining trend very lately. Growth of general terrorism and poor image of the country is one of the important factors behind this poor performance of investment in the recent years. Although Bangladesh is enjoying a moderate growth rate in recent years, a recent study (by the author) shows that there is huge discrepancy in the level of development and economic growth rates across different regions in Bangladesh. Investment activities are highly concentrated in the capital city and few other major cities in Bangladesh. Investors do not feel equally safe to invest in all areas of Bangladesh.

One of the main reasons for concentration of investment in the major cities is relatively greater presence of the law enforcing agencies and relatively less pressure for toll from local miscreants. Thus, the growth of terrorism by the local mastans has also contributed to unequal regional development of the country. Private investment had also been lower in the districts of Chittagong hill tracts and the southwestern parts of the country where the terrorist groups were more active. This point is substantiated by the information of per capita Bank advance in different divisions and selected districts in Bangladesh. Bank advance may be a good proxy for private investment. It is quite evident that bank advance is very unevenly distributed across different regions of the country. Per capita bank advance is quite low in the districts of Chittagong Hill Tracts. Same is true for the districts in the southwestern part of the country.

Chittagong Hill Tracts is one of the most potential regions in terms of its resource base and capacity to have positive impact on the overall development of the country. This is the region where country's main forestland is located. The region has enormous natural resources. The region is famous for its natural beauty. However, potential for its own development is far from being materialized. Terrorist activities in that region are one of the important factors in this regard. Development in the hill tract area has been achieved basically through government initiative. Private investment is much lower in this area. Foreign investors are also very much interested to take part in extraction of natural resource and contribute to development in this region. However, terrorism has discouraged foreign investment as well. Direct activity of foreigners remained halted in this area for about a year after the hostage incidence of the last year.

The southeast part of the country including the Hill Tracts has tremendous potential for tourism. However, growth of tourism is heavily obstructed by the lack of security in this region. Moreover, the government also had to drain huge amount of public money for military expenses to curb the terrorism in this area. The terrorist activities of the Islamic fundamentalist of more propaganda than its real existence and however, this propaganda is enough to create a negative image about the country so as to discourage foreign investment and tourism.

Impact of International Terrorism

Economy of Bangladesh has to incur heavy cost because of terrorist activities outside the country as well. Bangladesh and many other LDCs are now more integrated with global economy. Bangladesh has passed through a heightened pace of global integration in the 1990s. State of the global economy is likely to have stronger impact on the Bangladesh economy now than in any time in past. It is now widely recognized that, as far as developing countries and LDCs are concerned, global integration has both its opportunities and risks. Any terrorist activity that has a negative impact on our major trading partner and other collaborators can render a negative effect on the economy of Bangladesh as well. The classic example in this regard is the negative impact of terrorist attack of 11th September in USA. USA being our major export destination country, the September massacre in USA tolled the Bangladesh economy by a huge amount. The world economy has been facing a recession since the last quarter of 2000.

Bangladesh economy was also hurt by the recession. Even though a global recession was recognized in the first quarter of 2001, Bangladesh was able to maintain its steady performance of export growth. However, export performance of Bangladesh economy started to deteriorate since the fiscal year 2001-02. The situation became embarrassing since the terrorist incidence of September. Bangladesh enjoyed an impressive export growth in the last two decades. Export growth in real terms was more than 2.5 times than the growth of GDP. This stellar performance in export was mainly possible because of the impressive growth of RMG under the Multi-Fiber Agreement (MFA). However, despite a double-digit growth in export, export basket of Bangladesh remained quite concentrated. Export of readymade garments (RMG) alone accounts for three fourths of its export earnings. Export market of Bangladesh is not well diversified either. Some 45 per cent of RMG export of Bangladesh is directed towards US market only.

As a result, export of RMG from Bangladesh was heavily affected by the September incidence. In addition to global recession, terrorist attack had a tremendous negative effect on our export. RMG export destination country. As a result, overall export growth became negative for the first time in the history of fifteen years. One might argue that much of the negative export growth of Bangladesh is due to the global recession. However, a further look into this matter indicates the importance of September attack behind the negative performance of RMG export. Negative growth in RMG export is highest in the US market, negative growth in other countries are modest. While RMG exports to some of the major destination countries have declined, RMG export to some other major destination countries also experienced some positive growth. Actually, total RMG export to the 15 countries of the European Union marked a positive growth despite the global recession. On the other hand, RMG export to US market declined by more than 20 per cent.

Thus, the 11th September terrorist attack and consequent intensified recession in the US economy had a tremendous negative impact on our export. Because of the negative export growth, our GDP growth also declined from an accelerating trend in the recent years. September 11 terrorist attack affected our economy in much other indirect way. First, US resorted help from Pakistan to carry on war against Talibans of Afghanistan and in return, Pakistan received some additional benefits from US regarding export of RMG which the country otherwise would not have received. As a result many orders for RMG have been diverted from Bangladesh towards Pakistan. Thus, the gain of Pakistan is achieved through a cost of LDCs like Bangladesh. Imposition of restrictions on US visa for the citizens of country like Bangladesh may also have some negative impact. First it might lower the inflow of remittance to Bangladesh.

Second, it may minimize the exchange of knowledge and deprive the prospective Bangladeshi students to receive modern education. Foreign investment depends not only on the image of a country but also on the image of the region. Terrorism in the South Asian region may have some negative impact on the economy of Bangladesh as well by discouraging FDI. Moreover, development of tourism has a regional dimension. Terrorism in south Asia may render some negative impact on the growth of tourism in this region including Bangladesh. Terrorism has become an important concern in recent years. Although severity of terrorism is less in Bangladesh compared to some other South Asian countries, it still incurs heavy cost to the economy. Domestic terrorism has increased cost of doing business, reduced competitiveness and diminished the image of the country as a good place for investment. Terrorism by the miscreants due to general weakness in law and order situation is supposed to have the most widespread negative impact on the economy.

On the other hand terrorism by the Islamic fundamentalist, mostly being propaganda, also results in a negative image to the foreign investors and tourists. Terrorism in Chittagong hill tracts is a great hindrance for the development of this region as well as it's potential contribution to the economy. Bangladesh is also negatively affected by regional and international terrorism. In particular, the September attack in the USA had a strong negative impact on the export of Bangladesh economy, which in turn lowered the economic growth of the country. Although sometimes there is confusion between terrorism and act of freedom fighter by the counter groups, it is true that such activities render huge economic cost to the society. Hence, Bangladesh and all other nations should seriously work to minimize the terrorist activities. Dialogue must be encouraged instead of force, where possible.

Overall law and order situation must be improved through reforming the police force and rejuvenating the legal system that would help curb the terrorist activities by miscreants. Bangladesh economy is now heavily integrated with global economy. Terrorism itself has regional and international dimensions. Hence, the world must work together to fight against terrorism. State terrorism must be abandoned. Regional and global initiative is a must in this regard. There had been several initiatives and consensus about cooperation at regional level in South-East Asia as well as in Asia and Europe to combat terrorism. However, regional activities are far more limited in south Asia. SAARC should come forward to deal with issues like combating terrorism. This will not only minimize cost of terrorism, but also help to minimize tension in the region.

Islam and the West

It was not Jerusalem, Baghdad, Sarajevo, Grozny or Charar-e-Sharif. It was Oklahoma City, situated at the heart of the USA. A powerful car-bomb of thousands of pounds exploded on 19 April in the centre of the city. It shook buildings as far away as 30 miles and reduced 91- story huge complex housing government offices to rubbles. The pile up of charred bodies (137 could be retrieved, and more than 60 burnt to ashes), the scattered limbs of children, their bleeding bodies and heart rending cries presented a ravishing scene and it seemed as if a scene from formerly mentioned cities had been repeated there.

"I had seen all this happening in Sarajevo but could not even imagine of witnessing all this here in America", said one eye witness. The fact, however, is that calamities of even hundreds of Oklahomas put together can not equal the atrocities being committed since long in Sarajevo, Bosnia and Grozny all of which is witnessed silently (and perhaps with satisfaction) by America and Europe. According to the weekly *Newsweek*, "the misunderstanding that we are safe at least at our home has been buried forever under the debris of this sabotaged building in the heart of America".

Even without the tragedy of Oklahoma, there was little room for such a wishful thinking in America whose citizens exchange heavy fire in their infightings that result in the killing of 22 thousand innocent civilians annually, where a zeal of starts indiscriminate shooting all of a sudden and kills dozens of people without any reason, where government is unable to check this wide-spread use of fire arms. Yet, at the same time it plays policeman of the world whose energies and activities are aimed at efforts to deprive Muslim countries from not only of nuclear weapons but also of all conventional arms.

Delusion of the West

The Americans as well as the Europeans, since long, have made themselves to believe that they are so civilized and protectors of human rights that it is simply impossible to commit any terrorist activities. Only 'outsiders' do it. It is clear which 'outsiders' they mean. This kind of thinking has taken such a complete control of them that when the news of the Oklahoma went around, the common American immediately suspected Muslims to be behind this act of terrorism. Why? Obviously because their leaders and media have made them into believing that no one else than those 'born in the Middle East', Arabs and Islamic fundamentalists, could commit such acts. Those who hold responsible positions started issuing 'decrees' over TV, Radio and in the press.

Though without any evidence, they talked about "beards" and "black hair" of the accused. An innocent Muslim, an Arab-American, was subsequently arrested at London airport and extradited to USA. As a result there was an outrage against Muslims and hatred against them assumed new proportions. Muslim faced threats at mosques and at places of residence. Their friends turned away. There were slanderous outbursts along roadsides branding them as 'child killers'. All this did not fall under the category of terrorism as is described by America. The outcome was, however, the one which only terrorism could produce.

All Muslims, Americans as well as immigrants, remained in a state of harassment till the arrest of the 'real' culprit. Who was it? A purely white and native American, formerly a soldier who had taken part in operations in Iraq and had killed hundreds of Iraqis even though they had surrendered. This act of terrorism turned out to be a result neither of a fiery speech of any 'Sheikh Abdur Rahman', nor of the planning of any 'Yusuf Ramzi'. Nor was it an act of some individual, a brown man from Middle East, a fundamentalist. It was not even a protest or reaction of an oppressed against continued imposition of cruel and dictatorial regimes in the Muslim world, establishment of a Jewish state, Israel, at the heart of the Muslim land, displacement of Palestinians, burning and burying alive of thousands of troops in Iraq, shooting down of the Iranian plane, sabotaging the democratic revolution in Algeria or preventing Muslim societies from adopting Islamic way of life. It was not due to poverty or economic retardation, either. It was not instigated by Iran which calls USA "the biggest Satan" and whom USA has declared the most terrorist state of the world. It was also not done on the behest of any of the other four Muslim countries Sudan, Libya, Iraq, and Syria about whom USA annually completes the formality of declaring terrorist states.

It was also clear that the culprit was neither alone nor he suffered from mental disorders. They were not a few but hundreds of thousands of people, associated in a network in 30 states, organized and armed to the tooth and nail. They were educated and were not illiterate; civilized and white, not black or brown. They were using computers and internet and publishing booklets since long to propagate their ideas and techniques of bomb-making and terrorism. These people called their government 'big Satan' and regarded it as the foremost enemy of their rights and freedom. They declared it 'beast like' because of its tyranny and oppression. And a government which is bent upon rounding up 'Yusuf Ramzis' around the world and their extradition to America is either oblivious of these people or ignoring them.

This is the story of what the US claims to be the biggest terrorist act on its soil. However, it can be termed as the biggest act of terrorism only when we do not open the chapters of history since the arrival of Columbus till the tragedy in Oklahoma which relate stories of oppression, subjugation: racial exploitation of the Red-Indians, their ethnic 'cleansing', and their expulsion to 'protected areas'; burning alive of the blacks by racist organizations like Kuklux Klan. The Oklahoma tragedy, however, made one thing quite clear that though it is in the forefront of the campaign to declare Muslims and their countries as terrorists, the US itself is harboring a large number of terrorists on its own soil.

Once the identity of culprits was established, the misconception that only Muslims carry out such acts of terrorism should have been buried in Oklahoma. Propaganda against Muslims and Islam should have been stopped and those responsible for such vicious campaign should have begged apology from Muslims all over the world in general and the Muslims in America in particular. But this did not happen, nor is it going to happen. Continuous pumping into the balloon of 'Islamic terrorism' is a political necessity. The government and the media will, therefore, continue to follow the beaten path.

What would have been the situation if the culprits were Muslims? How the West would react if Muslims are found responsible for an Oklahoma-like incident in future? Even the imagination of this is dreadful. Such be the case, the hell would be let loose on Muslims as had been let loose to

Sikhs in India after the assassination of Indira Gandhi, or is being meted out to Muslims in India and in Bosnia, or had been done with the Jews in Europe, or is being done in Rwanda.

These dreadful possibilities are not imaginary. If the mood of the American society suddenly turned against Muslims after the Oklahoma tragedy, there is nothing strange in it. There was nothing strange either when mood of the West was bitter for Muslims during the Gulf war (as has been analysed by weekly *Time*) though nearly all Muslim rulers sided with the US for crushing a Muslim country. This all is because the picture of the Muslims, for political reasons, has been so painted in the West that a feeling of hatred and fear has become a part of their collective psyche.

That is why; Washington Post's Columnist Stephen Rosefield had the audacity to say "yes, Muslims were hastily held responsible. This is despicable and dangerous. Yes, I admit that the first thought that came to my mind was also that it was an act of Muslims. But our reaction is not the outcome of any ignoble prejudices. This is not an issue of the picture of Islam. It is based on facts [i.e. fault lies with the Muslims]. Muslims indulge in acts of terrorism; consider it as legitimate and Muslim governments' back terrorist activities. We cannot close our eyes in the name of friendship and fair play. Though it is now known that the Americans too can be terrorists, [what is different with us is that] our government is against them." [In subdued words, he admits] "Yes, our government should desist from acts of unlawful killings abroad which are termed as acts of terrorism and which damage our moral reputation."

The Western Dualism

The big question is: What is the reality? While adamantly raising this question about Jesus Christ, Roman ruler Pontess Pilot had ordered his crucification. Perhaps today's successors of the Roman rulers have decided to crucify Muslims and Islam after holding them responsible for terrorism.

It is difficult to define terrorism and what constitutes it. This ambiguity is being exploited by the powerful countries. A lot of hue and cry was raised about ambiguity in the blasphemy law and the German Chancellor chose to himself raise the issue during his meetings with the Pakistani rulers. It is worth noting that though nobody has so far been punished under this law, a full-blown campaign against the law is on. Terrorism is really a strange crime for which not only the individuals but the whole nations and followers of a religion are being targeted and victimised; deceitful and fraudulent methods are employed to hijack and arrest the accused (which itself is terrorism), and on the other hand there is no definition for it under any law. Neither is it a crime under any international law nor any punishment is prescribed for it. According to the author of the most authentic book on this subject, the definition of terrorism is not only ambiguous but is non-existent, rather impossible.

If there is any definition, it is highly controversial because this is not a legal but a political issue. The politically motivated definition is aimed at condemning the accused more than defining the crime itself so that despicable actions against the opponents could be justified and the demands of the biased view and political interests are fulfilled. This self-centerd approach teaches that terrorism which serves own interest should be regarded as legitimate while the one which does not serve this purpose is illegitimate and heinous crime. Today's liberation fighter is tomorrow's terrorist and today's terrorist is tomorrow's Prime Minister [e.g. Afghan Mujahideen, Israeli Prime Minister Ben Gurian, and Kenyan President Jomo Kenyata]. If the terrorists are from amongst own ranks, their acts and motives would be viewed with sympathy and efforts are undertaken for the way out and solution.

The crime would be considered as of an individual and the community would not be held responsible for it. This would be the attitude when the terrorists are, for instance, Americans. However, when terrorism goes against own interests or the terrorists are political or civilisational adversaries, they would be declared formidable terrorists, liable to severe punishment. Their culture, their religion and whole of their country all would become culprits. This view is adopted when terrorists are found to be from amongst the Muslims.

To achieve their objectives, the powerful countries openly carry out military, economic or political actions against whomever they want and whenever, wherever they like. They target whole of the countries, as America did to Iraq, Panama and Haiti. They drop as many bombs they like, as Israel does in Lebanon and shelled at PLO headquarters in Tunis and Iraqi nuclear installations. American heavy bombardment on a small Cambodian territory outclassed the bombardment during the Second World War; US also bombed at the residential areas of Tripoli and Ben Ghazi and the residence of Col. Qaddafi. Using their agents in foreign lands, these countries topple governments, as CIA did to Dr. Musadiq's government in Iran.

They can organize homicidal attacks on the heads of states and leaders and get them killed, as they did to Chile's elected Prime Minister, Alliande, Cuban President Castro, Libyan President Qaddafi, Iranian Speaker Behishti and Prime Minister Ba-Hunar, Lebanon's Sheikh Fazlullah, Saudi King Faisal and General Zia-ul-Haq of Pakistan. They can force whole of the country, including its women and children, to suffer from protracted hunger and disease, as they are doing in Iraq. Since the authority of defining terrorism also lies with these powerful countries, they not only manage to keep their actions out of the definition of terrorism despite their being acts of overt state terrorism, they consider them to have been taken in the name of justice and fair-play and for the welfare of the humanity.

On the other hand, acts of hijacking, occasional bomb blasts and killings done by the oppressed, which have no other means to register their protest and draw world's attention to atrocities perpetrated upon them, are zealously projected as the worst forms of terrorism and all efforts are made to rally world support in favour of such a biased propaganda. Therefore, large scale massacre and arson by hundred of thousands of Indian forces in Kashmir, by Russian army in Chechnya, by Israeli forces in Beirut are considered normal and legitimate. Terrorists are Kashmiris, Palestinians, Chechens, and Pakistan if it wants to support the oppressed Kashmiris in their right cause of attaining the right promised to them by the world community.

Discrimination and Cruelty in the West

If the purpose is to find out reality, instead of being captives to illusion, then it is necessary to ascertain as to which extent the lives and properties, religion and places of worship of Muslims living in these very Western countries are safe. The use of force against and desecration of places of worship and graveyards should be declared as worst form of terrorism. There have been countless incidents of attacks on the mosques and graveyards and throwing of pork in Britain, Germany and other countries of Europe. But here again, the US tops them all. In Yoba town, 150 miles away from San Francisco in California, a beautiful mosque was built in a period of three years at a cost of one million dollars. It took two whole years in obtaining mere permission for its construction. Soon after its completion, inflammable chemicals were sprayed on it on September 01, 1994, and the whole mosque was burnt and reduced to ashes overnight.

America fervently propagates incidents of terrorism in other countries and also exerts pressure for condemning such incidents, its Press, TV and Radio, however, did not even bother to report this gruesome incident of arson. It was the Muslims themselves who raised and activated over the issue and the world knew about this tragedy. Neither Governor Peter Wilson nor any other government functionary uttered a single word about this heinous crime. When an inter-state parliamentary delegation of Muslims met with five officials of Foreign Affairs, they simply refused to take notice of the incident. Instead, they complained about the excesses of 'Muslim extremists' in Muslim countries. [Had a church been torched in Pakistan or some other Muslim country, then ...]. Earlier, when a Jew terrorist massacred innocent Muslims at al-Khalil mosque in Jerusalem, the response was equally apathetic.

Islam values human life more than the place of worship. Leave aside the series of attacks on Muslim in their homes and on roadside in Britain, Germany, France and Belgium, has any Muslim 'terrorist' ever been involved in acts like drowning and putting houses to torch and burning of people alive therein? On the other hand, Muslims living in the countries which campaign against terrorism continue to be the targets of such brutal and heinous crimes. And the media gets absolved of its duty by reporting such acts as incidents of 'racism', not terrorism. The victim is shown as a Turk, a Moroccan, not a Muslim.

On May 29, 1993, terrorists torched a Muslim house in Solingen, Germany. Two women and two girls were burnt alive; one jumped out of the window but succumbed to her injuries. This family was settled in Germany for the last 20 years. This was not the first incident of this kind (nor would it be the last!). In November, 1992, fire bombs were thrown at two Muslim houses in Molln, a city near Hamburg. A woman and two girls were burnt alive in their beds and nine persons, though with serious burns, survived. On May 01, 1995, at a rally of presidential candidate Li Pan in Paris, three 'skinheads' killed a Moroccan Muslim,

Ibrahim, by throwing him into the River Sen and then themselves melted away in the crowd [Had a Christian house been burnt in Pakistan, then...].

What did German Chancellor Kohl do when three Muslim women and five girls were burnt alive? He did not refuse to attend the funeral of the victims of arson in Solingen, nor did he go to their house. In fact he has never visited a Muslim house which has been a victim of such attacks. He does not even like to condemn such acts of violence.

When two Americans were killed in Karachi, America cried hoarse. FBI landed at Karachi and though without proof weekly Time did not feel shy in putting a caption "Islamic terrorism claims two lives." On the other hand, the European governments have failed to protect the Turkish diplomats and centers from Armenian and Kurd terrorism. During two days in June and November 1993, Kurdistan Workers Party carried out 75 terrorist activities a day against the Turks. Armenians too have been involved in similar activities. But both the media and the government have no grudge against or hatred for them, perhaps on the plea that Armenians and Kurds are oppressed. The question is: are Palestinians, Kashmiris and Algerians not oppressed?

Co-existence and Co-operation

We are not hesitant in admitting that some Muslims were involved, and are involved, in activities which are contrary to the acknowledged and sacrosanct principles of the security of life and property of innocent people, and some of these activities might have been carried out with the abetting of governments. These Muslims are certainly oppressed, weak and wronged, some have been driven out of their own countries and, therefore, are homeless for about half a century, their youths are being killed, women molest and houses burnt. Some are under the subjugation of such rulers who depend on foreign support for the prolongation of their rule, who are guilty of perpetrating oppression as well as plundering the national wealth for their own luxury and for the pleasure of their Western masters. According to the Western philosophy of crime and punishment, all crimes of such people deserve to be declared as legitimate acts.

On the other hand we have no hesitation in saying that in the light of Islamic teachings their activities are anti-Islamic and they should refrain from indulging in them. These activities do not serve Islamic cause. Human life is so precious according to Islam that "murdering an innocent person is just like the massacre of the whole of humanity" (Surah al-Ma'idah). A Muslim is the one who protects others' life, property and honor through his deeds and speech (Sahih al-Bukhari). This applies equally to both Muslims and non-Muslims. Even if a polytheist (*mushrik*) asks for protection during Wartime, he has to be provided protection and led to his own place. (Surah al-Tauba). Killing of someone who is asking for peace and reconciliation is forbidden. Setting a prisoner free is desirable.

There is no room for beating him while tied up. Excesses against women, children, the old, the handicapped and the sick and burning of the crops and the factories is not allowed even during the times of war. We also do not believe in the argument that "your committing a crime sanctions our committing it". Though the activities of Muslims which the West considers as acts of terrorism are, in fact, nothing as compared with similar activities of the West itself, we, however, do not think such a comparison would be of much use here.

We just want to ask the US and the Western rulers, intellectuals and the media to stop the dangerous game of fanning hatred against Islam and the Muslim. The fire they are igniting may even wrap them. They have slyly branded Islam as fundamentalism (which is, in fact, a Christian term) and fundamentalism as terrorism (in other words, a triangle:

Islam-Fundamentalism-Terrorism). This slyness, however, is not going to do any good either to them or to the world at large. Incidents of poisonous nerve gas in Japanese trains, bomb blasts in World Trade Centre and Oklahoma should suffice to show the extent to which the oppressed and the dedicated to a cause can go. They may not necessarily be Muslims, however.

It is they who try to convince the world that Islam and Muslims are a real threat. In the policy paper of the state department (October, 1985), Robert Oakley writes: indigenous terrorism too is a serious problem. The FBI and the law enforcing agencies would not let it grow out of control [Oklahoma tragedy has exposed how capable they are!]. Real threat of large scale terrorism is, however, from abroad, especially from 'Moslem'. Out of 52 documentaries telecast by ABC Nightline in 40 months during 1985 -1988, 48 were focused on the Middle East. But when *Newsweek* reviews the incidents during seven days before the Oklahoma tragedy, it show Muslims' involvement in only three of the total 13 cases. As a result of fanning such hatred, the confrontation between West and Islam is getting worse and the hatred for America is spreading among Muslims. Now, this hatred is no more restricted only to the fundamentalists, it has encircled the most liberal and secular intellectuals, journalists and leaders.

Muslims can establish good relations with the West on the basis of mutual respect and tolerance. For this, the foremost priority of Muslims is that they have the right to lead their lives in accordance with Islamic teachings. If it is accepted, then well and good otherwise, Muslims will not hesitate even in laying down lives in the struggle for having this right. The Muslims living in the West would certainly be well-wishers of their countries and respect the laws in vogue there. Muslims' second priority would be to get rid of their despotic rulers who are Western agents and dance to the tune of their masters. They would regain their right to use their wealth and resources according to their own free will. They would follow their own model for development. This does not mean that they would necessarily work against Western interests. In today's world, economic and scientific progress is possible only through co-operation, but the West would have to end its policy of exploitation.

In this framework, if the West does not insist on keeping the Muslims under their political and economic domination the Islamic movements, the fundamentalists and ordinary Muslims can prove good friends of America and the West. They are not 'sworn enemies' of America.

We fear if America and the West insisted on their policy of enmity and hatred for Islam and the Muslims, they will achieve nothing except regrets. Mr. Robert Macknamara, the architect of the Vietnam War during Kennedy-Johnson regimes, has recently published his 'confession of guilt'. After paying the price of 60,000 American and 3,300,000 Vietnamese lives and billions of dollars, he says: alas! Our action was a mistake; a big mistake... the reason was that we were totally ignorant of the history, culture and the politics of those people. Lest some other Macknamara has to say the same after paying even more dearly, when opportunities are lost.

6

Terrorism and the Law of War

Trying Terrorists as War Criminals

OnNovember13, 2001, President Bush signed a Military Order pertaining to the detention, treatment, and trial of certain non-citizens as part of the war against terrorism. The order makes clear that the President views the crisis that began on the morning of September 11 as an attack "on a scale that has created a state of armed conflict that requires the use of the United States Armed Forces." The order finds that the effective conduct of military operations and prevention of military attacks make it necessary to detain certain non-citizens and if necessary, to try them "for violations of the laws of war and other applicable laws by military tribunals."

The September 11 attacks clearly violated numerous laws and may be prosecuted as criminal acts, as past terrorist acts have been prosecuted in the United States. The unprecedented nature of the September attacks and the magnitude of damage and loss of life they caused have led a number of officials and commentators to assert that the acts are not just criminal acts, they are "acts of war." The President's Order makes it apparent that he plans to treat the attacks as acts of war rather than criminal acts. The distinction may have more than rhetorical significance. Treating the attacks as violations of the international law of war could allow the United States to prosecute those responsible as war criminals, trying them by special military commission rather than in federal court.

The purpose of this report is to identify some of the legal and practical implications of treating the terrorist acts as war crimes and of applying the law of war rather than criminal statutes to prosecute the alleged perpetrators. The report will first present an outline of the sources and principles of the law of war, including a discussion of whether and how it might apply to the current terrorist crisis. A brief explanation of the background issues and arguments surrounding the use of military commissions will follow. The report will then explore the legal bases and implications of applying the law of war under United States law and precedent for its application by military commissions. The report will conclude with an analysis of the President's Military Order of November 13, 2001.

Some observers have expressed concern that treating terrorist acts as acts of war may legitimize the acts as a lawful use of force and elevate the status of the perpetrators and terrorist networks to that of legitimate state actors and lawful combatants. However, it may be argued that an application of the law of war to terrorism does not imply lawfulness of the conflict, nor does it imply that perpetrators are not criminals. Terrorists are not members of armed forces for the purpose of the law of war and do not, by definition, conduct themselves as lawful combatants. Under this view, those who participate directly in unlawful acts of war, including those with command influence, may be treated as war criminals and if captured, are not entitled to prisoner-of-war (POW) status under the Geneva Conventions. As suspected war criminals, they may be tried by any nation in its national courts or by a military commission convened by one nation or many.

Under the terms of the President's Military Order of November 13, the President has the option to order the trial of accused terrorists, whether captured overseas or on U.S. territory, by military commission. It is argued by some that it would be unworkable, for instance, to try Osama bin Laden in federal court under established rules of procedure and evidence. A public trial, some argue, could be used to the terrorists' advantage by allowing them to force the government to release sensitive information. A trial of suspected terrorists could also become an "international media circus," raising possible concerns for the safety of judge and jurors. Such a trial could be lengthy and subject to multiple appeals, during which a conviction could be overturned on a technicality. It might be impossible to empanel an impartial jury anywhere within the United States, some observers have argued.

Observers have expressed concern that invoking the law of war against terrorists in this instance could lead to the use of a similar approach to combat other societal ills upon which rhetorical "wars" might be declared. This tactic, they argue, could allow the government to establish military tribunals to try drug dealers, for example, without ordinary due process of law. Other opponents of using military commissions argue that secret trials could deny due process and that the resulting verdicts would lack legitimacy in the eyes of the international community. A review of legal precedents indicates that the authority of the Commander in Chief to try war criminals in occupied territory is well settled.

Similarly, there is substantial precedent for establishing military tribunals to try enemy belligerents who are charged with violating the law of war, especially individuals captured overseas. Determining who qualifies as an "enemy belligerent" for acts committed on U.S. territory, however, would likely present greater constitutional difficulties. The President's order appears to be broader than the authority cited by previous Presidents, and may cover aliens in the United States legally who are citizens of countries with which the nation is at peace. It may also be seen as conflicting with certain acts of Congress.

Ancillary Issues

The President's order raises some possible related considerations. For example, section 1(d) of the order finds that the United States' ability to protect itself and its citizens depends upon using the United States Armed Forces to "identify terrorists and those who support them, to disrupt their activities and to eliminate their ability to conduct or support such attacks." Does this finding authorize the military police to investigate certain crimes, possibly implicating the *Posse Comitatus* Act, which restricts use of the military to enforce civilian law? When civilian police are involved in terrorism investigations, must they follow the same standards that they apply to criminal cases? The use of military tribunals may also affect the United States' ability to extradite terrorist suspects captured abroad.

The order may also affect the rights and treatment of aliens. Because the current state of hostilities does not involve an enemy foreign state as such, the status of an alien as an "enemy alien" cannot be determined according to citizenship. The question may arise as to whether aliens subject to the order may be treated as enemy aliens, in which case the law of war may permit the irinternment but would also entitle them to the protections of the 1949 Geneva Convention IV. Under U.S. law, their detention may be authorisable only in accordance with the Enemy Alien Act.

Such an approach could also have an impact on available remedies for victims. Will there be any effect on the possible civil liability of terrorists to compensate victims? Would it matter if a particular victim was a government employee or some one located at a "military target" at the time of an attack? Will there be an effect on the liability of insurers? A decision to adopt a law of war approach to the terrorist acts currently at issue, or to future acts of international terror, could also have significant foreign policy repercussions.

Principles of the Law of War

As a subset of the law of nations, the law of war is a composite of many sources and is subject to varying interpretations constantly adjusting to address new technology and the changing nature of war. It may also be referred to as *jus in bello,* or law in war, which refers to the conduct of combatants in armed conflict, as distinguished from jus ad bellum – law before war – which outlines acceptable reasons for nations to engage in armed conflict. The rules overlap somewhat but remain conceptually separate due to the cardinal principle that *jus in bello* applies to both parties in a conflict, without regard to the lawfulness of the inception of the conflict. In other words, the party "at fault" retains the rights and responsibilities of the law of war, even if the armed conflict itself is unjustifiable under international law.

The law of war is also sometimes known as the "law of armed conflict" or "international humanitarian law" (IHL). The use of the terminology "armed conflict" reflects the applicability of the law to un-declared wars, in recognition of the reality that formal declarations of war may be largely a thing of the past. The term IHL is favored by some to emphasize the humanitarian purpose of the law, that is, to protect civilians to the extent possible in the event *jus ad bellum* fails to prevent an armed conflict.

Sources

Sources of the law of war include customary principles and rules of international law, international agreements, and judicial decisions by both national and international tribunals, national manuals of military law, scholarly treatises, and resolutions of various international bodies. Customary principles of international law apply universally. Treaties bind only those parties to them, unless they are seen to codify *jus cogens* principles, that is, have attained the common acceptance of nations. The other sources are generally treated not as binding sources of law, but rather as evidence that rules and principles have attained the common acceptance of nations to qualify as *jus cogens* norms.

The first attempt to codify the law of war is generally accepted to be the first Geneva Convention of 1864. The process continued with the Hague Conventions of 1899 and 1907 (also known as the "Law of The Hague") and when the Geneva Convention was revised and expanded into the four Geneva Conventions of 1949. The process has continued through the adoption of the additional protocols in 1977, and augmented with related treaties such as the Genocide Convention. The United States Army Field Manual (FM) 27-10, The Law of Land Warfare, codifies the Army's interpretation of the law of war, incorporating reference to relevant conventions and rules of the customary law of war, as well as relevant statutes.

Principles

The main thrust of the law of war requires that a military objective be pursued in such a way as to avoid needless and disproportionate suffering and damages. At the risk of oversimplifying the concept, three principles derived from the law of war may be applied to assess the legality of any use of force for political objectives.

Military Necessity

The use of force must be proportional in relation to the anticipated military advantage or as a measure of self-defense. The principle applies to the choice of targets, weapons and methods. This principle, however, does not apply to unlawful acts of war. There can be no excuse of necessity if the use of arms is not itself justified. In other words, military necessity can never be invoked to justify a breach of *jus ad bellum,* and it may not be invoked to justify a use of arms if there is no valid military advantage to be gained. However, responsibility for "collateral damage" to otherwise unlawful targets may sometimes be excused by military necessity.

Humanity

Lawful combatants are bound to use force discriminately. In other words, they must limit the retargets to valid military objectives and must use means no harsher than necessary to achieve that objective. They may not use methods designed to inflict needless suffering, and they may not target civilians. It is also unlawful to target facilities such as nuclear power plants, whose destruction would unleash even more destructive forces likely to cause unjustifiable civilian casualties and lasting environmental damage. However, there is an exception if the facilities are used to support "regular significant and direct military operations," especially if the facilities can be put out of production in such a way as to avoid unleashing disproportionately destructive forces.

Chivalry

Combatants must adhere to the law of armed conflict in order to be treated as lawful combatants. They must respect the rights of prisoners of war and captured civilians, and avoid behavior such as looting and pillaging. They may not conceal their arms and disguise themselves as non-combatants during battle or preparation for an attack. While a "ruse" may be permissible to maintain operational secrecy or obtain information about the enemy, "perfidy"– lulling the adversary into believing there is a situation under which the law of war provides protection – is not allowed. An example of perfidious conduct is the waving of a white flag to indicate surrender in order to ambush combatants. It is also forbidden to "kill or wound treacherously" enemy individuals.

Responsibility

The law of war had its origins when states were considered the only subjects of international law. Its original purpose was to define the rights and duties of states in wartime to facilitate the determination of the legal responsibility of states for their breaches. One of the more recent developments of the law of war is the notion of individual responsibility for conduct in war. Each soldier is bound to obey the law of war even if it means disobeying the direct order of a superior. Soldiers who obey unlawful orders are responsible for the violation along with whoever ordered it. Conversely, responsibility for war crimes may not be imposed upon groups of individuals based on an unlawful act committed by a member of the group. The notion of individual responsibility and justice through individual trials necessarily excludes the notion of collective guilt.

Protection of Civilians and Prisoners of War

Since the 1949 Geneva Conventions, the focus of the law of war has turned from rules of engagement to the protection of individuals. An individual's status as combatant or civilian is important for determining the forms of protection due under international law. Combatants are allowed to wage war but may also be attacked by the enemy. Civilians may not wage war, but unless and for so long as they directly participate in hostilities, may not lawfully be attacked.

POW

Members of the armed forces who fall into enemy hands during an armed conflict are protected by GC III and are treated as POWs. They may be interned under humane treatment as provided by the Convention, but they may not be punished unless convicted of a crime. If a POW is to be punished for a crime, he must first be convicted and sentenced by a court "according to the same procedure as in the case of members of the armed forces of the detaining Power." A POW may be confined awaiting trial for no longer than three months, and no trial can begin until three weeks after the detaining Power has notified the prisoner's representative and the protecting Power of the charges on which the prisoner is to be tried, where the prisoner is held, and where the trial will take place.

Civilians

Civilians who are citizens of a party to an armed conflict and fall into enemy hands either by residing as aliens in the territory of an opposing party or through capture by invading or occupying forces, are entitled to treatment in accordance with GC IV. They, too, may be interned if necessary but may not be punished unless convicted of a crime by a regular tribunal practicing the generally recognized principles of regular judicial procedure. Civilians who take direct part in the hostilities and fall into the hands of the adversary are treated as POWs until a competent tribunal determines that they engaged in unlawful combat. A captive may not be prosecuted for unlawful participation in hostilities unless such a determination has been made. Therefore, even in the case of unlawful belligerents, it would seem the law of war no longer permits trial by military tribunal without ordinary due process merely on the accusation that a person has engaged in unlawful combat.

Spies and Saboteurs

Spies and saboteurs do not receive the same protection. A spy is one who, in disguise or under false pretenses, penetrates into the zone of operations of a belligerent to obtain information with the intent of communicating that information to the hostile party. If captured, a spy may be tried and executed. However, if a spy rejoins the army of the hostile party as a lawful combatant, he is no longer a spy and is not subject to punishment for those acts if he later falls into the hands of the enemy. Sending spies behind enemy lines is legal under the law of war. Spies are not punished for criminal culpability so much as they are "deactivated" as a security measure. However, spies are entitled to a trial in accordance with the detaining power's applicable laws before they can be punished.

Saboteurs or enemy agents who penetrate into the territory of an adversary without openly bearing arms in order to perpetrate hostile acts are subject to similar treatment. However, such person is still a "protected person" for the purposes of the Geneva Conventions, and is entitled to a fair and regular trial as prescribed. It is unclear whether a saboteur retains the status of unlawful belligerent after rejoining the lawful forces or whether he becomes a lawful combatant, immune from punishment for the hostile acts. If sabotage is treated in a similar manner as spying during war, it may not be possible to characterize all "war criminals" as "unlawful belligerents" that are not entitled to treatment as POWs.

The Law of War Applied

The purpose of this section is to discuss the issues relative to whether the attacks of September 11 may be considered "acts of war" under international law, and if so, how those responsible might be treated under the law of war. The law of war may be applied only to acts that are part of an "armed conflict." A terrorist act is not seen to be an act of war unless it is part of a broader campaign of violence directed against the state. Where terrorist acts amount to no more than "situations of internal disturbances and tensions such as riots and isolated and sporadic acts of violence," the Hague and Geneva Conventions do not apply. Instead, peacetime domestic criminal laws and international conventions aimed at the repression of terrorism would come into play, obligating states parties to the agreements to try or extradite those believed responsible.

Armed Conflict

Because the terrorist organization allegedly behind the September attacks is not a state under international law and its members are not uniformed soldiers of any recognized army, there are conceptual difficulties in fitting their activities into the rubric of the international law of war. There are two recognized types of armed conflicts – international and internal. An international armed conflict involves two or more states, whereas an internal conflict involves a legitimate state engaged in conflict with an armed group that has attained international personality.

The nature of "internal conflicts" remains a matter of some controversy. While Additional Protocol I to the 1949 Geneva Conventions on the Protection of War Victims ("Protocol I") sought to extend coverage to non-international conflicts "in which peoples are fighting against colonial domination and alien occupation and against racist regimes in the exercise of their right to self-determination," it is not clear whether groups fighting for other causes were meant to be covered. At any rate, the United States did not ratify Protocol I, arguing that to recognize as combatants irregular groups – terrorists – would allow them to "enjoy many of the benefits of the law of war without fulfilling its duties, and with the confidence that the belligerent state has no real remedy under the Protocol to deal with this matter."

The use of force by private persons rather than organs of a state have not traditionally constituted "armed conflict." It has been suggested that the possible involvement of the governments of foreign states may make international terrorism an armed conflict for the purposes of the law of war. Some have maintained that state support of terrorism is a violation of international law. On the other hand, some jurists argue that states supporting the acts of third parties are not necessarily responsible for those acts merely by providing financial, political, or intelligence support. Only direct military support would qualify as an act of war under this view.

Viewing the situation pragmatically, it may not matter whether the initial attacks were perpetrated by state actors or a criminal enterprise. The existence of an armed conflict is effectively determined by the behavior of sovereign states. One international legal writer has concluded that a "state of generalized hostilities" accurately characterizes state practice regarding application of the law of war, raising the issue of the status of non-parties to the conflict as neutrals. Under this view, a factual determination of whether the fighting is persistent enough or of a sufficient magnitude to rise to the level of "armed conflict" in the view of the international community would suffice to settle the issue.

The present conflict does not fit squarely within the definitions of internal or international armed conflicts. The attacks on New York, Pennsylvania, and the Pentagon do not appear to have been part of an effort to take control of territory or install a new government, nor is it certain that they were carried out under the direction of another state. However, the sophisticated planning and execution believed necessary to have accomplished the attacks suggest that they were carried out by organized members of a quasi-military force. The political and ideological purpose ostensibly motivating the terrorist attacks arguably distinguishes them from "ordinary" criminal acts of violence. The magnitude of harm combined with the threat of more attacks appears to be considered sufficient to give rise to a right of self- defense, not only in the viewpoint of the United States, but by many other states and the United Nations. If the attacks are viewed as the opening volley to the United States' military response in Afghanistan, and the reactions of other nations are taken into account, an armed conflict in the "factual sense" could be said to exist.

The term "act of war" may be defined as "a measure of force which one party, using military instruments of power, implements against another party in an international armed conflict." Another definition is a "use of force or other action by one state against another" which "[t]he state acted against recognizes ... as an act of war, either by use of retaliatory force or a declaration of war." The September attacks were not "acts of war" in the traditional sense, because the perpetrators were not overtly acting on behalf of a state and because they did not employ conventional military weapons. However, the United States' reaction to the attacks is likely to be of greater significance than the technicalities for the purposes of applying the law of war.

Assuming the existence of an armed conflict, it is beyond question that the September attacks were part of it. Preparation for the attacks would also be covered, notwithstanding the fact that the hostilities had not yet technically begun. Recent cases of mail containing anthrax spores delivered to government representatives as well as civilians may also be "acts of war" If they were carried out as part of the same terrorist campaign. To label the attacks as "acts of war" does not imply that they are lawful. Although the principles of the law of war leave a great deal of room for interpretation, there can be little doubt, assuming such acts can be viewed as acts of war, that the attacks of September 11 were not conducted in accordance with the law of war. Even if one considers the Pentagon to be a valid military target, the hijacking of a commercial airliner is not a lawful means for attacking it. Acts of bioterrorism, too, violate the law of war, regardless of the nature of the target.

Assuming that the attacks may be considered acts of war, and that there is indeed an ongoing armed conflict, The Hague and Geneva Conventions come into play to determine the rights and responsibilities of participants, or "belligerents." Members of armed forces of a party to the conflict are classified as *combatants* unless they belong to a small class of members excluded from participation in combat, such as medical and religious personnel, who are designated as *non-combatants*. Other officials may under some circumstances attain combatant status if so designated by their state. All others are considered *civilians*, who are not ordinarily authorized to take part in hostilities. If captured, combatants are entitled to POW status and may not be criminally punished for acts of violence carried out lawfully in their role as combatants. Civilians who fall into enemy hands, however, may be punished as Criminals for participating in military hostilities, even if that conduct would have been legal for a combatant.

A member of an irregular or voluntary military is covered only if he is commanded by a person responsible for subordinates, he wears a fixed distinctive emblem recognizable at a distance, he carries arms openly, and he conducts operations in accordance with the laws and customs of war. Because terrorists do not follow these rules, they are not covered under the Geneva Convention as POWs. It should be noted that Protocol I art. 96 requires non-state belligerents, in order for their members to been titled to protected treatment under the Protocol, to file a declaration with the Swiss Government accepting the obligations of the Protocol.

If al Qaida can be viewed as an irregular army, then, no member of al Qaida would be entitled to POW treatment. On the other hand, if al Qaida is a political organization, only members who engage in war like activities are unlawful combatants. Other members, as well as civilians who give them aid that doesn't amount to direct participation in hostilities, do not lose their status as civilians. Members of al Qaida captured in Afghanistan may be entitled to POW or civilian status, depending upon the circumstances of their capture. If they are members of the armed forces, they must be treated as POWs, even if they are accused of previously violating the law of war or carrying out a terrorist act. GC III requires that a POW who is not accused individually of committing a crime be detained in accordance with appropriate guarantees of rights and humane treatment. POWs accused of a crime may be tried and imprisoned in the same manner that a member of the armed forces of the detaining power would be treated.

A civilian member of al Qaida captured in Afghanistan without having participated in the hostilities may be detained only in accordance with GC IV. If that individual is suspected of having committed a crime, he or she is entitled to a regular trial.

A civilian who has engaged in hostile or belligerent conduct is still a protected person, although one not entitled to POW treatment. A civilian captured within the United States who is "definitely suspected" of activities hostile to the national security, such as sabotage and espionage, is not entitled to claim such rights and privileges under GC IV that would be "prejudicial to the security of the state." However, such persons must nevertheless be treated with humanity and if subject to trial, "shall be granted the full rights and privileges of a protected person" under GC IV.

Legal Bases for Establishing Military Commission

United States law in corporate the international law of war. The United States adheres to the law of war through incorporation of the customary rules and treaty provisions into regulations of the armed forces. The Law of Land Warfare, FM 27-10 may be viewed as an embodiment of the United States Army's interpretation of the law of war on land. Although the manual is not considered binding upon courts and tribunals interpreting the law of war, those provisions of the manual that are neither statutes nor the text of treaties to which the United States is a party may be considered as evidence of the custom and practice of the law of war.

Military jurisdiction is recognized from two sources: "that branch of a country's municipal law which recognizes its military establishment" and "that which is derived from international law, including the law of war." The U.S. military exercises its jurisdiction through the use of courts-martial, military commissions, provost courts, and other military tribunals.

A military commission consists of a panel of military officers convened by military authority to try enemy belligerents on charges of a violation of the law of war. It is distinct from a military court martial, which is a panel set up to try U.S. service members (and sometimes civilians accompanying the armed forces) for violations of the Uniform Code of Military Justice. U.S. service members charged with a war crime may be tried before court martial or in federal court.

President Bush's order authorizing the use of military commissions for the trial of terrorists cites the President's authority under the Constitution as well as the laws of the United States, including the congressional authorization to use military force in response to the September 11 attacks, as well as 10 U.S.C. There is no express language in the Constitution and very little mention in the legislative authorities cited that clearly authorizes military tribunals; however, there is historical precedent that may form a basis for an interpretation of the authorities to support the order.

The Constitution

The Constitution empowers the Congress to declare war and "make rules concerning captures on land and water," to define and punish violations of the "Law of Nations," and to make regulations to govern the armed forces. The Constitution further empowers the Congress to make all laws "necessary and proper" for the execution of all powers under the Constitution. The Congress also has the power to regulate the jurisdiction of the courts and to establish such inferior tribunal as it deems necessary.

Generally, the power of the President to convene military commissions flows from his authority as Commander in Chief of the Armed Forces and his responsibility to execute the laws of the nation. Under the Articles of War and subsequent statute, the President has at least implicit authority to convene military commissions to try offenses against the law of war. Articles 18 and 21 of the UCMJ recognize the concurrent jurisdiction of military commissions to deal with "offenders or offenses designated by statute or the law of war." Statutory offenses for which a military commission may be convened include only aiding the enemy, 10 U.S.C., and spying, 10 U.S.C. Case law suggests that military commissions could try as enemy belligerents those accused of committing war crimes even if they hold U.S. citizenship. Recognized hostilities with foreign enemies may qualify to invoke the law of war even where no declared state of war exists. Congress has thus recognized the authority to convene military commissions, and has delegated to the President the authority to set their rules of procedure, both trial and post-trial.

Congress has not, however, provided a definition of the offenses under the law of war over which a military commission might exercise its jurisdiction, nor has it explicitly identified many statutory offenses for which the accused might be tried by military commission.

Precedent

Most of the United States' experience with military commissions relates to occupied territory or conditions of martial law. Although the current crisis does not fit the typical circumstances associated with war crimes committed by otherwise lawful combatants in obvious theaters of war, there is some precedent for convening military commissions to try enemy belligerents for conspiring to commit violations of the law of war outside of any recognized war zone.

War with Mexico

The use of military commissions by the United States dates back at least until the war with Mexico in the 1840's.

During the occupation of Mexico in 1847, General Winfield Scott convened "councils of war" to try Mexican citizens accused of violations of the law of war, such as committing guerrilla warfare or enticing American soldiers to desert. Despite the lack of statutory authority, General Scott relied on his own power under the law of war as the occupier of territory to issue the order.

Civil War Cases

In April 1863, Union Army General Order Number 100 declared that military commissions could prosecute "cases which do not come within the Rules and Articles of War, or the jurisdiction conferred by statute on courts-martial" by using the common law of war. Military commissions tried more than 2,000 cases during the war and reconstruction period. However, after the war, the courts limited the jurisdiction to areas occupied by United States forces and governed by martial law and limited the jurisdiction to genuine violations of the law of war. After the outbreak of the Civil War, Congress enacted the Act ofMarch3, 1863, relating to habeas corpus, and regulating judicial proceedings in certain cases authorizing the suspension of habeas corpus during the Rebellion.

The President issued the following proclamation:

That during the existing insurrection, and as a necessary means for suppressing the same, all rebels and insurgents, their aiders and abettors, within the United States, and all persons discouraging volunteer enlistments resisting militia drafts, or guilty of any disloyal practice, affording aid and comfort to rebels, against the authority of the United States, shall be subject to martial law, and liable to trial and punishment by courts martial or military commission. Second. That the writ of habeas corpus is suspended in respect to all persons arrested, or who now, or hereafter during the Rebellion shall be, imprisoned in any fort, camp, arsenal, military prison, or other place of confinement, by any military authority, or by the sentence of any court martial or military commission.

The government sought to prosecute members of a group called the Sons of Liberty, an organized group of conspirators operating in Indiana who had allegedly been hired by Confederate officials to destroy the North. The "Supreme Grand Commander of the Sons of Liberty" was convicted by a military commission and sought review by the Supreme Court, which held it had no constitutional or statutory authority to review military commissions.

However, his co-conspirator Lamdin P. Milligan, who was convicted and sentenced to death on charges of conspiracy against the government, giving aid and comfort to the enemy, inciting insurrection, disloyal practices, and violation of the law of war, was granted his petition to the Court for *habeas corpus*. The Supreme Court recognized military commission jurisdiction over violations of "laws and usages of war," but stated those laws and usages ".can never be applied to citizens in states which have upheld the authority of the government, and where the courts are open and their process unobstructed" The Supreme Court explained its reasoning:

It will be borne in mind that this is not a question of the power to proclaim martial law, when war exists in a community and the courts and civil authorities are overthrown. Nor is it a question what rule a military commander, at the head of his army, can impose on states in rebellion to cripple their resources and quell the insurrection. Martial law cannot arise from a threatened invasion. The necessity must be actual and present; the invasion real, such as effectively closes the courts and deposes the civil administration.

However, in 1865 the Attorney General found that co-conspirators charged in the assassination of President Lincoln could be tried by military commission, despite the fact that the courts were operating in Washington, D.C. His opinion emphasized the difference between "open and active participants" in war and "secret, but active participants" in violation of the law of war.

One of the men tried was Dr. Samuel Mudd, sentenced to life in prison for aiding and abetting after the fact the conspiracy by providing medical assistance, lodging, and horses to John Wilkes Booth and a co-conspirator. Dr. Mudd later received a full pardon for his work in battling yellow fever in the prison. His great-grandson filed an application with the Army Board for Correction of Military Records asserting his great-grandfather was innocent of the charges and that the military commission lacked jurisdiction to try a citizen of Maryland when the courts were fully functional. The Board recommended the conviction be set aside, but the Secretary of Defense denied the application. The United States District Court for the District of Columbia dismissed the appeal, finding that "if Dr. Samuel Mudd was charged with a law of war violation, it was permissible for him to be tried before a military commission even though he was a United States and Maryland citizen and the civilian courts were open at the time of the trial."

Other Conflicts

In 1864 the United States made a treaty with the Modoc Indians in which the tribe agreed to remain on a reservation in the State of Oregon. United States troops were subsequently sent out to cause them to return to the reservation after they had left it. A conflict ensued, and soon thereafter the Indians allegedly murdered several local citizens and their families. More fighting between the U.S. troops and the Modoc Indians broke out. The U.S. detachment sent forth several emissaries to negotiate a peaceable conclusion. During the negotiations, the Modocs "treacherously assassinated" two negotiators and severely wounded the third. Captain Jack, the leader of the Modoc tribe, was captured along with most of his tribe, and the military sought the Attorney General's opinion as to whether the accused might be tried by military tribunal. The Attorney General agreed that they should be tried by the military commission, although he found that :

It is difficult to define exactly the relations of the Indian tribes to the United States; but as they have been recognized as independent communities for treaty-making purposes, and as they frequently carry on organized and protected wars, they may properly, as it seems to me, be held subject to those rules of warfare which make a negotiation for peace after hostilities possible, and which make perfidy like that in question punishable by military authority.

World War I

President Wilson did not use military commissions during World War I to try individuals for war crimes committed within the territory of the United States. Military authorities sought to try Pable Waberski, a Russian national sent by the Germans to "blow things up in the United States," by military commission. Waberski was arrested upon crossing the border from Mexico into the United States and charged with "lurking as a spy" under article 82 of the Articles of War. The Attorney General opined in a letter to the President that the jurisdiction of the military was improper.

He had not entered any camp, fortification or other military premises of the United States. He had not, so far as appears, been in Europe during the war, so had not come through the fighting lines or field of military operations. Martial law had not been declared at Nogalesor there about snore any where in the United States and the regular federal civilian courts were functioning in that district and throughout the United States with at least their normal efficiency.

The Attorney General cited *Ex Parte Milligan* for the proposition that offenses committed outside of the field of military operations and by a person not a member of the military where regular civilian courts were functioning were not subject to the jurisdiction of a military tribunal. The Attorney General therefore found that the words "or elsewhere" in Article 82 of the Articles of War were not constitutional. The law of war, the opinion stated, defined a spy as [a] person who, without authority and secretly, or under a false pretext, contrives to enter within the lines of an army for the purpose of obtaining material information and communicating it to the enemy; or one who, being by authority within the lines, attempts secretly to accomplish such purpose.

According to the Attorney General, Waberski, therefore, was not a spy according to the laws of war and, if guilty of any criminal offense, was triable only by the regular civilian criminal courts. It seemed plain to the Attorney General that "Congress cannot constitutionally confer jurisdiction upon a military court to try and sentence any man not a member of the military forces and not subject to the jurisdiction of such court under the laws of war or martial law." He explained to the President:

> If he could constitutionally betrayed by court-martial, then it would logically follow that Congress could provide for the trial by military courts of any person, citizen or alien, accused of espionage or any other type of war crime, no matter where committed and no matter where such person be found and apprehended.

In 1920, Congress reenacted Article of War 15 with the addition of the wording "by statute or" before the words "by the law of war." The words "or elsewhere" remain in article 106 of the UCMJ.

World War II

The post-World War II response to war crimes included both national and international military tribunals. While the Nuremberg war crimes tribunal was the most visible venue in the European theater, the number of national military tribunals far exceeded the number of trials conducted in the international tribunals. The Supreme Court confirmed the authority of the President, under his power as Commander in Chief of the Armed Forces and as delegated to him by Congress to try accused war criminals in occupied territories even though hostilities had ceased. The Supreme Court granted *habeas corpus* review to General Tomoyuki Yamashita, who had been sentenced by military commission to be hanged for atrocities committed by troops under his command. However, the Court declined to review the merits of the case or the sufficiency of evidence.

Yamashita argued, among other things, that no charge was stated against him under the law of war, because the military command did not allege that Yamashita committed or ordered the offenses of his troops against the civilian population in the Philippines that formed the basis for the charges. The Supreme Court disagreed, noting he had been properly charged for his breach of duty by failing to control the operations of the members of his command, permitting them to commit the specified atrocities. General Yamashita also argued that he was entitled to a trial using the same procedures as would be applied in courts martial, according to article 63 of the GenevaConventionof1929. The Supreme Court interpreted article 63 as applying only to offenses committed during captivity, 152 and therefore declined to examine the procedural rules applied by the military commission.

Less established was the authority to try enemy saboteurs caught within the territory of the United States during war. After eight Nazi saboteurs were caught by the Coast Guard, the President issued a proclamation that all such enemy saboteurs would betrayed by military commission. The eight German saboteurs (one of whom was purportedly a U.S. citizen) were tried by military commission for entering the United States by submarine, shedding their military uniforms, and conspiring to use explosives on unknown targets. In the case of *Ex Parte Quirin,* the Supreme Court denied their writs of *habeas corpus,* holding that trial by such a commission did not offend the Constitution and was authorized by statute.

Despite the fact that the civil courts were open and functioning normally, the Court held that the charge made out a valid allegation of an offense against the law of war for which the President was authorized to order trial by a military commission. The Court also distinguished *Milligan,* noting that he had not been a part of or associated with the armed forces of the enemy, and therefore was a non-belligerent, not subject to the law of war. The Court did not explain where it would draw the line:

We have no occasion now to define with meticulous care the ultimate boundaries of the jurisdiction of military tribunals to try persons according to the law of war. It is enough that petitioners here, upon the conceded facts, were plainly within those boundaries, and were held in good faith for trial by military commission, charged with being enemies who, with the purpose of destroying war materials and utilities, entered, or after entry remained in, our territory without uniform – an offense against the law of war. We hold only that those particular acts constitute an offense against the law of war which the Constitution authorizes to be tried by military commission.

The Court declined to apply the language of the Articles of War to determine whether the procedures comported with the statute, but the Justices were unable to agree whether Congress had not meant to apply the Articles of War to military commissions or whether the Articles could be interpreted to support the procedures used. In 1945, President Roosevelt issued a new military order establishing rules for convening military commissions to try enemy saboteurs, in which he clarified the applicability of some of the Articles of War. There was no occasion to test the new order, however. When Congress incorporated the Articles of War into the UCMJ in 1950, it included Article of War 15, "Jurisdiction of courts martial not exclusive", as Article 21 of the UCMJ to "preserve existing Army and Air Force law which gives concurrent jurisdiction to [other] military tribunals...".

Other Rulings on Military Courts

The Supreme Court has issued several more recent opinions limiting the authority of military courts-martial to persons reached pursuant to constitutional powers to regulate the armed forces. The Court held that an honorably discharged former soldier could not be tried by court martial for a crime he allegedly committed while stationed overseas. The Court also set aside the military conviction of a civilian dependant of a service member stationed overseas for a capital crime, at least during time of peace when the United States was not occupying the country in which the crime took place. The Court extended that ruling to civilian dependants overseas charged with non-capital crimes, voiding the conviction by court martial of a military wife charged with involuntary manslaughter.

The Court later ruled that civilian employees could not be tried by court martial, even for crimes committed overseas. While these more recent cases seem to demonstrate a trend toward limiting the jurisdiction of military courts martial, they may have little bearing on the jurisdiction of military commissions to try enemy belligerents under the constitutional war powers. The validity of any military commissions that might be convened pursuant to the President's Military Order of November 13, 2001, therefore, will likely depend in large part on whether the defendants are legitimately classified as "enemy belligerents" and "unlawful combatants," or whether they are merely alien civilians.

Analysis of President's Military Order

The Military Order issued by President Bush, and the circumstances under which it was issued, differ substantially from the World War II precedent used in *Quirin*. Perhaps the most obvious difference is that war had been formally declared by Congress against foreign states. It should be remembered that the law of war has undergone significant changes since the *Quirin* case was decided, most notably with the 1949 Geneva Conventions. While the importance of a formal declaration of war has faded since World War II, the law regarding the treatment of enemy civilians and combatants has progressed significantly.

Wartime Basis

President Roosevelt issued Proclamation 2561 under the caption "Denying Certain Enemies Access to the Courts of the United States" on July 2, 1942, after the capture of the eight Nazi saboteurs. On that same day, the President issued a Military Order appointing a commission of seven general officers to try the named defendants for "offenses against the law of war and the Articles of War." The order cited the President's authority as President and Commander in Chief, the Constitution and statutes of the United States, and specifically Article of War 38.

Proclamation 2561 does not mention Congress' declaration of war against Germany. The findings state simply that the safety of the United States demands that all enemies who enter U.S. territory "as part of an invasion or predatory incursion" or have entered "to commit sabotage espionage or other hostile or war like act" should be promptly tried in accordance with the law of war. The "invasion" language appears to be borrowed from the Alien Enemy Act, which states that during declared war between the United States and any foreign nation or government, or when an invasion is perpetrated by any foreign nation or government, and the President makes a proclamation of the event, the President may "direct the conduct to be observed, on the part of the United States toward the aliens who become liable [as alien enemies"]. The use of this language suggests that Proclamation 2561 might have been intended as a proclamation pursuant the Alien Enemy Act. On the other hand, a review of contemporaneous Presidential proclamations shows that President Roosevelt ordinarily cited specific statutory authority to support actions taken.

President Bush's Military Order of November 13 relies in large part on the congressional authorization to use force, which gives the President the authority to use all necessary and appropriate force against those nations, organizations, or persons he determines planned, authorized, committed, or aided the terrorist attacks that occurred on September 11, 2001, or harbored such organizations or persons, in order to prevent any future acts of international terrorism against the United States by such nations, organizations or persons.

The resolution does not address military tribunals explicitly, but could be interpreted as a broad authorization to exercise the President's power as Commander in Chief of the Armed Forces to prosecute an armed conflict. The Congress stopped short of declaring war, which would have automatically triggered a number of statutes, 172 including the Alien Enemy Act. The President could invoke the Act by proclamation without a declaration of war if "a predatory incursion" has been perpetrated by a hostile nation. Since the current armed conflict does not involve a hostile state as such, the Act is probably not applicable nor very practical, since it would only allow the President to direct the treatment of "natives, citizens, denizens or subjects" of the hostile state.

Jurisdiction

While the 1942 proclamation defined the acts subject to prosecution by military tribunal, the new order defines a class of non-citizens whose members are subject to military trial upon the President's determination. The President must first determine that the person is or ever has been associated with terrorist acts or organizations, and that it is in the interest of national security to subject that person to the order. The President has complete discretion once those determinations are made. Alien terrorists and violators of the law of war might not be subject to the order; citizen terrorists and war criminals are never subject to the order.

Proclamation 2561 pertained to "subjects, citizens or residents of any nation at war with the United States or who give obedience to or act under the direction of any such nation" who are accused of certain offenses. Thus, U.S. citizens who acted as enemy agents were covered by the proclamation. However, violators of the law of war outside the territory of the United States, or those who entered the United States lawfully, fell outside the language of the Proclamation.

The M.O. of November 13 applies only to non-citizens. It should be noted that aliens, even those lawfully admitted to the country, do not necessarily enjoy the same constitutional rights as citizens with regard to freedom from unreasonable seizures of their persons. During time of war, aliens who are citizens of hostile nations may be summarily detained and deported, and their property may be confiscated under the Alien Enemy Act. They may also be denied access to the courts of the United States if they would use the courts to the advantage of the enemy or to impede the U.S. prosecution of a war.

Even during times of peace, nonimmigrant aliens may be subjected to different treatment based on their nationality. In deportation proceedings, deportable aliens probably have no constitutional right protecting them from selective deportation and the First Amendment does not provide protection against removal based on association.

Aliens who have entered the country and established a connection to it, however, are protected by the Constitution, though their rights may differ from those of citizens. In criminal proceedings, such aliens receive full due process under the Constitution. Whether certain non-enemy aliens may be subjected to criminal punishment or detained indefinitely for their suspected association with terrorist groups is uncertain.

Offenses Triable by Military Commission

Military commissions trying enemy belligerents for war crimes apply directly the international law of war, without recourse to domestic criminal statutes unless such statutes are declaratory of international law. Proclamation 2561 limited the predicate offenses to entering the United States surreptitiously during war and "committing or attempting or preparing to commit sabotage, espionage, hostile or warlike acts, or violations of the law of war." The proclamation did not contain any definitions of the offenses. The eight saboteurs were charged with violations of the law of war and articles 81 and 82 of the Articles of War, as well as conspiracy to commit the foregoing. Therefore, the possibility that the language "hostile or warlike acts" was meant to include offenses that were not already included in the term "violation of the law of war," possibly causing the proclamation to exceed the statutory limit on jurisdiction, was not addressed.

President Bush's M.O. is ambiguous as to which offenses may be tried by military commissions. While the President's authority to try as saboteurs those responsible for the September11 attacks appears to be supported by precedent, the M.O. could be construed as a grant of authority to detain and perhaps try persons not suspected of direct participation or complicity in those attacks. The order allows the President to subject a non-citizen to trial by military tribunal if he determines that person is or was a member of al Qaida or committed, participated, aided and abetted, or conspired in any terrorist act, even those unrelated to al Qaida's campaign of terror against the United States. The order appears to apply to any act of terrorism during the "relevant time" and anywhere in the world, so long as damage or injury to United States persons was intended or caused. The order may also include persons who are protected under the Geneva Conventions and are entitled to due process in accordance with international law. A court could construe the order as incorporating those standards in order to avoid conflict with U.S. treaty obligations.

Section 4 of the order provides that "[a]ny individual subject to this order shall, when tried, be tried by military commission for any and all offenses triable by military commission...." (Emphasis added). This language could be construed as impliedly limiting the offenses to those validly tri able by military commission pursuant to 10 U.S.C. under the relevant circumstances, which would sharply narrow the scope of the order. Such an interpretation would lead to the conclusion that the language in section 2 confines the offenses triable to only those war crimes that are committed by non-citizens who fit the definition in section 2. In other words, the offenses in section 2 are not necessarily the offenses for which the defendant will be tried, but rather, are to be used by the President to determine whether an individual may be subject the order. Violations of the law of war by others could still be tried by military commission, but such a commission need not comply with the M.O. of November 13.

If the order is interpreted to be consistent with the congressional authorization for the use of force and 10 U.S.C. 821, incorporating by reference the law of war, the order would not permit the trial of individuals for terrorist acts unless the acts occurred as part of the present armed conflict (including preparation therefore) and they are violations of the law of war. Therefore, the language "at the relevant time" in Section 2(a)(1) should probably be construed to mean during and related to the present armed conflict with terrorist forces emanating from Afghanistan.

Authority to Detain

The President's order could be construed to authorize detention of persons for violations of statutes not expressly triable by military commission, based solely on a determination that the accused belongs to the class of persons subject to the order. Some language in the order could be construed to authorize detention of such persons even though they are not charged with any crime at all.

The authority to detain suspected war criminals is arguably implicit in the power to authorize their trial by military commission. Unless the authority is an inherent power of the Executive, it must flow either from statute or from the law of war. Although the language of the order could be construed to allow the indefinite detention of persons subject to the order without any charge, an interpretation that incorporates the authority it cites would lead to a different conclusion. The order could not consistently with 10 U.S.C. 821 authorize detention of persons who are neither unlawful combatants accused of violating the law of war nor persons accused of violating 10 U.S.C. 906.

The law of war does not permit punishment of enemy civilians, non-combatants, or combatants (even unlawful ones) for crimes for which they bear no individual responsibility. Therefore, their detention is likewise not authorized except as provided for by statute or convention. It might be argued that Congress implicitly allows the President to detain non-citizens without explicit statutory authority, because the President is expressly prohibited by statute from detaining citizens except in accordance with statute. However, in this case such an argument may be less persuasive because Congress, in enacting the USA

PATRIOT Act, placed express limits on the authority of the President to detain aliens for national security purposes. It is arguably insufficient for the President to issue a determination that an alien is subject to the order, unless the determination also contains an allegation that the detainee has committed a violation of the law of war. The interpretation of international law regarding responsibility for the acts of others through indirect participation may be necessary to justify detention of any alien suspected of conspiring with or aiding terrorists in ways that fall short of violating the law of war as an unlawful belligerent.

Jurisdiction of Other Courts

A featureof the November 13 M.O. not apparent in the Proclamation or Military Orders issued by President Roosevelt is language that appears to divest the federal and state courts of jurisdiction over any offense committed by a person subject to the order. Indeed, the order appears to strip the jurisdiction of foreign courts and international tribunals to hear appeals, even indirect appeals, of persons detained or convicted under the order.

To the extent that the order would affect the jurisdiction of state and federal courts over crimes, especially those not triable by military tribunal under statute or the common law of war, it may be judged to be overbroad. Congress' acknowledgment of concurrent jurisdiction over certain crimes to courts martial and military commissions does not imply that the President has the power to create exclusive jurisdiction in the military tribunals for offenses that might by statute be tried in another court.

The President would not seem to have the constitutional authority to regulate the jurisdiction of courts or convene inferior tribunals unless so authorized by act of Congress. Article 21 of the UCMJ recognizes the military commissions' jurisdiction to try only "offenders or offenses that by statute or by the law of war may be tried by military commissions, provost courts, or other military tribunals." Therefore, references to "offenses" and "crimes" in the order most likely must be understood to refer to "offenses against the law of war" and "war crimes," or to those offenses mentioned expressly by statute as triable by military commission.

Review and Appeal

Like FDR's Proclamation, the Bush M.O. directs that "individuals prosecuted by military tribunal shall not be privileged to seek any remedy or maintain any proceeding, directly or indirectly, or to have any such remedy or proceeding sought on the individual's behalf." The government argued unsuccessfully in the *Quirin* case that this language deprived the Court of its opportunity to afford the petitioners a hearing. In light of that decision, the order will not likely be interpreted to deprive persons of their right to seek *habeas corpus* relief in federal court, if they would ordinarily have such rights. It is unclear what avenue of redress other than a petition to file a writ of *habeas corpus* the order is meant to block.

If a court agrees to hear a petitioner's *habeas corpus* challenge to a conviction by military commission, it will not likely order the prisoner released or set aside the verdict "without the clear conviction that [the detention and trial] are in conflict with the Constitution or laws of Congress constitutionally enacted." Such a hearing would not inquire into the guilt or innocence of the prisoner, or question the decision of the tribunal, but only whether the tribunal was lawfully convened to hear the case.

The Bush M.O. also denies persons subjected to it the privilege of seeking any remedy in foreign courts or international tribunals. While the language would have no internationally recognized effect on the jurisdiction of foreign courts or international tribunals, it could be interpreted to revoke rights detainees would have under international law, including treaties to which the United States is a party. For example, a detainee claiming POW status has the right under GC III to protest perceived violations of his rights to the Detaining Power, the Protecting Power, and to humanitarian organization.

This right may not be denounced by the POW, nor may it be revoked or unnecessarily limited by the Detaining Power. A court or federal agency may interpret the language of the order as an indication that the President wishes to super cede parts of the Geneva Conventions, possibly binding the courts and federal agencies to disregard decisions of an international tribunal or efforts to intervene on the prisoner's behalf by his state of nationality or an international humanitarian organization.

The Military Commission Statutes

The Supreme Court has construed the UCMJ as broadly delegating power to the President. This authority may be further delegated to a field commander or any other commander with the power to convene a general court-martial. Statutes authorize prosecuting persons for failure to appear as witness, punishing contempt, and accepting into evidence certain depositions and records of courts of inquiry. The proceeding is exempt from statutory requirements in other court proceedings for a speedy trial. The rules pertaining to release and detention pending certain judicial proceedings likewise do not apply. Military commissions are also excluded from the definition of "agency" in title 5, which exempts them from, among other things, responding to requests for information under the Freedom of Information Act and challenges under the Administrative Procedures Act.

While the President may set the rules of procedure and evidence for military tribunals and need only apply "the principles of law and the rules of evidence generally recognized in the trial of criminal cases in the United States district court" where he considers it practicable to do so, he may not apply rules contrary to or inconsistent with the UCMJ. Where Congress has included military commissions in parts of the UCMJ regulating courts martial, the President may not apply a contrary rule. The taking and use of depositions, for example, must adhere to the provisions of Article 49 of the UCMJ.

Procedural Rules

As a non-Article III court, a military commission would not be subject to the same constitutional requirements that apply to Article III courts. Defendants properly before a military commission, like defendants before a court-martial, would likely have no right to demand a jury trial before a court established in accordance with rules governing the judiciary. There is no right of indictment or presentment under the Fifth Amendment, and there may be no protection against self-incrimination or right to counsel. While Congress has enacted procedures applicable to courts-martial that ensure basic due process rights, no such statutory procedures exist to define due process rights for defendants before military commissions. Procedural rules and evidentiary rules are prescribed by the President and may differ among commissions. Courts-martial are conducted using the Military Rules Subject to the statutory provisions above, the President may establish any rules of procedure and evidence he deems appropriate.

Search for an International Standard

Although there may be little judicial review available to persons convicted by U.S. military commissions, it would seem necessary to provide for trials that will be seen as fundamentally fair under both U.S. and international standards regarding the application of the law of war. Telford Taylor noted in evaluating World War II war crimes trials:

It is of the first importance that the task of planning and developing permanent judicial machinery for the interpretation and application of international penal law be tackled immediately and effectively. The war crimes trials, at least in Western Europe, have been held on the basis that the law applied and enforced in these trials is international law of general application which everyone in the world is generally bound to observe. On no other basis can the trials be regarded as judicial proceedings, as distinguished from political inquisitions.

There is some historical precedent from which an international norm regarding procedural rights for accused war criminals might be derived. The Nuremberg Tribunals provide a good starting point, as further refined by the International Criminal Tribunals for Yugoslavia and Rwanda. Perhaps the most recent embodiment of the requirements of the international law of war is to be found in the procedures of the not-yet-operational International Criminal Court established by the Rome Statute.

The evidentiary rules used at Nuremberg and adopted by the Tokyo tribunals were designed to be non-technical, allowing the expeditious admission of "all evidence [the Tribunal] deems to have probative value." This evidence included hearsay, coerced confessions, and the findings of prior mass trials. While the historical consensus seems to have accepted that the war crimes commissions were conducted fairly, some observers argue that the malleability of the rules of procedure and evidence could and did have some unjust results.

Protocol I to the Geneva Convention provides, in article 75, a list of basic guarantees that may be viewed as a baseline for an international standard of due process:

Article 75.-Fundamental guarantees 1.

1. In so far as they are affected by a situation referred to in Article 1 of this Protocol, persons who are in the power of a Party to the conflict and who do not benefit from more favorable treatment under the Conventions or under this Protocol shall be treated humanely in all

circumstances and shall enjoy, as a minimum, the protection provided by this Article without any adverse distinction based upon race, color, sex, language, religion or belief, political or other opinion, national or social origin,wealth, birth or other status, or on any other similar criteria. Each Party shall respect the person, honor, convictions and religious practices of all such persons.

2. The following acts are and shall remain prohibited at any time and in any place whatsoever, whether committed by civilian or by military agents:

a. Violence to the life, health, or physical or mental well-being of persons, in particular:
   (i) Murder;
   (ii) Torture of all kinds, whether physical or mental;
   (iii) Corporal punishment; and
   (iv) Mutilation.

b. Outrages upon personal dignity, in particular humiliating and degrading treatment, enforced prostitution and any form of indecent assault;

c. The taking of hostages;

d. Collective punishments; and

e. Threats to commit any of the foregoing acts.

3. Any person arrested, detained or interned for actions related to the armed conflict shall be informed promptly, in a language he understands, of the reasons why these measures have been taken. Except in cases of arrest or detention for penal offences, such persons shall be released with the minimum delay possible and in any event as soon as the circumstances justifying the arrest, detention or internment have ceased to exist.

4. No sentence may be passed and no penalty may be executed on a person found guilty of a penal offence

related to the armed conflict except pursuant to a conviction pronounced by an impartial and regularly constituted court respecting the generally recognized principles of regular judicial procedure, which include the following:

a. The procedure shall provide for an accused to be informed without delay of the particulars of the offence alleged against him and shall afford the accused before and during his trial all necessary rights and means of defense;
b. No one shall be convicted of an offense except on the basis of individual penal responsibility;
c. No one shall be accused or convicted of a criminal offence on account of any act or omission which did not constitute a criminal offence under the national or international law to which he was subject at the time when it was committed; nor shall a heavier penalty be imposed than that which was applicable at the time when the criminal offence was committed; if, after the commission of the offence, provision is made by law for the imposition of a lighter penalty, the offender shall benefit thereby;
d. Anyone charged with an offense is presumed innocent until proved guilty according to law;
e. Anyone charged with an offense shall have the right to be tried in his presence;
f. No one shall be compelled to testify against himself or to confess guilt;
g. Anyone charged with an offence shall have the right to examine, or have examined, the witnesses against him and to obtain the attendance and examination of witnesses on his behalf under the same conditions as witnesses against him;
h. No one shall be prosecuted or punished by the same Party for an offence in respect of which a final judgement acquitting or convicting that person has

been previously pronounced under the same law and judicial procedure;

i. Anyone prosecuted for an offence shall have the right to have the judgement pronounced publicly; and

j. A convicted person shall be advised on conviction of his judicial and other remedies and of the time-limits within which they may be exercised.

5. Women whose liberty has been restricted for reasons related to the armed conflict shall be held in quarters separated from men's quarters. They shall be under the immediate supervision of women. Nevertheless, in cases where families are detained or interned, they shall, whenever possible, be held in the same place and accommodated as family units.

6. Persons who are arrested, detained or interned for reasons related to the armed conflict shall enjoy the protection provided by this Article until their final release, repatriation or re-establishment, even after the end of the armed conflict.

7. In order to avoid any doubt concerning the prosecution and trial of persons accused of war crimes or crimes against humanity, the following principles shall apply:

a. Persons who are accused of such crimes should be submitted for the purpose of prosecution and trial in accordance with the applicable rules of international law; and

b. Any such persons who do not benefit from more favorable treatment under the Conventions or this Protocol shall be accorded the treatment provided by this Article, whether or not the crimes of which they are accused constitute grave breaches of the Conventions or of this Protocol.

8. No provision of this Article may be construed as limiting or infringing any other more favorable provision granting greater protection, under any

applicable rules of international law, to persons covered by paragraph 1.

7

Competing Approaches to Fighting Terrorist

The three papers in this collection of readings resulted from a conference entitled "Beyond the U.S. War on Terrorism: Comparing Domestic Legal Remedies to an International Dilemma." The conference was sponsored by the John Bassett Moore Society of International Law, University of Virginia School of Law, in cooperation with the Strategic Studies Institute, U.S. Army War College, and was held on February 25-26, 2005. Over 160 people participated in the conference conducted at The University of Virginia. Conference participants included representatives from government agencies involved in the U.S. war on terrorism, students and faculty members from other universities participating in fields related to the topic of the conference, and members of the local community and the University of Virginia.

The conference program was designed to discuss international legal remedies to terrorism in terms of:

1. The importance of definitions for war and terrorism,
2. The evolution of U.S. political and legal responses to terrorism,
3. The long and rich European experience,
4. The lessons from Latin America about terrorism and the dangers of oppressive reactions,

5. The Islamic world's role in and reaction to terrorism, and
6. The relationship between terrorism and the law of the battlefield. A panel, with members drawn from diverse backgrounds, was dedicated to each of these six topics. Key insights from the conference are:
   1. Competing definitions of terrorism and war yield different diplomatic, legal, and military consequences. The definition a policymaker chooses is a key consideration.
   2. The United States defined the September 11, 2001, attacks as acts of war rather than crimes outside a war context. The resulting response was due in part to a lack of legal flexibility in U.S. law, not understanding the power imbedded in criminal categorization, and reliance on structural changes for solutions.
   3. European countries have a long history of individually and collectively responding to terrorism through their legal systems, and the United States could profit from examining those responses.
   4. Latin America has a long history of contending with terrorism in a context of guerrilla warfare.
   5. Strategists and policymakers often incorrectly view the Islamic world as homogeneous and unchanging in its relationship to the West and to terrorism.
   6. Policy formulation could benefit from the many historical examples, some in U.S. history, of problems associated with applying laws of war to insurgencies and other irregular warfare.
7. The United States should avoid:
   1. Limiting it by adopting overly simple definitions;

2. Characterizing offending groups by a tactic used and forgetting they have many other dimensions;
3. One-dimensional reactions to attacks; and,
4. Underestimating the value of legal solutions to international problems.

The three papers herein represent presentations addressing the first three conference themes and reinforce all the key insights except 4, 5, and 6. In the first paper, Mr. Paul Pillar clearly articulates issues associated with basic concepts of terrorism and why definitions have diplomatic, legal, and military consequences. He cautions us to remain aware that the American perspectives about terrorism, and those of our friends, are the products of our particular cultures and histories. While we should learn from others' experiences, we must avoid their perceptual traps as readily as our own. Mr. Pillar concludes by wisely pointing to the shared goals of international law and counterterrorism operations to minimize human suffering, even in situations where the likelihood of suffering is increased, such as war. If we can keep that goal in mind, our motivation to save innocent people from future terrorism is more likely to outweigh revenge, expanding influence, and other less noble motivations.

In the second paper, Mr. Michael German illustrates why he believes the U.S. reaction to terrorism is not just inadequate, but rather, by being incorrect, our strategy compounds the problem. By defining activity as terrorist warfare rather than criminal behavior, we enhance perpetrators' status and provide them the legitimacy that they seek. The author's experience as an undercover Federal Bureau of Investigation agent has given him valuable insights into terrorists' desire for legitimacy among their supporters, sympathizers, and others who have potential to become part of those two groups. He discusses how these groups develop strategies to create overreaction by authorities and to avoid their most feared outcome, being labeled as mere criminal gangs.

He likewise discusses the patterns of governmental overreaction that must be avoided if the government's legitimacy is to be preserved; fortunately, the U.S. Constitution provides an effective structure to avoid overreaction by guaranteeing individual rights and requiring open-source and transparent methods for criminal prosecution. Secrecy and increased governmental power is not the solution. He convincingly argues that his conclusions about domestic terrorists are applicable to their international counterparts and that the legalistic approach that has proven effective within the United States would be equally effective internationally. Finally, Dr. Shawn Boyne discusses Germany's recognition of the Islamic terrorist threat, but rejection of the metaphor of war in favor of its constitutional law framework. That commitment provides for the same civil liberty protections for all acts, whether or not committed by citizens and without regard for motivation.

She convincingly argues that the German approach is a consequence of its relatively long and active history of dealing with domestic terrorism and more recent internal debates. Germany decided, in contrast to the United States, not to view the September 11, 2001, attacks as the beginning of a war, but through the lens of German and international law. Germany's response was not to create new law, but to strengthen resources to investigate and enforce existing laws. Logically, its military forces were provided specifically for Afghanistan, mostly in non-combat roles, and not for the general war on terrorism. Germany's legalistic stance was not sufficient to avoid making difficult choices about the balance between internal security and civil liberties and may mean that democracies must remain vigilant in protecting human rights, no matter which tactics they choose to fight terrorism. At a minimum, the United States should view the German solution as an alternative to its own and compare its relative effectiveness for security and potential costs in civil liberties for its citizens.

Perceptions of Terrorism

Of the two sponsorships of this event, most Americans immersed in the vocabulary of what is commonly called a "war on terrorism" probably would find the military one easier to understand. The role of international law is more likely to elude their understanding. But international law speaks directly to the core of what international terrorism is all about. Indeed, one way in which terrorism can be defined is as a violation of international law, and in particular of the laws of war. Think about what terrorist's do what behavior makes them terrorists. They commit or threaten violence against innocent noncombatants, including civilians who have no connection with an armed force and are not themselves engaged in warfare. That is a key defining behavior, one that all terrorists share.

And in addition, many terrorists commit such specific acts as taking civilians as hostages, committing reprisals against civilians or their own prisoners, abusing their prisoners up to and including murdering them, disregarding any concept of neutral territory and inflicting suffering on the citizens of neutral countries, and violating what is supposed to be the inviolability of embassies, diplomats, and other accredited representatives. All of these violate the laws of war as codified in The Hague and Geneva Conventions negotiated during the 19th and 20th centuries. This observation alone suggests that a great deal of value exists in viewing international terrorism through a legal lens.

It also suggests that there is a significant role for international cooperation, including cooperation that, like the conventions on the laws of war, center on certain legal concepts. And one could make many other points that would lead to the same conclusions. I am not going to posit prescriptions for a counterterrorist strategy, however.

Instead, I will offer a few observations about how we Americans tend to think about terrorism and counterterrorism, and also how some non-Americans tend to think about it. I make these observations in the spirit of what this symposium is about, and in the hope that some additional introspection about our own thought processes and what shapes them will sharpen our skills in self-criticism and enable us to combine the best of our own thinking and that of our foreign friends.

The first observation is that the perception that most Americans have of the terrorist threat they face, and of how it has waxed or waned, is not the same as how the actual terrorist threat has waxed or waned. The national mood regarding this topic needs to be clearly distinguished from the objective reality. This is important in thinking about what the September 11, 2001 (9/11) attack meant to the United States, and to counterterrorism, and what changes it did and did not mark. For 31/2 years now, it has been common currency in public discussion in this country to say that that particular terrorist attack was one of the biggest epoch-defining discontinuities in American history. We speak of a "sea change" and a "new era" and how things will never be the same again. And there is no question that in terms of the public's mood and response, and the policy response, it *was* a huge discontinuity certainly in terms of counterterrorism, but also in terms of many other matters related to the suddenly and dramatically increased American preoccupation with terrorism.

For the American public, the danger from international terrorism seemed much, much higher on September 12, 2001, than it had on September 10. But the actual terrorist threat to this country did not suddenly increase. In one sense, one might say that the threat remembering that "threat" means the prospect or possibility of *future* harm had actually gone down, because the long-planned 9/11 operation, once it was carried out, became part of our past and no longer was in our future. The threat of jihadist Islamist extremists a broad and diffuse movement of which bin Ladin and al Qaida were to become the most infamous part, but only a part had been present for some time, and certainly for most of the 1990s. Think about the first Islamist terrorist attack on the World Trade Center, the one that occurred 12 years ago.

The objective of Ramzi Yousef, the leader of that attack, and his fellow conspirators was nothing less than to topple the twin towers and kill thousands. That they failed to do that and another group of conspirators succeeded 8 years later had to do partly with the better financing for the latter plot but mostly with the greater effectiveness of the particular tactic that the later group devised. The difference involved technical issues such as the effects of burning jet fuel on steel girders. It did not involve differences in ideology, motivations, the intent to do the United States severe harm, or the roofs of the underlying hatred. If Yousef had solved his technical problems, we would have had our sea change, our epoch-defining moment, 8 years earlier.

Those in this country whose job it was to deal with the objective reality of that threat, and not just with public moods and perceptions, were well aware of that reality. A substantial record including not just of work and communications within our government, but of such available measures as public testimony at the time by the Director of Central Intelligence or later statements and memoirs by former senior officials, make it abundantly clear that the strategic threat that would be most dramatically manifested in the 9/11 attack was fully appreciated well before then.

But it is a fact of politics and public policy, because it also is a fact of human nature, that it often requires a calamity to muster the support for major new initiatives or major expenditures on behalf of a public good. That is true of the stoplight that does not get installed at an intersection until after a child is struck by a car while crossing the street. It is true of dealing with some natural disasters, such as the tsunami warning system in the Indian Ocean that will only now be erected after the tragic event of last December. And it was true for the United States of major new expenditures in aviation security, and going to war half a globe away in Afghanistan, sufficient support for which could be gathered only after a disaster as shocking to Americans as 9/11.

We Americans, in focusing our attentions and our energies on the threat of the moment, tend to over-emphasize the newness and the discontinuities of recent events. We tend to underplay, or be unaware of, the historical continuity that those events so often represent. That is true of our perceptions of terrorism, which have a long pedigree. One could go far back in history, such as to the "assassins" of the medieval Islamic world, or the terror of the French Revolution, to gain some appreciation of the long-standing roofs of the concepts and even the vocabulary that we apply to the terrorism that concerns us today. Even without going that far back, there are patterns in the waxing and waning of international terrorism that it behooves us to understand, because it provides a context for what we face today.

David Rapoport, one of the veterans of American studies of terrorism, has written about four "waves" of modern international terrorism. The first was the anarchist wave, which featured Russian revolutionaries who openly called themselves "terrorists" and whose activities began in the 1870s and continued until World War I. The second was the anti-colonialist wave, which lasted from the 1920s until the completion of most decolonization in the early 1960s. The third was the "New Left" wave, which arose at the time of the Vietnam War and diminished to only remnants of its former self as the 20th century drew to a close. And the fourth, which has overlapped the third, has been the "religious wave" which began with the Iranian revolution and Afghan jihad against the Soviets in 1979.

Studying, or at least becoming aware of, these kinds of historical patterns could help significantly in sorting out our thinking and our policies toward current terrorist problems. It would help us to understand what really is new and what is not, what accounts for the rise and the decline of terrorist phenomena, how these phenomena are roofed in the global politics of their era, and how much longevity we can expect from threats that we may make significant sacrifices to combat. It would help us to differentiate the tactic of "terrorism" from the political or religious trends that may underlie a particular wave. And it might help prevent either despair or false hopes when we realize that these sorts of waves have tended to persist for 40 years or so, but that there is no reason not to expect still more waves of terrorism, of as yet unknown character, even after the current wave declines.

I am not arguing for a kind of determinism in which we are content merely to float and bob on historical waves. Rather, the point is that the broader context and perspective that are too often sorely lacking in discussions of international terrorism in this country would usefully inform a host of policy questions about countering it.

The lack of awareness of this type of history is not surprising. What Russian anarchists were doing in the late 19th century or what Kenyan Mau Mau were doing in the 1950s did not directly affect America, so naturally we Americans do not commonly factor those episodes into our thinking about terrorism. But there is a further sense in which historical waves and patterns have truncated or distorted our thinking about terrorism, and that has to do with our own political history. Our concern, or lack of concern, about terrorism has to a large degree reflected changing patterns in the political climate in the United States, the dominance at different times of different parties or ideologies, and preoccupations with particular sets of non-terrorist issues.

Historian Philip Jenkins has explored some of these patterns in his book, *Images of Terror*. He points out there was, in fact, a brief but intense American focus on that first wave of terrorism, the anarchist wave, near its end right after World War I. This was partly a reaction to a series of anarchist and communist bombings and other crimes, highlighted by the detonation in September 1920 of a bomb on Wall Street that killed 40 people. Our government's response was a campaign of arrests and deportations that was severe enough to elicit a critical reaction from the likes of the American Civil Liberties Union. This was the era of the Red Scare, and the prevailing public mood that was defined by that scare was a reaction not only to the terrorist attacks themselves, but to a larger fear of, and animosity toward, those who were known as "the Reds." There was something similar with a later "Brown scare" a concern over Nazis and fascists during the run-up to World War II.

Contrast those scares, and our current overriding concern about terrorism, with what was going on in this country in the early- to mid-1970s. There was a lot of terrorism occurring in the United States at that time, at the hands of both domestic and foreign terrorists. The attacks included, just to name some of them:

- A series of attacks by the leftist Weather Underground, which targeted police stations, corporate offices, and federal offices, including the U.S. Capitol, where the group set off a bomb in a bathroom.
- Assassinations of police officers in several major cities, as well as other attacks, by the Black Liberation Army.
- A campaign of assassinations, bank robberies, and kidnappings in California by the Symbionese Liberation Army.
- Dozens of bombings and other attacks by Puerto Rican militants, carried out on the U.S. mainland as well as

Puerto Rico, including the bombing in 1975 of the Fraunces Tavern in New York City.

- The assassination of an Israeli colonel in Washington, DC, in 1973, an act claimed by the Popular Front for the Liberation of Palestine.
- A terrorist campaign by Croatian extremists in 1975 and 1976, including a bombing at LaGuardia Airport that killed 11, the placing of a bomb in Grand Central Station, and the hijacking of a TWA jet out of New York.
- A car bombing in Washington, DC, in 1976 by Chilean intelligence, in which former Chilean ambassador Orlando Letelier was killed.
- And a campaign of bombings in the Miami area, beginning in 1975 and including dozens of attacks, perpetrated by anti-Castro Cubans.

That's just a partial list of the terrorism taking place in the United States during a 3 or 4-year period. Imagine anything like that taking place during the last 3 1/2 years, in our current climate. Imagine just the prospect, or fear, of anything like that taking place in our current climate. Where was our "war on terrorism" then? Where were the recriminations, the finger-pointing, the commissions of inquiry? Where was the 1970s version of the Patriot Act? The great difference in the national response to the terrorism of the 1970s and the terrorism represented by 9/11 is in large part due, of course, to the lethality of that latter event being orders of magnitude greater than that of anything taking place during the 1970s. But the breadth and frequency of the terrorism, right here in the United States during the 1970s¯with Americans, not just foreigners, getting killed certainly would warrant, by today's standards, far more of a response than did take place.

The other major reason why there was not such a response was, again, the temper of the times. And in those times, with the Watergate affair in the process of becoming one of the most compelling and wrenching chapters in American history, and stories of abuses of power and excesses involving U.S. security services, as showcased in forum such as the Pike and Church committees, whatever concern there was about terrorist threats was eclipsed by concern over what our own governmental institutions were doing. Far from there being a constituency for something likes a Patriot Act to expand the powers of those institutions, the impetus was instead to curtail, or at least more tightly control, those powers.

Our counterterrorist policies, perspectives, and rhetoric have served, and have been shaped by, various other political and ideological needs and trends, not just the need to stand up to terrorist threats. That is as true of our current perspectives and rhetoric as it was of the earlier eras I mentioned. I am not going to take the time to discuss specifically the political and ideological factors that operate today, but let me mention one other need more of an intellectual, as well as a rhetorical one that is part of what is at play in how we think and talk about terrorism post-9/11. We seem to have a yearning to identify and demarcate eras, and to define each one in terms of a single, overriding goal or principle.

During our modern history, the Cold War served this purpose admirably for four decades, with the era defined in terms of a competition with a single superpower foe. In the decade following the collapse of the Soviet Union, pundits, politicians, and political scientists struggled to come up with a comparably clear defining characteristic for the newest era, and for a name to apply to the post-Cold War era, other than "the post-Cold War era." The shock of 9/11 and the sudden surge in priority of counterterrorism solved the problem of those looking for a simple, era-defining characteristic. The era would be known as the era of warring against terrorism.

The rhetorical and intellectual simplicity of this kind of era-labeling has advantages, of course, but it also especially because simplification all too readily becomes oversimplification has disadvantages. And I think we Americans suffer more from the disadvantages than do some other peoples whose experiences have given them a better developed sense of historical continuity and complexity.

The business of demarcating eras gets to another deeply based and distinctly American way of thinking. We tend to see ourselves in a war, called the "war on terrorism," which we believe began in a clear, distinct, well-demarcated way on September 11, 2001. That way of looking at counterterrorism appeals to a long-established American perspective which goes beyond any one administration or political party for looking at foreign policy challenges and at how we deal with foreign threats in general. The American perspective of which I speak is a non-Clausewitzian perspective. It does not regard war as a continuation of politics by other means. Instead, it looks at war and peace as two distinct states, which involve different sets of rules, which require different magnitudes of resources and effort, and which have clear beginnings and ends that set off times of peace from times of war.

Admittedly, many people (at least the more thoughtful ones) who are comfortable in using the vocabulary of the "war on terrorism" would not describe things quite as starkly as this. But I am making the point starkly to clarify what is a pronounced tendency in the American way of confronting threats to our security.

Walter Russell Mead, in his book *Special Providence*, offers a perspective that can help to explain this American thought pattern. Mead describes several traditions in American foreign policy thinking, which he names after famous statesmen, that have been exhibited throughout the republic's history and that continue to shape debates over policies today. Some of these traditions are readily apparent in current policies, and discussions of policy, concerning terrorism.

For example, the principle that we need to encourage more freedom and openness in political and economic systems in other parts of the world, especially the Middle East, to change the milieu that breeds terrorism, is an expression of the Wilsonian tradition, which sees the United States as having an obligation to spread its democratic and social values throughout the world. We heard an eloquent statement of this viewpoint in President Bush's second inaugural address, in which he said the expansion of freedom in the world is "an urgent requirement of our nation's security."

The person who drives a fuel-efficient hybrid car with a bumper sticker that says "Terrorist Prevention Vehicle" a reference to American dependence on Middle Eastern energy supplies, and the unavoidable connection between that dependence and the question of dealing with the Middle Eastern roofs of international terrorism is referring to issues of concern to the Hamiltonian tradition, which places particular importance on America's economic links to the outside world.

But the tradition that is most readily apparent in the current American perspective toward confronting terrorism is the Jacksonian tradition, the most militant and populist of the traditions. It is less an ideology than an expression of a folk community one that resides today primarily in middle class suburbia and includes security moms, NASCAR dads, and some of those other political animals on whom the pollsters and pundits like to focus. And at the core of this tradition are certain values centered on honor and valor, and a belief in the need to use arms and use them vigorously when needed to counter threats to Americans' security.

Mead completed his book shortly before 9/11, but some of his discussion of the Jacksonian tradition describes with almost eerie accuracy the American reaction to that event. Jacksonians, for example, believe in extending honor to enemies who fight honorably, but not to dishonorable enemies who fight dirty which certainly would include terrorists. In dealing with the latter, the same rules do not apply a principle that gets to the heart of such current issues as the treatment of detainees.

But what I want to highlight is this tradition's conception of war and non war as two distinct states. "Jacksonians," writes Mead, "see war as a switch that is either on or off. They don't like the idea of violence on a dimmer switch." This is a view that is very comfortable with the idea of a "war on terrorism" that suddenly began one day 3 1/2 years ago. It is uncomfortable with the idea of counterterrorism as a long-term effort that already had been going on for years before 9/11; that concerns a variety of groups, movements, and issues; that uses a variety of policy tools with varying levels of intensity and violence; and that will have to continue into an indefinite future and as Secretary Rumsfeld and other senior officials have correctly reminded us will not have a definite end.

However valuable the Jacksonian tradition has been in mobilizing and energizing the American people, this simple, dichotomous war/no war outlook toward counterterrorism has perceptual, analytical, and semantic disadvantages. It tends to throw several different issues and concepts into a single pot, obscuring the distinctions among them. Much perhaps most of the discourse in this country (from both supporters and critics of the current administration) that refers to a "war on terrorism" fails to make clear at the outset whether the reference is to a metaphorical "war" meaning a major national effort against something, akin to a war on drugs or war on poverty or a literal war, meaning application of military force and various other things that go with it, such as application of the laws of war. Much discourse also has failed to distinguish among the concepts of "war" as a way of characterizing the nature of a threat, a way of expressing the seriousness of the threat, and a way of countering the threat. Those are three different things.

The viewpoint of an on-off, war or no war, switch also tends to miss how much continuity there has been in U.S. counterterrorist policy. Like Mead, I wrote a book that came out shortly before 9/11. The opening sentence in that book referred to how combating international terrorism was a "major objective of the United States." Two sentences later, I mentioned how the fight against terrorism was often referred to as none other than a "war." How soon we forget. The common American way of looking at "war," and a failure to distinguish among the different usages of that term I mentioned a moment ago, have resulted in many words being uselessly expended on such debates as whether terrorism is best described as "war" or "crime." One has only to look at something like the military tribunals at Guantanamo to realize that is a false dichotomy, and that military actions and the use of some kind of criminal justice system are not two separate and mutually exclusive approaches to the problem. And one has only to look at the last several issues of the State Department's annual report on international terrorism, and specifically at the principles of U.S. counterterrorist policy that have been restated each year in that report in essentially unchanged form, to realize that. One of those principles to quotes from the most recent of those reports, a statement of the current administration made amid our "war on terrorism" is "Bring terrorists to justice for their crimes."

My overall point about the American perspective toward terrorism is that it unavoidably has a lot of baggage and blinders. It is a perspective that has as much to do with our history and culture, our politics and our ideologies, as with the terrorist threat itself. We need to realize that, and to reflect on that, as we consider ways to make our fight against terrorism even more effective. And we need to realize that being the target of 9/11 does not give us a monopoly of wisdom on thinking about international terrorism. We could learn a lot from others. Others, of course, have their own baggage and blinders, some of them similar to ours, and others based on their own histories and foreign policy traditions different from ours.

One pattern in foreign reactions to terrorism akin to our reaction to 9/11 that shows up repeatedly is that it takes actual attacks and casualties, not just intelligence about a threat, to get publics and governments serious about counterterrorism. As an example from recent years, Saudi Arabia has shown a level of commitment to counter-terrorism over the past 2 years substantially greater than it did before a series of attacks beginning in May 2003 demonstrated how much harm terrorism could do to Saudi Arabia's own citizens, not just to foreign interests in the kingdom.

That is a recent example, but some of our European and other allies have been attending the school of hard terrorist knocks for much longer. They have been there, learned lessons, and taken actions well in advance of some of the corresponding steps taken by the United States. One thinks, for example, of the attack by Palestinian terrorists at the 1972 Munich Olympics, where an unsuccessful operation by German security elements ended in confusion and tragedy. In response to this failure, the Germans created an elite counterterrorist commando unit that performed brilliantly 5 years later in a rescue of hostages from a hijacked airliner in Somalia. The United States would not follow suit until the next decade, after its own rescue failure at Desert One in Iran in 1980. The terrorist threats that several European states faced from leftist groups in the 1970s and 1980s also led them to enact new laws relating to police and investigative powers again, well ahead of some of the corresponding debates and legislation in the United States.

The Europeans' experiences with a variety of terrorist threats also have helped them to understand that terrorism is a tactic that has been used, and will continue to be used, by many different groups. They know from first-hand experience that Islamist terrorism is not just al Qaida that Middle Eastern terrorism is not just the Islamists, and that terrorism that can strike their homelands is not just from the Middle East. The leftist wave was the main terrorist worry for many of them. But think also, for example, of France during the latter stages of the Algerian war for independence in the early 1960s, in which Paris had to deal both with terrorism from the Algerian nationalists and with a wave of attacks within France itself from the anti-independence Secret Army Organization.

The terrorist threats that some Europeans as well as others, in countries ranging from Peru to Sri Lanka have had to confront have been in an important sense even more serious and the lessons from them thus more trenchant, than what we have faced in the United States. Yes, 9/11 was far more lethal and destructive than any other single attack of modern international terrorism. And yes, the United States continues to be the most salient terrorist target on the globe. But even 9/11 was not a strike at this country's territorial integrity, or a strike with a chance of bringing down our fundamental institutions, as distinct from bringing down buildings that may house them. Al Qaida's campaign against the United States has been mostly a way of waging a civil war within the Islamic world.

With the terrorism against some of our friends and allies abroad, it has not just been a matter of getting caught up in someone else's civil war. The Basque terrorism that Spain has faced, for example, has been an attempt to use violence to do nothing less than carve a chunk out of Spain and this in a country in which separatist sentiments may be not far below the surface (not just in the Basque country, but also elsewhere), and where a bitter and bloody civil war is still within the living memory of some Spaniards. Just across our northern border, some 35 years ago, Quebecois extremists were using terrorism to try to tear Canada apart, before the Canadian government responded with draconian measures to crush them. In the British Isles, there is a still unresolved issue of the capacity to commit terrorism (the so- called "decommissioning of arms" issue) on the part of the Irish Republican Army, whose objective in its terrorist campaigns, notwithstanding more recent political agreements, has been to tear apart the country whose full and formal name is the United Kingdom of Great Britain and Northern Ireland.

Beyond the separatists, the reach of terrorism all the way to the central political institutions of European countries has been demonstrated by, for example, how close that Secret Army Organization came on more than one occasion to killing the president of France, or by the Italian Red Brigades abducting one of Italy's leading politicians (a former prime minister, Aldo Moro) and depositing his dead body for the world to see in the trunk of a car. Think about those sorts of episodes the next time you may be tempted to regard the Spanish or Canadians or others of our allies as inexperienced wimps when it comes to terrorism.

While we learn what useful lessons we can from our foreign friends, we also have to be careful not to fall in line with some of their less helpful parochial ways of using or manipulating the terrorist issue. Whether it is Israel dealing with the Palestinians, Russia confronting the Chechens, India handling the Kashmiris, or China facing the Uighurs, a natural tendency is to apply the vocabulary of the "war on terrorism" if for no other reason than to win support from the United States to issues that have to do with much more than just terrorism itself. This is not to deny the interests we do share with those or other foreign interlocutors on terrorist-related matters only to caution that we need to be aware, as well, of the ways in which our interests or values may diverge.

I close by returning to the subject of international law on the conduct of war. Its basic purpose is to minimize human suffering to minimize it even among the hatreds and conflicts that give rise to wars in the first place. I prefer to think about counterterrorism in the same terms. Its purpose what ought to be the purpose of any "war on terrorism" is to minimize terrorist attacks, and thereby to save the lives and limbs, and minimize the suffering, of innocent people. To stay true to that purpose and to pursue it with focus, skill, and clarity, both we and our foreign friends need to be aware of the various historical, cultural, political, and ideological influences on our respective ways of thinking about terrorism. We need to try to strip away, as well as we can, any extraneous objectives that grow out of those influences, whether it is to restore one's honor, exact revenge, expand one's influence, or anything else, other than saving innocent people from future terrorism. That is not easy, but we ought to try.

Squaring the Error

I have taken as the title to my paper a phrase that British counterinsurgency expert Sir Robert Thompson used to critique American military strategy in Vietnam during the 1960s. When the military force applied in Vietnam failed to achieve the desired results, rather than reevaluate the strategy, we simply doubled the effort, and in doing so, squared the error. If the terrorist attacks of September 11, 2001 (9/11), taught us anything, it is that doing nothing in response to terrorism is unacceptable, and there is no doubt but that we are now making great efforts. But we also have to recognize that terrorism is a complex problem, and an incorrect response may compound our problems rather than resolve them, regardless of the amount of effort we apply to the task.

In the *Art of War*, Sun-Tzu counsels that we must both know our enemy and know ourselves to ensure victory. Knowing ourselves is the easy part. We are a constitutional democracy; a nation of laws, a free and open society in which individual rights are inalienable, and government power is limited. Global terrorism threatens us by exploiting the very freedoms and openness that define us as a democratic society. Government's primary obligation in a hostile world is to protect its citizens.

But the efforts now underway to protect us from terrorism are changing America and changing the world in ways that actually assist the terrorists, because in the midst of all this change, very little effort has been made to truly understand terrorists. This is where I think my experience might be helpful since I have been on both sides, living simultaneously as a terrorist and a counterterrorist. In the early 1990s, working as a Federal Bureau of Investigation (FBI) undercover agent, I spent over a year with white supremacist extremist groups engaged in a racial holy war.

A few years later, after the Oklahoma City bombing, I spent another 6 months undercover with militia groups in the Pacific Northwest. I later served as a counterterrorism instructor at the FBI National Academy, but it is my experience working within terrorist groups and seeing the world from their perspective that has most influenced my understanding of the nature of the threat we are facing. My repeated success using constitutionally sound, proactive law enforcement techniques to infiltrate terrorist groups and prevent acts of terrorism convinces me that a criminal law approach to counterterrorism can be effective.

In my experience, terrorism, quite simply, is what "they" do to "us". Terrorist groups almost never refer to themselves as terrorists, but rather as soldiers, revolutionaries, holy warriors. And governments, no matter how oppressive, conduct only counterterrorism operations. You'll never see a Department of Terrorism on a government's organizational chart. As bodies pile up on both sides, each sees himself as the victim. In addition, terrorist acts are often so heinous they are seen not only as unjustified, but as unjustifiable. Anyone suggesting a rationality supporting the terrorist's behavior is branded a sympathizer, which chills intelligent discourse about the roof causes of terrorism and the behavior of terrorists.

This again is where my experience helps. I am clearly not a terrorist sympathizer. The terrorists I befriended all went to prison because I betrayed them. Now some could argue that my experience with domestic terrorists, particularly right-wing extremists, is irrelevant to a discussion focusing on Islamic terrorism because right-wing extremists are just lightweights and amateurs compared to al Qaeda. I would simply remind them that, while al Qaeda failed in their first attempt to bring a building down in the United States, right-wing extremists succeeded in Oklahoma City, and, while no weapons of mass destruction (WMD) were found in Iraq, a cyanide bomb capable of killing every person in a 30,000 square-foot building was discovered in a storage locker in Noonday, Texas. We ignore domestic terrorists at our peril.

"Amateurs" is probably a fair description of them, though, in the sense that they never had state sponsorship like al Qaeda enjoyed with the Taliban. But that they are able to continue operating without financing and without a safe haven arguably makes them a more formidable threat, not less of one. I often hear terrorism expert's remark that al Qaeda's evolution into decentralized cells after the invasion of Afghanistan is a sign of organizational genius, but they are really just imitating the leaderless resistance and lone wolf strategies right-wing extremists pioneered decades ago. Nobody ever called them geniuses.

More to the point though, as a criminal investigator, I did not focus on the ideology of the group I was investigating, mainly because the First Amendment to the U.S. Constitution guarantees their right to their beliefs, but also because their beliefs were not going to hurt anyone, while the bombs they were making were. So I focused on the methodology; what the terrorists were doing to accomplish their criminal goals. I found the methodology is essentially the same for all terrorist groups, regardless of ideology. Hitler and Stalin had diametrically opposed ideologies, but the totalitarian regimes they established were remarkably similar in the methods they used to hold power. It is the same phenomena with terrorists.

Three universal truths about terrorists are: First, terrorists are unhappy with the status quo; second, terrorists lack the political power to alter the status quo through legitimate, peaceful means; and finally, terrorists lack the military power to force a change. A terrorist has a very black and white world view that divides "us," the virtuous and pure, from "them," the corrupt and unclean. Terrorists see the world at a tipping point, and their goal is to devise an attack that will alter the status quo; that will throw the world into chaos, a cleansing war, a jihad. White Supremacists call it RAHOWA, short for Racial Holy War. Charles Manson called it Helter-Skelter. Whatever they call it, the terrorists believe that out of the chaos, their people will rise and dominate, either because God, or simply justice, is on their side.

They recruit in the places they find people who are similarly unhappy with the status quo: in prisons, among the unemployed. They seek idealistic young students eager to make a mark in the world. Typically there is a cleansing ritual to symbolize the separation of the group from the corrupt society; dress and dietary requirements are established, sexual taboos are either strictly enforced, or, as in the case of the Weather Underground, ceremonially violated. Sometimes there are physical manifestations of separation; neo-Nazi skinheads shave their heads, jihadists grow beards.

I have heard Richard Clarke, the former White House counterterrorism official; describe the jihadist movement as a series of concentric circles, with the smallest circle in the center representing hard-core al Qaeda members and the outer circles representing varying levels of support for the movement. I think this analogy is helpful, but my version is a little different in that it is generic to any terrorist group rather than specific to one. Imagine a series of concentric circles with the hard-core terrorist group at the center. In the next circle are supporters, who assist the group but do not participate directly in terrorist attacks.

The third circle contains people who sympathize with the cause but who do not actively support the terrorists. In the fourth circle are people who the terrorists consider part of their "us" community, but who do not identify themselves as part of a community represented by the terrorist group. White supremacists refer to this group as "sheeple," whites who do not believe in a Jewish conspiracy to destroy their race. The fifth and final circle represents "them," the population of others that support the status quo and benefit from it. Outside the circle is the oppressive force; the government, the Jewish conspiracy, communism, capitalism, the New World Order, whatever the terrorists are against.

The core terrorist group must do something in order to gain influence among its supporters. This can be something positive, like promoting sobriety or ridding a neighborhood of a criminal element that has been exploiting it, a further cleansing of the community. Getting attention from sympathizers in the next circle requires bolder action on behalf of the community, perhaps assassinating a corrupt police officer who has been shaking down the local businessmen. Now this is a critical stage for the terrorists because at this point they look very much like a gang of criminals and if the government can brand them as criminals, it will be very difficult for them to retain support among sympathizers and impossible to gain any support among the sheeple in the fourth circle.

This is also a critical stage because moving to the next level of influence requires outside assistance, and that assistance can only come from one source: their enemy. To accomplish their goals, terrorists need to trigger a severe government reaction, one that will impact the innocent in the community as well as the guilty, to stir resentment and validate the terrorist's propaganda that "they" are persecuting "us." The over-reaction will divide the population along the lines the terrorist wants them divided, driving the sheeple in the fourth circle to the cause of the terrorist. This strategy is laid out in Carlos Marighella's "Mini-manual of the Urban Guerilla," a virtual how-to guide for terrorists. That a how-to guide for terrorists exists surprised me when I started working in counterterrorism, and I think it underscores what truly is an intelligence failure on the part of our government. Osama bin Laden has followed the how-to guide to a tee, and we fell far too easily into the role of the oppressor, just as it was scripted.

If you have seen Gillo Pontecorvo's film, "The Battle of Algiers," lately, you might have noticed that my description of the development of a terrorist organization mirrors the first part of the movie in which the National Liberation Front, known by its French acronym FLN, starts a terrorist campaign against French colonial forces in Algiers. It is often dismissed as propaganda, but I think it has tremendous intelligence value because the original screenplay was actually written by an FLN terrorist, Yacef Saadi. In the film, as in real life, the security forces do overreact to the terrorist attacks, uniting the Algerian community behind the FLN.

The French military resorts to torturing detainees to develop intelligence and they succeed in breaking the FLN, but the political fallout from the abuse energizes the Algerian resistance, undermines French support for the effort, and alienates the international community. France wins the battle of Algiers, but loses the war for Algeria. This is the crucial final stage of a terrorist campaign, when the people in the fifth circle start to believe their government is unjust and incapable of solving the terrorist problem. The film was made in 1967 but here, almost 40 years later, we find ourselves on the brink of that final stage, divided at home, alienated from allies abroad, fighting an enemy all over the globe that can strike when and where it wants.

Marighella's genius is that he understands that governments are compelled to overreact to terrorism: "The government has no alternative except to intensify its repression. The police networks, house searches, the arrest of suspects and innocent persons, and the closing off of streets make life in the city unbearable." Written in 1969, is this applicable to our current situation? How about this quote from Osama bin Laden shortly after 9/11: "I tell you freedom and human rights in America are doomed. The U.S. Government will lead the American people and the west in general into an unbearable hell and a choking life." Just as a terrorist's actions are designed to speak to his community, the government has an audience it must answer to as well. When a terrorist attack occurs, the victim population rightly questions why the government charged with protecting it has failed and the people demand more effective security. The easiest way for the government to satisfy this constituency, their own "us" in that fifth circle, is to take restrictive measures against "them" by expanding the powers of the security services.

Creating an effective security service is fairly easy. Militarize the police and consolidate military, intelligence, and law enforcement functions under one central authority. Make that authority accountable only to the executive branch of government. Authorize "emergency" powers that suspend traditional protections of personal liberties. Permit extra-judicial detentions and the use of coercive investigative techniques. Establish a tribunal system separate from the normal criminal justice system and allow the use of secret evidence. Ignore inconvenient international treaties and conventions. Restrict travel. Encourage people to inform on their neighbors, to report all suspicious activity, and then follow-up on every report to reinforce the perception that the government is in control. Gather and retain intelligence on the general population. Most importantly, give the security services the power to operate in secret so no one will know what the true security situation is, and so mistakes and abuses can be hidden. There are plenty of examples we can use as models; authoritarian regimes throughout history are defined by the effectiveness of their security services. But unchecked power and freedom from public accountability always lead to abuse, which undermines the legitimacy of the governing authority. The effectiveness of these security solutions tends to be short-lived and ultimately illusory.

This is Marighella's trap: measures we take to win each battle make it more likely we will lose the war. The good news is we can avoid the trap, not by increasing the power of the security services, but by increasing their efficiency. To be truly effective, a counterterrorism program must be efficient, not only in that its resources are used wisely, but in that all of the counterterrorism efforts are directed squarely at the terrorists. But increasing efficiency is much more difficult than simply increasing power. Governments by their very nature tend to be bureaucratic and inefficient. Luckily, our founding fathers created a mechanism that compels efficiency in government: the U.S. Constitution. We need to recognize that our Constitution and the freedoms it guarantees are not weaknesses, but rather the source of our strength. Nothing makes it more difficult for a terrorist to convince people that the government is oppressive and unjust than scrupulously protecting his rights in a public criminal trial.

First we need to take Sun Tzu's advice and get to know ourselves a little better by being honest about why our counterterrorism efforts before 9/11 were ineffective. In the wake of the attacks, officials in the Bush administration denied the government had any forewarning of the plot. A lack of intelligence was cited as the cause of the failure, so Congress acted quickly, passing the U.S. Patriot Act to give the administration powers it said, it needed to get the intelligence necessary to prevent another attack. Meanwhile, the administration resisted the investigations that ultimately revealed the true cause of the failure. It turned out that the government had a tremendous amount of intelligence and simply failed to respond to it, but by that time the idea that 9/11 was an intelligence failure had already taken roof. The intelligence reform train had left the station.

The issue was further confused when the Justice Department and the FBI blamed their lapses on their over-reliance on a criminal justice approach to counterterrorism, which also was simply not true. In fact, while domestic terrorism cases like mine were treated as criminal matters, the FBI has always handled international terrorism cases as counterintelligence matters. Each of the three FBI cases the 9/11 Commission cited as failed opportunities to prevent the attacks were intelligence investigations. FBI agents in New York actually were prevented from pursuing criminal investigations against two of the hijackers because managers at FBI headquarters misunderstood intelligence-sharing regulations. FBI managers, who denied Minneapolis agents their request to get a Foreign Intelligence Surveillance Act (FISA) warrant in the case of Zacarias Moussaoui, later admitted in testimony before the Senate Judiciary Committee that they did not even know the standard of proof necessary to obtain a FISA warrant. The Phoenix memo was never even read prior to 9/11. Bureaucratic inefficiency and managerial incompetence were the true causes of the breakdown, not a lack of intelligence and certainly not an over-reliance on criminal law enforcement.

In fact, proactive criminal investigations can be very effective in preventing terrorism, as my repeated success proves. That these cases are rare is not because the techniques are not effective, but because the FBI does not employ them effectively. A criminal law enforcement approach to terrorism has many inherent advantages that promote efficiency. By treating terrorists like criminals, we stigmatize them in their community, while simultaneously validating our own authority. Open and public trials allow the community to see the terrorist for the criminal he is, and successful prosecutions give them faith the government is protecting them. Judicial review ensures that the methods used are in accordance with the law, and juries enforce community standards of fairness. The adversarial process exposes improper or ineffective law enforcement techniques so they can be corrected. Checks and balances on government power and public accountability promote efficiency by ensuring that only the guilty are punished.

Finally, and this is perhaps counterintuitive, the exposure of proactive law enforcement techniques at trial is a force multiplier. Intelligence collector's focus on protecting sources and methods to ensure their continued availability, but this does not necessarily promote security as the three cases cited by the 9/11 Commission demonstrates. In each case, restrictions on intelligence-sharing caused the breakdown. If the presence of two al Qaeda terrorists in the United States was broadcast to state and local law enforcement, or if the Phoenix memo was distributed to flight schools around the country, perhaps the outcome would have been different. Protecting this intelligence did not protect national security.

When I was undercover, I was present during the planning of dozens of terrorist attacks. In almost every case, the one thing that stopped the terrorists from following through on their plans was the fear they had been compromised by an infiltrator. If a terrorist knows that every new recruit is a possible agent; if every old friend might have been turned; if communications over the phone, or over the radio, or over the internet are vulnerable to interception, his ability to operate effectively is greatly restricted. Certainly the terrorist will modify his behavior to try to avoid law enforcement detection, and this will require the government to constantly adapt and develop more effective techniques, but this is not a bad outcome.

Our security services do need to be improved. Congress needs to improve oversight and enact criminal laws to assist law enforcement in dealing with this threat, and some of the provisions in the Patriot Act and Intelligence Reform Bill are helpful. But overall, the reorganization and reform of the security services will fail because the real problems that led to 9/11 are not addressed, and bureaucratic inefficiency and managerial incompetence continue to hamper our counterterrorism efforts. After 3 years and 170 million dollars, the FBI still does not have a functioning computer system.

The worst part of these reforms, though, is that they increase the government's power to operate in secret, beyond judicial or congressional oversight, and beyond public accountability. After failing us once, the security services should be more accountable, not less.

We also need to better understand our enemy, and to do this, we need to use more efficiently the intelligence we already have. I spent over a year-and-a-half living undercover with right wing extremists, but despite my many requests, I was never operationally debriefed by the Domestic Terrorism Unit. I recorded hundreds of hours of conversations with real terrorists, selecting targets, planning attacks, and discussing motives and methods. These tapes were used as evidence in public trials, but they have never been analyzed for their intelligence value. If someone had bothered to listen to these tapes in the early 1990s, they would have heard right-wing extremists discuss the possibility of crashing a messenger air liner into a military installation to start the race war.

Contrary to popular opinion, from the terrorists' perspective, 9/11 was a political disaster for the jihadist movement. The scale of the attack was so horrible, the world united in solidarity with the United States to stop terrorism. Even many jihadi supporters could not accept that Muslims did something so terrible, and they dreamed up conspiracy theories suggesting Israel planned the attack to frame Muslims. In Tehran, the heart of the most anti-American Muslim state, there was a spontaneous candlelight vigil in sympathy for the victims. Other Muslim countries with a history of antagonism toward the United States, such as Pakistan and Syria, agreed to assist us. When diplomatic efforts failed to convince the Taliban to arrest and extradite al Qaeda criminals, the international community supported a military intervention to remove the Taliban from power and al Qaeda, "the base" of the jihadist movement, was destroyed. But when we departed from the rule of law, both our own Constitution and our obligations under international conventions, when we antagonized and alienated the international community, we undercut our success and handed a victory to the terrorists.

What we have to realize is that this is not a struggle of ideologies; it is not Islam against Christianity or fundamentalism versus secularism. This is a battle for legitimacy, and as such, it is one that we should easily win. As an open and free democracy regulated by the rule of law, we offer a future of peace and prosperity that the jihadist movement does not. Its resort to terrorism is a sign of weakness, not of strength. We need to avoid the trap of demonizing our enemies, of dividing the world between "us" and "them" as the terrorist does. As former Weather Underground member Brian Flanagan said in a recent documentary, "if you think that you have the moral high-ground . . . you can do some really dreadful things."

That goes for both sides. Respect for the rule of law, international conventions, and treaty obligations will not make us weaker, it will engender international cooperation and good will that make it impossible for extremist movements to prosper. I have heard commentators suggest that we are losing the propaganda battle in the Middle East, but that misses the point entirely. The term "propaganda" connotes a fabrication or a spinning of facts to support one's position, and that is exactly what we must not do. In a battle for legitimacy, honesty and accountability are the most effective ammunition.

Terrorism will never go away, and free and open societies will always be especially vulnerable. But we do not win by becoming less free and less open. Ironically, al Qaeda does not have the power to destroy the United States of America. But we do. By playing into a script written by terrorists we have indeed squared the error.

Preserving the Rule of Law in a Time of Terror

Media coverage concerning the state of the U.S. partnership with Germany has focused primarily on Germany's opposition to the Iraq War. In fact, for some commentators, the litmus test of the state of German-American relations is whether or not Germany, at any point, will send military forces to Iraq. This narrow inquiry has overshadowed an equally, if not more, important difference of opinion between the two countries. While the United States elected to invoke both the metaphor and tools of war in response to the September 11, 2001 (9/11) attacks, Germany has chosen to frame its response within the strict bounds of both German and international law.

While both sides of the Atlantic share a common vision that terrorism must be prevented, the German response to terrorism has been strongly shaped by unique historical and cultural forces. With the caveat that the construction of history and culture is an ongoing process, this essay will explore how Germany's prior experience with terrorism and war has helped to shape its current response to terrorism. The goal of this analysis is not to critique or evaluate Germany's response, but rather to appreciate some of the factors that have helped to define it. Toward that end, this chapter will review Germany's prior history in dealing with domestic terrorists, the country's post-9/11 legislative initiatives, and the recent debate about the role of torture that occurred within Germany.

Germany's Prior Response to Terrorism

From a post-9/11 standpoint, Germany's prior experience with domestic terrorism offers an intriguing example of the inherent tensions in balancing security interests and civil liberties. Between the late 1960s and the early 1980s, a host of terrorist groups challenged the authority of the German government through a campaign of terror defined by the kidnapping and murder of prominent members of German society, as well as bombings and other violent criminal behavior. Ironically, the decisive deployment of violent tactics by groups that included the Red Army Fraktion (RAF), the Revolutionary Cells (RZ), and the June 2nd Movement commenced as the energy behind Germany's student movement began to dissipate.

In contrast to the antiwar protest movement in the United States that occurred during the same period, the primary grievance articulated by German protestors in the late 1960s was the legislature's debate concerning amendments to the German Constitution or Basic Law which would enable the government to assume extraordinary powers in the case of an emergency. The protest movement, which included students, trade unionists, intellectuals, and other liberal groups, alleged that the governing Christian Democratic Union (CDU) planned to use the legislation to return Germany to a police state. The election of Social Democratic Party (SDP) member Willy Brandt as Chancellor and the Soviet invasion of Czechoslovakia in 1968 triggered the decline of the student movement. Frustrated with the protest movement's direction and decline, individuals who sought to bring down the German government launched a campaign of terror that began with the bombing of the Springer publishing house.

For more than a decade after the Springer bombing, the German legislature seemed to respond to each highpoint of violence by enacting new legislation. Without a doubt, some Germans feared that the onslaught of terrorist activity would cause German history to replay itself. However, the decisive factor that shaped the legislative responses was not the actual threat that these groups posed to German security but rather the nature of the political struggle between Germany's political parties. In some cases, the politicized nature of this response led the government to unnecessarily restrict civil liberties. Some of the most egregious actions included using databases to profile not only terrorists but also left-leaning citizens, as well as subjecting millions of civil service applicants to loyalty screenings.

In addition, new legislation that criminalized the act of forming a terrorist organization did not require law enforcement officials to possess reasonable suspicion before initiating an investigation. German prosecutors subsequently used this legislation in some cases to broadly target government dissent. Another new provision banned "anti-constitutional" action, which was defined as any behavior likely to disturb the peace. After the highpoint of domestic terrorism passed in the autumn of 1977, there was increasing opposition among the public and the liberal media to further governmental restraints on civil liberties. Between 1978 and 1989 a group of SDP deputies, as well as members of the Free Democratic Party (FDP), began to oppose additional encroachments on the rule of law. Critically, German civic pride and confidence in the Basic Law grew throughout the 1970s.

This development led to an uneven liberalization of Germany's internal security policy that included the repeal of the criminal code section that banned propagation of "anti-constitutional" action in 1981. Most importantly, by the mid-1980s, the German public had adopted a more tolerant attitude toward political protest and a more discriminating and suspicious attitude toward state action that intruded on civil liberties. The changed nature of German public opinion during this period was reflected in the fact that the Bundestag defeated additional security measures introduced by the CDU and modified the "loyalty oath" provisions governing civil service employment.

The German Reaction to 9/11

In the immediate aftermath of 9/11, the German government expressed its strong support for the United States. Germany's Minister of the Interior, Ofto Shily, stated that it was not just America that was attacked, but democracy itself, as New York was "a symbol for the desire for freedom in this world." At the same time, Germany did not view the attacks as a prelude to war. This sentiment mirrored the public opinion of many Germans who did not believe that it was feasible to "win a war" against terrorism by using military means. From a policymaking perspective, this framing represented a choice by the German government to develop its response to terrorism within the existing framework of German and international law. This policy contrasted sharply with the decisions made by U.S. policy makers to push, if not cross, the legal envelope in developing strategies to combat terrorism.

Although the German legislature enacted two broad anti-terrorism packages after 9/11, the primary focus of this legislation was not to create new laws, but to reform existing law and to increase the amount of resources devoted to identifying and prosecuting terrorists. A prime example of this was the changes made to Section 129 of the German Penal Code. Although this legislation was originally intended to punish Germany's domestic terrorist groups, after 9/11 the legislature enacted changes that extended the reach of the statute to terrorist organizations operating within any member state of the European Union (EU). In cases where a personal or geographic connection to Germany exists, the reach of the statute extends to terrorist groups located outside of the EU.

Enhancing the resources and information-gathering roles of Germany's key state security agencies was also a key focus of the legislative changes. As in the United States, German legislators recognized that there was an urgent need to improve the information flow between state agencies. Germany's determination to frame its response strictly within its existing rule of law framework led legislators to limit attempts to expand law enforcement's investigatory powers. For example, the legislature refused to give German law enforcement agencies "initiatory investigative" power which would have allowed law enforcement to commence investigations to gather evidence to form an initial suspicion of a suspect. Moreover, the German government has resisted further attempts to increase the power of the Federal Crime Office (*Bundeskriminalamt*).

As the result of the reorganization of German law enforcement and intelligence operations instituted after World War II, each of Germany's 16 *länder* (states) possesses its own police and intelligence agencies which are responsible for terrorist investigations within its own jurisdiction. While Interior Minister Ofto Shily has tried to centralize Germany's security operations in Berlin to investigate terrorists more effectively, Shily's plans have often been blocked by members of his own government. In addition, efforts to create a central database of Muslim fundamentalists have encountered strong resistance by both government officials and privacy groups. Such attempts to relax of criminal procedure and constitutional standards have challenged Germany's commitment to the rule of law.

Although Germany contributed military forces to the International Security and Assistance Force in Afghanistan,

Germans do not consider that deployment to be part of the U.S.-led global war against terrorism. In keeping with the peacekeeping and reconstruction-focused mission of the German forces, Germany has strongly resisted efforts to integrate the United Nations (UN) force with American military forces. While many Germans supported the deployment of military forces to Afghanistan, they are less eager to support the use of those forces in combat operations.

In sum, in designing responses to terrorism German policymakers are still haunted by the legacies of the government's abuse of power during World War II. In addition, memories of government overreaching in combating domestic terrorism in recent decades have caused the government to exercise caution in increasing the investigative powers of security agencies. Finally, the highly decentralized structure of German security operations, itself a legacy of the postwar period, has also hampered efforts to centralize security operations.

The Debate about Torture

As the prior discussion demonstrated, the fact that Germany is committed to placing strict legal limits on its response to terrorism has not shielded the government from making difficult choices regarding the balance between security interests and civil liberties. Moreover, although the German media has criticized the war in Iraq as a violation of international law, the German press also has investigated reports of human rights abuses allegedly committed by members of Germany's law enforcement community. Most notably, within the past 18 months, a vigorous debate has occurred within the German press and the government concerning the use of torture as an interrogation tactic in serious criminal cases.

Last fall, Frankfurt Deputy Police Chief Wolfgang Daschner stood trial on charges that he had ordered a subordinate to threaten to use force against a suspect in a child kidnapping case. Although Daschner issued the order hoping that the threat would allow him to save a child's life, the threat violated Germany's Basic Law (*Grundgesetz*) which states that "[p]ersons in custody must not be subjected to mental or physical mistreatment." The issue of torture is taken very seriously in Germany not only for historical reasons, but also because Germany's most fundamental constitutional right is the right to human dignity. Article 1 of the *Grundgesetz* states that: "the dignity of the human person is inviolable." Law enforcement officials who violate the ban on torture face a potential 10-year prison sentence.

Despite the clarity of Germany's ban on the use of torture, the predicament facing the Deputy Police Chief generated sympathy from several prominent German officials. The President of the State of Hessen went on record stating that the Deputy Police Chief's actions were "personally understandable." The head of the German judges' federation, Geert Mackenrofh, voiced support for Daschner, stating that "there are situations that cannot really be resolved by legal means, and in which legally protected rights have to be weighed." These comments generated a substantial backlash from the media and other government officials. An editorial in the *Kölner Stadtanzeiger* pointed out that the German debate about torture did not involve the use of torture during wartime, but rather by a crime punishable under the penal code and went on to argue that:

> It is therefore all the more important we continue to press for the upholding of the ban on torture. This debate has shown how easily prepared we are to shed the principles of the rule of law . . . The protective film under which we keep human dignity safeguarded as a cherished possession has proven itself to be wafer thin.

Germany's problems with the unlawful use of force have not been restricted to a single incident. Within the past 2 years there has been a series of allegations against members of the German military, the Border Protection Police, and law enforcement officials concerning the excessive use of force. These accounts include a report published by the Council of Europe charging members of the German Border Police with using unnecessary violence when deporting foreigners, as well as allegations that German military officers tortured recruits during basic training by pretending to be Arab terrorists. These allegations have been particularly disturbing for Germany given that the German press harshly criticized the U.S. treatment of prisoners at the Abu Ghraib prison in Iraq as a violation of the Geneva Conventions.

Perhaps the lesson that democratic governments should take from the German experience is that governments must be vigilant in protecting human rights regardless of the particular tactics that they elect to fight terrorism. As the German example illustrates, the simple fact that Germany has chosen to respond to 9/11 by relying primarily on its existing criminal justice system has not prevented some public officers from committing human rights abuses.

A key challenge for democracies today is how to preserve human rights while protecting their security interests. In the best of circumstances, the nature of how terrorists operate challenge governments that attempt to craft effective counterterrorism strategies that protect human rights and civil liberties. To preserve the rule of law in a time of terror, it has become increasingly important that governments ensure that systems are in place to discover, investigate, and prosecute human rights abuses. This requires an ongoing commitment at all levels of government, as well as an aggressive media that is unafraid to shine the light on government transgressions. Absent this level of commitment, democratic governments run the risk that the most important casualty of the war on terror will be their commitment to the rule of law itself.

8

International Law Enforcement Academies (ILEA)

As we approach the 21st century, it has become imperative that we develop and implement an international training programme to confront the global challenges facing us with the escalation of international crime and terrorism. For the first time in history we must prepare, enable and empower police officers with little or no experience, to operate within a democratic framework in which they must both maintain social order and preserve civil and human rights. It is imperative that the brotherhood of law enforcement professionals be willing and able to stem the corrosive tide of organized crime. In mid-1994, the Federal Bureau of Investigation (FBI) Director Louis J. Freeh and a delegation of top United States law enforcement professionals traveled throughout Central and Eastern Europe. The purpose of the trip was to meet law enforcement colleagues in the region and discuss methods to attack transnational criminal activity.

Mutual assistance and training were quickly identified as two areas that would have an immediate, significant impact. It was in this context that the concept of an International Law Enforcement Academy (ILEA) facility for the region was first developed. The ILEA initiative is a multinational effort organized by the United States, the Government of Hungary, and other international training partners. United States federal law enforcement agencies and the Department of State (DOS) are engaged in a cooperative effort to provide assistance to our police colleagues in the emerging democracies.

These law enforcement agencies are the Federal Bureau of Investigation (FBI), Drug Enforcement Administration (DEA), United States Secret Service (USSS), Bureau of Alcohol, Tobacco, and Firearms (BATF), United States Customs Service (USCS), Internal Revenue Service (IRS), the Department of State Diplomatic Security Service (DS), the Department of Energy (DOE), and the Federal Law Enforcement Training Center (FLETC). Other countries engaged in this international partnership by providing instructors for ILEA programs including Canada, Great Britain, Ireland, Italy, Germany, Russia, Hungary and the Netherlands.

In addition, representatives from the European Union and the Council of Europe have participated in the development and operation of the ILEA. The partnership developed between the law enforcement agencies of the United States and the Hungarian National Police, serves as a model for international law enforcement cooperation. As full partners in the ILEA initiative, both countries contributed financial and personnel resources to ensure that the ILEA would be successful.

ILEA Facilities

The site chosen for the ILEA was an existing training and education center for the Hungarian National Police (HNP). The facility was built in 1910 as a military post for Hungarian Cavalry Units. Experts in the design of classroom and dormitory facilities were utilized to create a plan for optimum use of existing facilities. The plan called for a comprehensive renovation of a classroom building and two dormitories. Approximately $2.5 million (US dollars) was furnished by the DOS and the FBI, with an additional $500,000 (US dollars) furnished by the government of Hungary to accomplish the extensive renovation. The buildings identified for the ILEA, although structurally sound, were in need of renovation to bring the facility up to a more modern standard. An agreement between the Hungarian Ministry of Interior, HNP, DOS and the FBI was signed regarding the development of the ILEA and was subsequently authenticated by an exchange of Diplomatic Notes between Hungary and the U.S.

The ILEA International Curriculum Committee (ICC)

Curriculum development for the ILEA project has, and continues to be, a needs-driven process. In February 1995, the first meeting of the ICC was convened at the future site of the ILEA in Budapest, Hungary, to develop curriculum for the program. In attendance at this historic meeting were police officials from the participating countries of the Czech Republic, Estonia, Hungary, Poland, Lithuania, Russia, Slovakia, and Ukraine as well as the potential partner countries of Canada, Denmark, Norway, Sweden, Italy, and Great Britain. Also participating in the meeting were representatives from the United Nations Crime Prevention Bureau of Vienna and the European Union (Euro customs). The U.S. delegation included representatives from the FBI, DEA, and the U.S. Department of Treasury. The ICC was co-chaired by the University of Virginia (UVA) and John Jay College of Criminal Justice in New York.

The ILEA curriculum evolves through biannual ICC meetings, which are scheduled in Budapest and in the United States. At these meetings, the ICC receives input on crime problems and training needs from the countries attending the next session and receives a critique of the course from the countries attending the current session. The makeup of the ICC varies from meeting to meeting, but has always included a representative number of European participants.

The International Faculty

No permanent instructional staff is present in Budapest. Lecturers for the various courses are primarily practitioners who come to Budapest to present their area of expertise and then return to their home country. Law enforcement professionals from the United States, Canada, Great Britain, Germany, Ireland, Italy, Russia, Hungary, and the Council of Europe representatives from Belgium and France, have collaborated to ensure that the ILEA program is relevant to the needs of the international law enforcement community.

ILEA Management

The overall management structure of the ILEA is composed of an on-site program manager from the FBI, a deputy program director from the USSS, a senior Hungarian police liaison officer who serves as a deputy, and two contract support employees (Hungarian citizens). An ILEA steering committee, located in Washington, D.C., provides policy guidance, and the International Training Section at the FBI Academy, Quantico, Virginia, provides operational support. Supporting the ILEA program manager is a class coordinator, who is a federal law enforcement official chosen on a rotating basis from one of the agencies participating in the ILEA program. Assisting in the overall ILEA management effort is the input generated from the regular meetings of the ILEA ICC. The ILEA program manager is a FBI agent assigned to Budapest on a term assignment. The ILEA steering committee is composed of members from all participating law enforcement agencies, chaired by a representative from DOS.

The committee is charged with the responsibility of establishing and reviewing ILEA policies and procedures, prioritizing requests for use of the facility, and addressing any issues and problems that may arise. The rules established to govern committee operations provide equitable representation for all agencies and countries involved. In addition to the steering committee, an executive policy board was created. This board is composed of cabinet level officials from DOS, the Department of Treasury and the Department of Justice. Because of the international nature of ILEA operations, the makeup of the ILEA steering committee has provisions for an international component, possibly staffed by representatives from the embassies of countries who are active partners in the ILEA initiative. The current management structure provides a flexible, adaptable mechanism and process to address and resolve issues related to ILEA activities.

ILEA Funding

To operate the ILEA, the FBI utilizes two separate DOS funding agreements: Freedom Support Act (FSA) funds and Support for Eastern European Democracy (SEED) Act funds. The FBI is reimbursed through DOS in accordance with the guidelines set forth in the Interagency Agreement between DOS and the FBI. It is the FBI understands that funding for ILEA; Budapest falls under the Foreign Assistance Act which specifies the amount of aid individual countries will receive under that Act. In this case, DOS funding for ILEA is limited to those countries comprising the Russian Federation and Newly Independent States. The following is a list of countries eligible to receive FSA and SEED funds: FSA-Armenia, Moldova, Azerbaijan, Russia, Belarus, Tajikistan, Georgia, Turkmenistan, Kazakhstan, Ukraine, Kyrgyzstan, Uzbekistan, SEED, Albania, Lithuania, Bosnia-Herzegovina, Macedonia, Bulgaria, Poland, Croatia, Romania, Czech Republic, Serbia-Montenegro, Estonia, Slovakia, Hungary, Slovenia, Latvia.

Student Selection

The comprehensive student selection process for the ILEA eight-week program involves the vetting of prospective students within their own organizations, according to the criteria established by the first ICC. These criteria are:

- Be nominated by their country without regard to race, color, or sex.
- Be at least 25 years of age.
- Be a regularly appointed, full-time law enforcement officer with a minimum of five years of substantially continuous law enforcement experience, who agrees to remain in law enforcement a minimum of three years after graduation.
- Be in excellent physical condition, certified for strenuous physical exertion and regular participation in physical training and defensive tactics.
- Be of good moral character and reputation and outstanding in the law enforcement profession.
- Have at least a high school equivalency, with some level of university experience desirable. The candidate should show aptitude and interest in academic achievement.
- While no regular background investigation is possible, records are reviewed to ensure there is no information, which would preclude acceptance.

ILEA Eight-Week Program

The opening of ILEA in April 1995 was an important step toward establishing a mechanism for regional law enforcement training in Eastern Europe. The ILEA is similar to the domestic FBI National Academy (FBINA) program in the United States, conducted with simultaneous translation to eliminate an Academy requirement for students to speak English. The ILEA program is an eight-week personal and professional development program, conducted for up to 50 students in each of five sessions per year.

The focus for this program is not on technical skills, but rather on leadership, personnel and financial management issues, human rights, ethics, the rule of law, management of the investigative process, and other contemporary law enforcement issues. At ILEA, police officers from Eastern Europe, Russia and the Baltic States are trained in techniques used to combat modern criminal activity, including organized crime and terrorist groups. As of June 19, 2001, 31 sessions will have been provided to a total of 1,396 students representing 25 countries, with the largest number of students coming from Hungary. The ILEA facility also hosts specialized training and seminars sponsored by various U.S. law enforcement agencies. By June 2001, an additional 4,384 law enforcement officials, representing 26 countries, have attended the specialized training.

9

Tension between India and Pakistan

Improvement in the relations between India and Pakistan will continue to look a mirage till some miraculous changes take place in the behavior and approach of the powerful states *vis-à-vis* smaller nations and their problems. Both India and Pakistan remain at loggerheads, since their independence, In spite of their history of deadly wars, poverty and diseases. Despite writing documents of peace after each battle, they could not make any progress towards peace or normalization of relations during the last 54 years. On the contrary now the nuclear capability of both these countries poses a great danger to a huge population of millions of human beings in this sub continent. In fact the road to peace passes through Kashmir which is blocked by India. How unfortunate?

India opens each time some new Pandora's Box to belie all hopes of peace and reconciliation for the suffering humanity of our region. India has chosen a horrendous path of militarism to resolve the Kashmir dispute with Kashmir and Pakistan. Every time India, in order to silence the people of Kashmir, enacted draconian laws and now the Government of India has put a new law on its statute-book, called Prevention of Terrorism Act(POTA), which gives police sweeping powers to detain a person and seize and confiscate his/her property as a terrorist. According to the Indian dictate now anybody expressing his faith in the right of self-determination or advocating human rights sanctity is a terrorist and is liable to detention or prosecution any time on flimsy grounds. India justifies her barbaric steps against Kashmiris in the name of so called "proxy war by Pakistan", but at the same time India rejects any UN monitoring of the inside situation. India is allergic to third party mediation over Kashmir. It is strange that India is not ready to show any proof of foreign interference to the United Nations or to allow the monitoring teams of the "US led coalition against terrorism" to visit Kashmir.

The Government of India has enhanced her military budget only to crush the 20th century freedom struggle and intensify human rights abuses, thus adding fuel to fire in Kashmir and elsewhere. The systematic ethnic cleansing of minorities, especially those of Muslims in Gujarat—loot, arson and gang rape of their women in broad day light under the patronage of the Government and law enforcing agencies is a living example of religious fanaticism and terrorism in India. One day the world will have to discover with surprise a poisonous cobra of cast/race fanaticism with wings of terrorism hidden in higher Indian castes-equally threat to all other cultures, religions and races in the world. For the world it is better to wake up now and it should not attribute everything to the slogan of Jehad in the Muslim world. West claims to be liberal and secular. Is there any scope for a secular culture in a racial and cast system like this, we find in the beliefs of Balthakrey like leaders and followers.

Kashmiris in Kashmir follow for centuries a culture of co-existence between cultural groups of Muslims and Non-Muslims and despite separate religious beliefs, there is no notion of, no room for racial/cast supremacy or discrimination in Kashmir. On the contrary Indian ruling class is a racial class and wants to govern by racialism. This is the roof cause of tension between India and Pakistan over Kashmir and this much hidden phenomenon might start a war between the two countries.

The high profile emissaries of the world are one after another paying visits to both India and Pakistan to defuse the tension. But the world has not achieved as yet any substantive success in this regard and western citizens have been directed by their Governments to leave this region. At the same time this dilemma has some other aspects.

Financial Times, says, the arms dealers see bonanza in Pak-India stand off. It writes, while the international community calls for restrain on the Indo-Pak border, Governments led by the UK & USA are jockeying as never before for a bigger slice of Indian budget.

In March this year (2002) India launched a new military intelligence agency to bring the existing army, navy and air force networks under one roof. The Defense intelligence Agency (DIA) is modeled along western lines and will be headed by an army Gen, as per a defense ministry announcement.

The Indian Government has also enhanced intelligence funds to boost the activities of its different networks and establish the most modern spying and counter spying system. Mr. B L Kak A well known Indian columnist throws some light on its statistics in the Indian Express. Some excerpts of the report are given below:-

"A substantial increase in the annual outlay of country's intelligence agencies has been made available in the budget proposal of 2002-03. The 209-page document titled "Expenditure budget 2002-03 made public by the Finance Minister mentioned only one outfit, namely Intelligence Bureau(IB), as the Governments secrecy-for the-sake-of-secrecy policy prevented Mr. Yashvant Sinha from disclosing details of the enhanced financial outlay for other intelligence agencies, particularly the Research And Analysis

Wing(RAW), Military intelligence(MI), BSF intelligence Organization. More money for all intelligence agencies will also lead to an increase in the Source fund during the 2002-03 financial years over the revised allocation during 2001-02.

The total plan and non-plan allocation for the IB during 2002-03 has been fixed at Rs. 349.10 crores. Equally striking feature of the 2002-03 budget allocation of the Ministry of Home Affairs is a substantial amount of money (Rs. 341.79 crores) earmarked for the prestigious organization, known as SSB (Special Security Bureau).

Of the financial allocation of the order of Rs. 10743.20 crores earmarked for the Home Ministry, Border Security Force (BSF) will get Rs. 2607.24 crores as against the revised outlay of Rs. 2289.55 crores during 2001-02 financial years. Similarly the Finance Minster has proposed Rs. 1998.79 crores for the central reserve Police Force. (CRPF), Rs. 97.69 crores for the national security Guard (NSG), Rs. 446.67 crores for Indo-Tibetan Border Police (ITBP), and Rs. 719.17 crores for Assam Rifles.

"A substantial increase has been brought in the allocation of funds for indo-Pakistan Border works, from Rs. 91.95 crores in 2001-02 to Rs. 186. 99 crores during the 2002-03 financial years. According to Mr. Yashvant Sinha, provision has been made to check inflow of arms and ammunition from across the Indo-Pakistan Border. With a view to meeting the financial requirements on India's representation 157 missions and posts abroad, the finance minister has proposed Rs. 787.82 crores during the next Financial Year as against Rs. 759.92 crores in 2001-02.

The Ministry OF External Affairs will for the next financial Year get a total of Rs. 3238.34 crores as against Rs. 2830 crores during 2001-02. A sum of Rs. 785.01 crores has been earmarked as special diplomatic expenditure during the next Financial Year, as against Rs. 690.01 crores in 2001-02".

This is only a little bit of India's security preparedness, but the hidden agenda is much greater in as for as the aggressive designs are concerned. India tries to gain maximum out of the US slogan of war against terrorism. In fact, India wants to annihilate Kashmiris by labeling them as Al-Qaida members. It is only a lame excuse, otherwise till recently India called Kashmiri freedom fighters as misguided youth.

There is also the fear of adopting by India, the pre-emption doctrine of America. Peter W Galbraith a former ambassador to Croatia is not wrong when he says, "NO place is the risk greater than in South Asia. If India adopted the American doctrine of pre-emption, it risks a nuclear war, with devastating consequences for the world."

It is in this background that India is not ready to start negotiations with Pakistan when the later has repeatedly offered unconditional talks to the former. India is not ready to pull back troops from attack positions on Pakistan's border unless Pakistan meets her irrelevant demands or till so called Assembly elections in Kashmir. Does India want that Pakistan should ban struggle of the people of J&K people for their brothers across the LoC? No-that can not happen. As for the movement in Srinagar, it is an internal struggle of Kashmiris. Pakistan can not join hands, with India to stop the call for freedom in Kashmir. India is suppressing the armed struggle in Kashmir, would she instead recognize peaceful political fight of Kashmiris for their birth right-the right of self-determination? India's stand off, bellicosity, refusal to hold talks with Pakistan, curbing of peaceful political activities inside Kashmir by extreme repressive laws, human rights abuses, thrusting farce polls on Kashmir, and making ridiculous proposal of joint India Pak patrolling of LoC, and recently the custodial brutal murder of a Pakistani soldier by India on the border, indicates that the tensity in India-Pakistan relations will increase further, as India will remain in search of any excuse to attack Azad Kashmir.

Because, the political cry against India inside Kashmir is not in anybody's hands. Over 80000 graves of martyrs spread all over Kashmir are enough to remain as centers for uprising-not necessarily armed. Will people forget their beloved martyrs? Therefore, India should not blame Pakistan for everything in the valley. Such intransigent approach towards regional dispute will never help India stop the music against her in the occupied territory. Redeem your historical pledges with Kashmiris and stop there bloodshed. That is urgently required. And remember Children born in turmoil are of a different mettle as compared with the people who died before it.

Net benefits

Apart from the contemporary fad of announcing one's presence in the www, there is surprisingly little initiative shown by government agencies or by private enterprises to exploit the Net even at half its potential. More often than not in our country a web-site sits there just doing nothing except that gives owner the feel of being fashionable. They are there simply because their respective owners think that they would look silly without being on the Net as is the contemporary wont, never having realized the negative impact of a site is not strategically designed. Because a comatose web-site with nothing but routine information or details of self aggrandizement costs them a great deal of lost visitors - people who come, see, get turned off by the platitude and go away never to come back.

Being online is much more than dishing out drab details that do not interest or entertain any one except the agency owing it. The content of the site must be compatible with the objective of the site owner, besides being unique in character to retain viewer's interest, or to stimulate his easy interaction .But what we see in practice is that most of the web-site particularly those of government agencies are not too sure of their objective and therefore start out without a well defined strategy which reduces the site to a dull bulletin, resulting in wasted efforts.

Having to waste the advantage of such a powerful medium is no less than a cardinal sin for any organization, particularly for those who often grumble about infrastructural handicaps in reaching out to the people or to the focus groups.

At a time when one of the avowed priorities of any democratic government is transparency and free access to information for the public, the internet assumes a very crucial role in terms of both reach and irretrievability. It is particularly so to such areas as are relatively left behind in infrastructural adequacy for various reasons. Against this backdrop it is heartening to see initiative taken by the State Police in that direction with special focus on police-public interface. It augurs well that the particular content of the site has been drawing quite a handful of visitors some of them with frank and discerning observations within a short period of time. The palpable shift of focus of Assam Police towards improved police - public interface is a laudable initiative which was long overdue and in which the web-site may play the role of an important catalyst.

The very fact that public is offered a forum to voice their frank opinion over matters relating to their own safety ,security and grievances is a very welcome departure from the familiar posture of menacing virulence, the Police have so long been identified with-much to the consternation of the people . If properly nourished over a period of time this may lead to very significant achievements in terms of police public symbiosis which is so much indispensable for either of the two in a liberal democracy. This is not to suggest that police-public symbiosis alone will it together eradicate crime from the society. On the contrary, the stark reality is that a crime free society is an impossible dream. But in a civilized society crime can and must be contained to tolerable limits and also crime as a phenomenon should be viewed in the social perspective, since the criminals are as much a part of our social firmaments as the rest.

As such, policing becomes progressively onerous, adding newer dimensions to the problem. Unlike familiar patterns of social violence where the victim and the criminals are usually related in some way or the other, the targets of contemporary terrorism are chosen at random. The most effective bulwark, therefore, against modern terrorism is a healthy symbiosis between the public and the police, which provides the basis of social policing. The traditional belief that the key to control of crime is the criminal's justice system, must now be reviewed in the light of emerging social convolutions and the changing pattern of crime in the form of terrorism and white - colour offences. It obviously calls for more active participation of the members of the society .since every person is a potential victim of such violence. Needless to say that it is however mandatory for the police to perform the pivotal role in creating an environment of confidence for the public to come forth and supplement the efforts of the law enforcing agency.

The initiative of Assam Police to that direction - however humble may be for the present - is a positive move to which a section of the society is already seen to have offered their proactive response. It hardly needs to be emphasized that the people at large are thoroughly averse to any form of violence form whatever source, which is pretty much evident from some of the observations found in the discussion forum of the Police website. People have begun to realize at a great cost the futility of shedding innocent blood for an illusion pursued by handful desperadoes who throw all qualms to the wind to justify their means of chasing an autistic dream. To illustrate the point a few quotes from the site will help. The public must rise to the occasion one writes Peace is not a commodity which can be packaged and sold for public consumption. It is a perception which grows as a result of our joint efforts. We want peace and we are loath to give it away because a handful few happen to hold our 'Sonor Asom to ransom.'

One only wishes that other agencies of the government also take cue from Assam Police to dispel public apprehensions about their activities and thereby bringing in transparency to their dealings. It is about time that our policy makers mould their hackneyed mindset for new ideals to take roof, in keeping with the changing priorities before it is too late to retrieve them from the morass of obsolescence. This is not to mean though, that going digital alone would purge them of all their accumulated rusts and make them any sprightlier to rise to the occasion, unless they learn to read the writings on the wall and do some self introspection as to the chasm between what is expected of them and what they are actually delivering . Until then one can only keep one's fingers crossed and hope for the best, lest the map of Assam in world at last be replaced by a skull and cross bones, for all time to come.

10

The Homeland Security and Posse Comitatus Act

The quotation above is the much-discussed Posse Comitatus Act in its entirety. That is it! That is all there is to it. Seldom has so much been derived from so little. Few articles written about the act and its implications cite the law as it is written, leading one to believe that the authors have never taken the trouble to go to the U.S. Code and see for themselves or to look up the legislative history of the act or to read the exceptions in the law. As a result, much of what has been said and written about the Posse Comitatus Act is just plain nonsense.

The Posse Comitatus Act is often cited as a major constraint on the use of the military services to participate in homeland security, counterterrorism, civil disturbances, and similar domestic duties. It is widely believed that this law prohibits the Army, Navy, Air Force, and Marine Corps from performing any kind of police work or assisting law enforcement agencies to enforce the law. This belief, however, is not exactly correct.

What is correct is that new rules are needed to clearly set forth the boundaries for the use of federal military forces for homeland security. The Posse Comitatus Act is inappropriate for modern times and needs to be replaced by a completely new law.

The law was enacted originally on 18 June 1878. It was amended in 1959 to make it applicable to Alaska. It was amended in 1994 to remove an upper limit of $10,000 on the fine that was in the original act. As shall be noted later, in recent years Congress has enacted other laws that specify when the Posse Comitatus Act does not apply. The biggest error is the common assertion that the Posses Comitatus Act was enacted to prevent the military services (Army, Navy, Air Force, and Marine Corps) from acting as a national police force.

Colonel Richard Hart Sinnreich, in an otherwise admirable piece, opined thusly in an article in the 12 December 2001 Washington Post:

The American aversion to a military gendarmerie was formalized after Reconstruction in the Posse Comitatus Act of 1878, which severely restricts the use of active military forces in domestic law enforcement.

Reconstruction was the 12 years from 1865 to 1877 when the U.S. Army occupied the defeated Southern states. Major Craig T. Trebilcock, U.S. Army Reserve, in his Journal of Homeland Security article "The Myth of Posse Comitatus," does a good job at pointing out that the use of military personnel to enforce the law is in fact allowable, but makes a mistake when he says:

The Posse Comitatus Act was passed to remove the Army from civilian law enforcement and to return it to its role of defending the borders of the United States.

Another gross misinterpretation of the Posse Comitatus Act was made on 13 December 2001 in the Washington Times, which reported that Provost Marshal William J. Bolduc of the Walter Reed Army Medical Center reduced the police powers of the civilian police force at that facility because they were bound by the Posse Comitatus Act. The story said:

The Posse Comitatus Act of 1878 prohibits members of the U.S. armed forces or employees of the U.S. military from enforcing laws on civilians [emphasis added].

Sinnreich, Trebilcock, Bolduc, and most commentators who opine on this law are wrong. The Posse Comitatus Act was not, as they assert and as most people believe, enacted to prevent members of military services from acting as a national police force. It was enacted to prevent the Army from being abused by having its soldiers pressed into service as police officers (a posse) by local law enforcement officials in the post-Reconstruction South.

The Story of the Posse Comitatus Act

The law was enacted as a result of the election of 1876, which was the event that ended the period of Reconstruction after the Civil War. The law was enacted to overturn an 1854 opinion of the attorney general. The story is bound up with the conflict within the United States about slavery and the Union.

The posse comitatus doctrine comes from English common law. Posse comitatus means, literally, the "force of the county"; the posse comitatus is that body of men above the age of 15 whom the sheriff may summon or raise to repress a riot or for other purposes. In 1854, Caleb Cushing, attorney general for President Franklin Pierce, blessed the posse comitatus doctrine and opined that marshals could summon a posse comitatus and that both militia and regulars in organized bodies could be members of such a posse.

This was done to improve the enforcement of the Fugitive Slave Act of 1850. Among other things, this meant that the United States was responsible for expenses incurred by U.S. marshals in employing local police, state militia, or others in apprehending and safeguarding fugitive slaves.

The Cushing Doctrine meant that even though the armed forces might be organized as military bodies under the command of their officers, they could still be pressed into service by U.S. marshals or local sheriffs as a posse comitatus without the assent of the president. This doctrine was merely the opinion of the attorney general and was not subjected to judicial or legislative review prior to its enunciation. The Cushing Doctrine encouraged the use of the Army and Navy as police forces, and it was used widely in the West, where the Army was the only armed force available to assist local officials to enforce the law along the turbulent frontier. It had little effect in the South during the period before the Civil War and came into prominence there only during Reconstruction.

During Reconstruction, the Army exercised police and judicial functions, oversaw the local governments, and dealt with domestic violence. In effect, the Army governed the 11 defeated Confederate States and was the enforcer of national reconstruction policy during all or part of the period. Before the Civil War, the militia under state control was used to control local disorders throughout the United States, but during Reconstruction, there was no effective militia in the defeated states, so the Army protected the people (especially the newly emancipated slaves) and dealt with disturbances. This use of the Army was validated by the Civil Rights Act of 1866, which empowered U.S. marshals to summon and call to their aid the posse comitatus of the counties, or portions of the land or naval forces of the United States, or of the militia. As the former Confederate States were readmitted to the Union, the status of the Army changed, but its role remained much the same.

After 1868, when all but three of the Southern states had reentered the union, the problem became one of how to obtain assistance from the Army to enforce the law. In response to a desperate plea from a U.S. marshal in Florida, the Attorney General of the United States, William M. Evarts, cited the posse comitatus doctrine that gave U.S. marshals and county sheriffs the right to command all necessary assistance from within their districts, including military personnel and civilians, to serve on the posse comitatus to execute legal process.

Evarts' decision led to numerous requests by marshals and county sheriffs for troops to use in enforcing the law, all without presidential approval. This met with some resistance from the Army, and the War Department said that the obligation of individual officers and soldiers to obey the summons of a marshal or sheriff must be held subordinate to the paramount duty as members of a permanent military body. The troops were to act only in organized units under their own officers and would obey the orders of those officers. In 1871, President U. S. Grant sought to provide a basis for the use of troops other than posse comitatus. In accordance with Grant's policy, the War Department issued general orders saying that the forces of the United States may be committed and shall be employed to assist the civil authorities in making arrests of persons accused of crime, preventing the rescue of arrested persons, and dispersing marauders and armed organizations.

By the end of Grant's second term, the South was ready and able to end U.S. Government control over their states. In the election of 1876, the Democratic candidate, Samuel J. Tilden, won a majority of the popular vote, but the Republican candidate, Rutherford B. Hayes, ended up with a majority of one vote in the Electoral College. The election was disputed and finally determined by a deal in which Tilden would concede the election if Hayes agreed to end Reconstruction. Accordingly, Reconstruction ended in 1877 with the inauguration of Hayes as the 19th president. Federal troops in the South were no longer used to enforce the law, and the Southerners became masters in their own states for the first time since the end of the Civil War.

Congress passed the Posse Comitatus Act in 1878 in a dispute over the use of federal troops by U.S. marshals in the South. Based on precedent, Attorney General Charles Devens took the position that the U.S. Judiciary Act of 1789 authorized U.S. marshals to raise a posse comitatus comprising every person in a district above 15 years of age, "including the military of all denominations, militia, soldiers, marines, all of whom are alike bound to obey the commands of a Sheriff or Marshal." However, Congress had become disenchanted with the habit of U.S. marshals and sheriffs to press Army troops into their service without the approval of the commander in chief.

The Southerners in particular questioned this policy. Ironically, the posse comitatus doctrine had been postulated in 1854 by Attorney General Cushing to help Southerners enforce the Fugitive Slave Act. Now it was being used to contest the Ku Klux Klan. On 27 May 1878, Representative J. Proctor Knoft of Kentucky introduced an amendment to the Army appropriations bill; the amendment eventually became the Posse Comitatus Act. In passing the act, the Congress voted to restrict the ability of U.S. marshals and local sheriffs to conscript military personnel into their posses. They did not vote to preclude the use of troops if authorized by the president or Congress.

Somehow, in the past 125 years, the meaning of the Posse Comitatus Act has been stood on its head. Clearly the exposition above demonstrates that the intent of the act was not to preclude the Army from enforcing the law but instead was designed to allow the Army to do this only when directed to do so by the President or Congress. The official history of the use of the military services to enforce the laws says:

Some of those who opposed it [the Posse Comitatus Act] in the Congress charged that [it] was taking away from the president entirely the power to use troops to repress internal disorders except on request of a state governor or legislature, that President Washington could not even had dealt with the Whiskey Rebellion under its terms. This interpretation of the Posse Comitatus Act has often been raised by those protesting against federal troop's intervention in the many instances it has occurred since 1878. And indeed the question of what the real meaning of the Posse Comitatus Act was has been the subject of some dispute ever since its passage ... however ... all that it really did was to repeal a doctrine whose only substantial foundation was an opinion by an attorney general, and one that had never been tested in the courts. The president's power to use both regular and military remained undisturbed by the Posse Comitatus Act, and by the law of 1861 and the Ku Klux Klan Act that had in fact been substantially strengthened during the Civil War and Reconstruction Era. But the posse Comitatus Act did mean that troops could not be used on any authority than that of the President and that he must issue a cease and desist from proclamation before he did so. Commanders in the field would no longer have any discretion but must wait for orders from Washington.

The immediate impact of the Posse Comitatus Act was not felt very much in the Southern states because President Hayes had withdrawn the troops that had been occupying them. However, there was great impact in the West, where the Cushing Doctrine had been used a great deal by marshals and local sheriffs to call on local military commanders for assistance. Having to wait for presidential approval before troops could be used was disadvantageous given the turbulence common on the frontier.

The Effect of the Posse Comitatus Act

Before speculating on why this act is so misunderstood, it is useful to spell out exactly what the act as it is written does and does not do. The Posse Comitatus Act -

- Applies only to the Army and by extension the Air Force, which was formed out of the Army in 1947.
- Does not apply to the Navy and Marine Corps. However, the Department of Defense has consistently held that the Navy and Marine Corps should behave as if the act applied to them.
- Does not apply to the Coast Guard, which is part of the Department of Transportation and is both an armed force and a law enforcement agency with police powers.
- Does not apply to the National Guard in its role as state troops on state active duty under the command of the respective governors.
- May not apply to the National Guard (qua militia) even when it is called to federal active duty. The Posse Comitatus Act contains no restrictions on the use of the federalized militia as it did on the regular Army. It is commonly believed, however, that National Guard units and personnel come under the Posse Comitatus Act when they are on federal active duty, and this interpretation is followed today.
- Does not apply to state guards or State Defense Forces under the command of the respective governors.
- Does not apply to military personnel assigned to military police, shore police, or security police duties. The military police have jurisdiction over military members subject to the Uniform Code of Military Justice. They also exercise police powers over military dependents and others on military installations. The history of the law makes it clear that it was not intended to prevent federal police (for example, marshals) from enforcing the law.
- Does not apply to civilian employees, including those who are sworn law enforcement officers. The origin and legislative history of the act make it clear that it applies only to military personnel. In those days, there were no civilian employees of the Army in the sense

that there are today. In particular, no one envisioned that the Army would hire civilian police officers to enforce the laws at its facilities.

- Does not prevent the President from using federal troops in riots or civil disorders. Federal troops were used for domestic operations more than 200 times in the two centuries from 1795 to 1995. Most of these operations were to enforce the law, and many of them were to enforce state law rather than federal law. Nor does it prevent the military services from supporting local or federal law enforcement officials as long as the troops are not used to arrest citizens or investigate crimes.

In recent years, several laws have been enacted that grant specific exceptions to the application of the Posse Comitatus Act.

Title 18 U.S. Code, Section 831, provides that if nuclear material is involved in an emergency, the Secretary of Defense may provide assistance to the Department of Justice, notwithstanding the Posse Comitatus Act.

Title 10 U.S. Code, Chapter 18, authorizes military support for civilian law enforcement agencies for counter drug operations and in emergencies involving chemical or biological weapons of mass destruction. The Secretary of Defense may provide information, allow the use of military equipment and facilities, train law enforcement officials in the operation and maintenance of military equipment, and maintain such equipment. Support for law enforcement agencies may not impair military readiness, and military personnel shall not participate in searches, seizures, arrests, or similar activities unless such participation is otherwise authorized by law. (Military police personnel, for example, may enforce the law within their jurisdictions.)

If there were violations of the act, the culprits would not be members of the Army and Air Force who assisted local law enforcement agencies but rather the local law enforcement officials who required the troops to assist in the enforcement of laws or local military commanders who did so without obtaining Presidential authority. It is no wonder that there have never been any prosecutions under the law.

It is worthwhile asking why the original meaning of the Posse Comitatus Act has been transformed into its almost exact opposite. It is not the purpose of this article to solve this mystery, but it is useful to speculate on some of the motives of the people who have been involved.

Some cynics believe that the Department of Defense and the military services support the erroneous application of posse comitatus because they do not want to get involved in domestic emergencies. This appears to be the position of many active-component officers. In an address to the Fletcher Conference on 15 November 2001, General William F. Kernan, Commander in Chief, Joint Forces Command, presumably referring to the Posse Comitatus Act, said that there were limitations on the active components that restricted them from "doing those kinds of things, and rightfully so." General Kernan went on to propose an order of response to domestic emergencies that starts with the first responders, then the National Guard, and finally the Reserves and active components. This may be a logical order, but it is based on a flawed understanding of history.

The military services and the Army in particular, have been used on numerous occasions to enforce the law, notably in federal efforts to desegregate public schools and quell riots. One recent example of this was the use of active-duty Army troops, Marines, and federalized California National Guard troops to deal with the 1992 riots in Los Angeles prompted by the acquittal of police officers charged with assaulting Rodney King. Now that the Quadrennial Defense Review for 2001 has declared homeland security to be the primary mission of the Department of Defense, this aversion to the use of active components for domestic security may be weakened. In the meantime, however, some elements of the Department of Defense continue to hew to the line that it is improper for any element of the department, military or civilian, to enforce the laws in any fashion.

Americans have a general antipathy to the use of troops as police. This stems from British practice during Colonial times. There is a general feeling in the nation that policing is a local matter best done by police forces whose members are trained in law enforcement. Until recently there was also general opposition to a national police force as exists in most Western European nations. The Federal Bureau of Investigation (FBI) was until recently quite small and worked on cases that clearly were federal crimes.

In recent years, the number of federal crimes has increased, particularly in the field of civil rights violations, and now the FBI seems to be involved in many cases that formerly would have been handled under state law by local law enforcement agencies. The threat of imminent terrorist attack can only reinforce the trend to more and more federal laws and more and more federal police officers and prosecutors to deal with them. Americans appear to accept the increase in FBI jurisdiction but are unsympathetic to the habitual use of military personnel as police officers. In support of this feeling, persons writing on the Posse Comitatus Act may have addressed it as a legal bar to an unpopular possibility.

The lawyers have had a hand in transforming the Posse Comitatus Act from its original intent to what it may or may not be today. A substantial body of case law and judicial decisions pertaining to the use of military personnel to enforce the laws has been created. A casual review of these cases reveals confusion, inconsistency, and downright perversion of the original intent of the law. Much of this litigation has been prompted by persons averse to any role for military forces in law enforcement. Moreover, a significant body of policy and regulation has been created extra legally in the form of Department of Defense directives and military service regulations. These attempts to clarify the situation only add to the confusion. Most of them are based on a presumption significantly at variance with the law itself.

Finally, another reason for the misunderstanding and misapplication of this law is simply sloppy scholarship. It is apparent that many of the numerous authors who have written about this matter did not read the U.S. Code, studied the legislative history of the act, or consulted the two official histories prepared by the Center of Military History before airing their erroneous opinions. This appears to be one of those academic chain letters in which one set of unfounded conclusions is used as a source for derivative sets, which are accepted and passed along containing the original errors. In effect, the misinterpretation of the Posse Comitatus Act has become an urban myth that is widely believed without substantiation. This need not be.

Recommendation

The Posse Comitatus Act is not a general and universal proscription of the use of federal military forces to enforce or execute the law. The military services may do so and have done so when ordered by the president and pursuant to the authorization of Congress. Although the current interpretation of the act is the opposite of its original intention, it does discourage the military services from being used as a national police force-something we have wisely avoided up to now. The Posse Comitatus Act does not prevent the military services from supporting the police, nor does it preclude them from enforcing the law when so ordered by the president. It does preclude them from being the police in normal times.

It is time to rescind the existing Posse Comitatus Act and replace it with a new law. The old law is widely misunderstood and unclear. It leaves plenty of room for people to do unwise and perhaps unlawful things while trying to comply with their particular version. It certainly does not provide a basis for defining a useful relationship of military forces and civil authority in a global war with terrorism. The Posse Comitatus Act is an artifact of a different conflict-between freedom and slavery or between North and South, if you prefer. Today's conflict is also in a sense between freedom and slavery, but this time it is between civilization and terrorism. New problems often need new solutions, and a new set of rules is needed for this issue.

President Bush and Congress should initiate action to enact a new law that would set forth in clear terms a statement of the rules for using military forces for homeland security and for enforcing the laws of the United States. Things have changed a lot since 1878, and the Posse Comitatus Act is not only irrelevant but also downright dangerous to the proper and effective use of military forces for domestic duties.

Recent moves to beef up intelligence gathering in the wake of the September 11th terrorist attacks have civil libertarians concerned that law enforcement agencies will entangle many law abiding citizens and social justice groups in their surveillance missions. Intelligence networks are setting their sights on the Internet, which up to now has had no clear privacy guidelines. Under the provisions of the inaptly named anti-terrorism act, "USA-PATRIOT," the Federal Bureau of Investigation (FBI), National Security Agency (NSA), Central Intelligence Agency (CIA), and a number of other smaller law enforcement agencies are looking for ways to monitor the Internet and mine useful intelligence from it. And new technology makes it easier than ever to spy on the Internet.

Although law enforcement and intelligence agencies claim they are merely looking for information to counter future acts of terrorism, the definition of "terrorism" is being expanded to cover non-violent groups that have traditionally used the Internet to marshal resistance to corporate-inspired globalisation. Politicians are already painting dissent as "unpatriotic" and therefore somehow linked to terrorism.

Meanwhile, a phalanx of software companies, consultants, and defense contractors stand to reap billions of dollars over the next few years by selling surveillance and information-gathering systems to government agencies and the private sector.

Law enforcement agencies like the FBI already have at their disposal a massive information sharing network through which federal, state, local, and foreign police forces can exchange information on groups felt to pose a threat. The system, RISSNET, or Regional Information Sharing System Network, which existed before the September 11th attacks, recently gof a boost when Congress authorized additional money for it in the USA PATRIOT Act.

RISSNET is a secure intranet that connects 5,700 law enforcement agencies in all 50 states, as well as agencies in Ontario and Quebec, the District of Columbia, Guam, the U.S. Virgin Islands, Puerto Rico, and Australia. According to sources close to the Washington Metropolitan Police, data on targeted local groups such as the Alliance for Global Justice, the anti-World Bank/International Monetary Fund activist organization, has been shared with other jurisdictions through RISSNET.

RISSNET has also been used to coordinate the monitoring of the activities of anti-globalization protestors in Seattle, Quebec City, Philadelphia, Los Angeles, Washington DC and Genoa. For example, when the FBI seized network server logs from Independent Media Center (IMC) in Seattle during the April 2001 anti-free trade protests in Quebec City, RISSNET was used to coordinate activities across jurisdictional boundaries. The IMC, founded during the 1999 WTO protests, allows activists and independent journalists to post directly to its site.

State and metropolitan police intelligence units also monitor the web sites of activist organizations in their jurisdictions. All RISS intelligence is archived by an Orwellian-sounding entity called MAGLOCLEN or "Middle Atlantic-Great Lakes Organized Crime Law Enforcement Network." There are other regional RISS intelligence centers around the country with equally mysterious acronyms. MAGLOCLEN, a nerve center headquartered in Newtown, Pennsylvania, distributes political intelligence to all police departments hooked up to RISSNET.

MAGLOCLEN allows police investigators to link various activist groups and members through the Link Association Analysis sub-system, a relational data base that identifies the "friends and families" of groups and individuals. The Telephone Record Analysis sub-system can call up records of phone calls of targeted groups and individuals. A suspect group's banking and other commercial data can be monitored by the Financial Analysis sub-system. And through a system that would have been the envy of J. Edgar Hoover, police and federal agents can also call up profiles that provide specific information on the composition of organizations, including their membership lists. The Justice Department has instituted a project called RISSNET II, which directly links the individual databases contained within the various RISS centers.

The FBI also runs its own intranet called Law Enforcement On-line or "LEO," which allows it to communicate intelligence which selects other law enforcement agencies. In the aftermath of September 11th, the FBI is under pressure to open up LEO to more police agencies so they can have access to more real-time intelligence. If Attorney General John Ashcroft lifts restrictions placed on the FBI's collection of political intelligence, undoubtedly information on the First Amendment activities of American citizens will wind up in the Bureau's computer databases.

"There has been no indication that the FBI needs expanded spying powers," says Center for Constitutional Rights attorney Michael Ratner. "We should learn from history; spying on dissent is not only unlawful but it is abusive."

This kind of surveillance is not new. In the 1960s and 70s, the FBI's Counter Intelligence Program, known as COINTELPRO, was used to gather personal details on the lives and habits of a wide array of activists ranging from public figures like Dr. Martin Luther King, Jr., actress Jane Fonda and noted pediatrician Benjamin Spock, to members of local anti-war and civil rights groups. This information was often used to disrupt lawful organizing and protest activities.

A modern-day FBI list might include any group deemed "terrorist" by any law enforcement agencies, the military or criminal prosecutors. That could subject organizations as varied — and unconnected to terrorism — as Earth First, Greenpeace, the American Indian Movement, the Zapatista National Liberation Front, ACT UP, and their supporters to a wide array of high-tech surveillance and eavesdropping tools.

Chief among spy agency tools is an e-mail sniffing program known as Carnivore. Changes brought about by USA-PATRIOT allow federal law enforcement officials to petition a secretive federal court called the Foreign Intelligence Surveillance Court for warrants to tap phones, read e-mail, or break and enter into homes or offices to conduct searches and plant bugging devices. These spy activities can be carried out without proof that an organization has links to terrorists or foreign intelligence agencies.

To read e-mail the FBI can order an Internet Service Provider to place a special monitoring computer called Carnivore (now renamed Data Collection System 1000) on its network servers. The FBI can then select the e-mail of surveillance targets for capture and storage. Not content with this device, the FBI now seeks to expand its surveillance capability to the entire Internet.

Making a Buck off of Government Spying

Companies that are positioning themselves to help the government surveillance the web came out in force at a recent Homeland Security Conference in Washington. They included Oracle, Microsoft, Information Builders, Choice Point, Man Tech, AMS, and Booz Allen & Hamilton. Government speakers from civilian and military agencies all stressed that they urgently need the technology to store surveillance-derived intelligence and exchange it with other agencies. If these corporations step up to the plate on developing new surveillance, monitoring, and biometric ID systems, they stand to make billions.

Companies like Top Layer Networks, Inc. of Westboro, Massachusetts, are developing ways for the FBI to install surveillance systems at a few key Internet hubs which would allow federal agents to remotely flip a switch and pound a few keys to begin monitoring the e-mail or web-based mail of any targeted group or individual. According to chief Top Layer engineer Ken Georgiades, the firm is working with a number of partners to develop new standards for the legal interception of communications at the Internet Service Provider level and at higher gigabit speeds.

The higher gigabit intercept equipment would be placed at major Internet backbone hubs in strategic locations like Washington, DC, the San Francisco Bay Area, Chicago, Dallas, and Los Angeles. Georgiades said that the 1994 Communications Assistance to Law Enforcement Act (CALEA) does not currently extend to the Internet and only applies to telecommunications companies. However, the fact that Top Layer and its unspecified partners are ramping up to deliver CALEA-like wiretapping services for the Internet indicates the FBI sees the power of CALEA growing beyond phone lines to the web. And Georgiades pointed out that foreign governments are under no such constraints and can use Internet snooping equipment under existing current wiretapping laws.

David Banisar, Research Fellow at Harvard's Information Infrastructure Project, said such systems "set a dangerous precedent to allow law enforcement and intelligence agencies to run the communications system." He added, "These agencies take an over-inclusive view of who they think are the enemies and it's likely that civil and human rights groups will, again, be monitored for no legitimate reason."

The large defense and intelligence consulting and engineering firm Booz, Allen & Hamilton has not only developed the FBI's Carnivore capability but it has assisted the bureau in ensuring that all telecommunications companies engineer their systems to ensure they are "wiretap friendly." The companies are required by the Communications Assistance to Law Enforcement Act to ensure the FBI has access to all forms of telecommunications, including cellular calls.

What if a target decides to use encryption to protect their e-mail from interception? That is not a problem for the FBI. Booz Allen & Hamilton has helped develop a system code-named Magic Lantern, which permits a virus containing a key logging program to be secretly transmitted to a recipient. After installing itself on the target's computer, any time the target types in a password to decrypt a message, that same password is immediately picked up by Magic Lantern and transmitted to the FBI. Essentially, the FBI has a virtual master key to break any encryption program used by a surveillance target.

A companion program to Magic Lantern, code named Cyber Knight, is a relational database system that compares and matches information from e-mail, Internet relay chats, instant messages, and Internet voice communications.

Not to be outdone by the FBI, the CIA has also been extremely active in developing software than can dig deep within the Internet to harvest information. The CIA has relied heavily on its wholly-owned and operated proprietary Silicon Valley company, IN-Q-TEL, to fund research and development for Internet snooping software. IN-Q-TEL's President and Chief Executive Officer Gilman Louie are to keynote a January 2002 Las Vegas seminar on the use of emerging intelligence technology to search and analyze the web. He is to be joined by Joan Dempsey, the Deputy Director of the CIA for Intelligence Community Management. IN-Q-TEL's web page describes the aggressive attitude the CIA is taking toward ensuring new technologies come complete with the spy agency's seal of approval, "IN-Q-TEL strives to extend the Agency's access to new IT companies, solutions, and approaches to address their priority problems."

Assisting the government in its goals to gather massive amounts of personal information on citizens and non-citizens is a company that owes its very existence to the CIA. Oracle, Inc. Chairman Larry Ellison has offered to provide to the government free of charge the database software required to establish an interactive national ID card system. Oracle got its start when the CIA gave Ellison a contract in the 1970s to design a system to enable the agency to store and retrieve massive amounts if information in databases. Not coincidentally, the code name of that CIA project was "Oracle."

The rush by the government to monitor the Internet has the backing of a group of federal contract research facilities that have pounded out report after report warning about the threat of cyberspace to national security. These "think tanks" include Rand Corporation and Analytical Services Corporation (ANSER). They are assisted in this policy laundering effort by the Center for Strategic and International Studies, the K Street rest home for former Pentagon, intelligence, and State Department political appointees.

But all the technology in the world will not protect citizens from terrorist attacks, unless the government knows how to use the information effectively. As the government and a few selected companies and think tanks push for new surveillance laws and more monitoring of the Internet and telecommunications in general, the words of Mary Schiavo, the Transportation Department's former Inspector General and outspoken critic of lax airline security, are particularly poignant. Speaking in Washington on December 18, Schiavo pointed out that the "United States already had laws to prevent what happened on September 11th . . . they weren't being enforced."

11

The War on Terror, Intelligence and Law Enforcement Technology

The warfare that most of us trained for now seems likely to become more an artifact of historical interest than the reality we feared. Today, the objective of conflict is less to obtain a political outcome than to create the conditions necessary for stability and responsible participation in international affairs. Perhaps the most striking difference from the war that Carl von Clausewitz spoke of is that today's conflicts have no time horizon. Still, there are constants; one is the requirement for intelligence concerning the enemy.

History illustrates that intelligence is a critical element of success in conflict. Even so, when military conflict encompasses transnational threats that include terrorism, insurgency, organized crime, weapons proliferation, and weapons of mass destruction—all of which inevitably invite the complications of public corruption—intelligence takes on a new meaning and generates requirements unknown a few years ago. The reasons are many, with technology at the top of the list.

Even though intelligence remains a critical element of warfare, it is startlingly apparent that the Department of

Defense (DOD), even with a vast array of intelligence capabilities, is not able to produce and analyze all the vital information necessary. In an era when the enemy is supported globally and transnational capabilities for communications, financial transactions, and transportation confound the utility for direct application of force, and civilian agencies are key to obtaining vital elements of information for the success of the mission.

Indeed, modern technology has greatly improved the combat capabilities of the American fighting forces. Network-centric warfare is a significant technological advancement and a proven way of fighting both more efficiently and more safely. However, the object is no longer merely to win the fight. Today, the object is to win the peace, which means creating conditions that will lead to stable societies. For that, partnering the technologies and capabilities of law enforcement, particularly those found within the Federal Bureau of Investigation (FBI), with the military mission is necessary. Coupling the innovations and skills discussed in this article with true cooperation between civilian law enforcement and the U.S. military will undoubtedly lead to a more effective prosecution of the war on terror.

Communications

Advances in communications technology have made our lives more convenient, but they have also provided the means for terrorists and criminals to communicate more easily. Twenty years ago, cellular telephones were relatively rare, clunky, and inefficient. Today, they are marketed to grade-school children. Cell phones and satellite phones are used by terrorists just as commonly as they are by organized crime members. What does this mean? Take a clue from organized crime: The FBI has stated many times that the defeat of organized crime on the U.S. east coast could never have been accomplished without electronic surveillance.

The same is true of terrorism, but the task is now infinitely more difficult because of not only cell phones but also the Internet.

Members of al Qaeda may live in caves, but many of them are sophisticated and learned. Using skills unimagined only a few years ago, al Qaeda has set a standard for terrorists by embracing the Internet as a tool for organizing, training, and propagandizing. Although the Internet is not new, improvements in computer, communications, and storage technology have made it a medium of choice for networking, information-gathering, and anonymous activities. Moreover, it is so cheap—often free—that anyone can use it.

Using the skills of modern technocrats, al Qaeda has adopted online tactics that mirror its offline techniques for evading discovery. These tactics include instant messaging, chat, bulletin boards, and a constantly shifting collection of Web sites where propaganda can be posted. For example, in 2005, a Web server operated by the Arkansas highway office was hijacked and used to distribute 70 files, including videos featuring Osama bin Laden. Recently, a group believed to be al Qaeda's Web-based propaganda arm distributed a weekly state-of-affairs Web cast and is reportedly searching online for recruits to aid with the coverage. This means that the group and their recruits will be searching for more and more computers to hijack in order to distribute additional content.

Officials of all nations are faced with the prospect of choosing between sabotaging terrorist uses of the Web (commonly referred to as "whack-a-mole") or attempting to monitor them. Neither option yields a satisfactory response. On the one hand, nearly anyone can put up Web sites. On the other, monitoring the Web is like counting grains of sand on a beach, so vast are the opportunities and methods of communication over the Internet. Moreover, if the choice is to monitor, it begs the questions of who can do it and who has authority to do it.

The largest Internet providers are located in the United States. Hotmail and Yahoo! offer unlimited free accounts. Terrorists can, and do, use the Internet extensively, undoubtedly changing their free accounts as often as practicable. A terrorist in Pakistan can log into a Yahoo! account in the United States and communicate with a networked terrorist in Jordan. Chat rooms, instant messaging, anonymizers, and other attributes of modern communications make the life of a terrorist much more flexible. However, monitoring email requires a judicially approved warrant. This means that the military must depend on law enforcement, perhaps even that of many nations, to bring in that part of the intelligence puzzle.

DNA Testing

The FBI has a large suite of forensic capabilities that are germane to counterterrorism efforts worldwide. One of the most important capabilities is DNA testing. Precise identification of individuals, both alive and dead, is a critical need. To this end, the FBI has established a large inventory of DNA samples, both to identify persons when they are confronted and to confirm the identity of bodies resulting from conflict situations. For example, DNA testing confirmed a claim by the Pakistani government that Muhsin Musa Matwalli Atwah, an al Qaeda operative wanted by the United States in connection with the 1998 U.S. Embassy bombings, had been killed in an air strike by Pakistani forces near the border with Afghanistan. On the other side of the world, FBI DNA testing confirmed the death of the Philippines' "most wanted" terrorist.

However, as valuable as this identification capability is, there are more subtle uses for DNA. For example, even though the body of Abu Musab al-Zarqawi was identified by fingerprints, tattoos, and scars after he was killed in an airstrike, DNA samples were sent to the FBI crime laboratory in Quantico, Virginia. The DNA collected was then compared to other samples in an effort to help establish locales where al-Zarqawi had been and who had been with him.

Fingerprints

One of the most common forensic capabilities is fingerprinting. The FBI maintains an Integrated Automated Fingerprint Identification System (IAFIS), which comprises the largest biometric database in the world. It contains the fingerprints and corresponding criminal history information for more than 47 million subjects in the criminal master file. This information is submitted voluntarily by state, local, and Federal law enforcement agencies. With the ability to transmit fingerprints digitally, state and local authorities, as well as the military abroad, can send prints for comparison and receive electronic responses to criminal 10-print fingerprint submissions within 2 hours and civilian fingerprint submissions within 24 hours.

The ability to identify suspected terrorists and insurgents in Iraq and Afghanistan is a highly desirable capability. As early as April 2002, the Attorney General directed that terrorist fingerprints and biographical data be gathered internationally from military detainees, from cooperative international exchange programs, through legal attaches in Embassies abroad, and from domestic law enforcement sources. As of September 1, 2006, more than 19,000 such prints had been added. Today, when the U.S. military rounds up suspected terrorists, they are "booked" and fingerprinted, using the same tools that police in the United States use to check criminal backgrounds. Consequently, if those fingerprinted subsequently attempt to enter the United States, they will be flagged.

When a large group was rounded up in 2004 in Iraq, 44 were determined to have criminal records in the United States and 2 were sought on Federal warrants. In 2005, the Department of Defense created its own biometric database, the Automated Biometric Identification System (ABIS), modeled on IAFIS. To ensure quality and interoperability of all fingerprint data collected, DOD has directed that all acquisitions related to fingerprinting must conform to the same standards and be interoperable with the IAFIS system. Now, prints sent to ABIS are sifted through IAFIS, where they are screened and compared to the FBI's most-wanted terrorists lists. The value of that screening has been demonstrated several times when suspects were detained after their fingerprints showed they had been arrested before. In one case, suspected al Qaeda terrorist Mohamad al Kahtani was positively identified based on prints taken when he was denied entry to the United States in August 2001.

Improvised Explosive Devices

More deaths in Iraq are caused by improvised explosive devices (IEDs) than anything else. Additionally, IEDs have become the weapon of choice for terrorists worldwide. To address this threat, in December 2003, the FBI created the Terrorist Explosive Device Analytical Center (TEDAC). This center established a single Federal program responsible for the worldwide collection, complete forensic and technical analysis, and timely dissemination of intelligence regarding terrorist bombs. All information gleaned from TEDAC's analysis is shared throughout the law enforcement, intelligence, and military communities. Additionally, using break-through technology, FBI technicians are beginning to identify the locales where the devices are made and even who is making them. According to a 5-year accounting of FBI progress in transformation, 56 bomb-makers were identified through TEDAC analysis.

These analyses suggest that there is a relatively small number of master bomb-makers, and those identifications have resulted in the capture of some, while others who were identified are being sought. The FBI also runs a Large Vehicle Bomb Post-Blast Crime Scene School that replicates a 2002 bomb blast overseas that killed more than 200 people.

Students do not watch the explosion; they pick up the actual pieces from the scattered wreckage that set the forensic groundwork for a criminal or terrorist investigation. They then learn how to identify the vehicle that blew up. The post-blast school started as a basic lesson on working a car-bomb scene—from forensics and equipment to crime scene mapping and processing—but it evolved to a graduate level curriculum in 1998, so law enforcement and military investigators with plenty of bomb-scene experience can get practical training in the devastation created by large-vehicle explosions.

The FBI has sponsored more than 70 classes around the Nation—and 2 overseas—since the school was launched in 1998. The size of the explosions limits where the course can convene; a 6,000-pound bomb, for example, might spread a field of evidence across 225 acres. Fortunately, the U.S. military has provided bases with huge barren acreage for the classes and even vehicles to blow up. Bomb technicians deploying to Iraq and Afghanistan get first crack at the maximum 50 slots in each class.

Financing

The technology that allows us to pay our bills online or send money to a child at college also permits the transfer of funds to or between terrorists. If those funds can be stopped short of their ultimate goal, the means to finance the terrorist fight against military forces can be curtailed. To do so, however, requires investigations at a great distance from the battlefield and often involves the authorities of several nations. It also requires information developed in the conflict zone—information that may be best recognized and evaluated by law enforcement personnel. However, the situation is complicated for two reasons. First, money laundering is not illegal in most nations. Second, and of immense importance, transactional data are not required to "follow the money." That means anonymous transfers of money are both possible and likely. Where do authorities have to look to find the sources of terrorism financing? Donors, nongovernmental organizations, and criminal enterprises all fund terrorist causes.

The Detroit U.S. Attorney's Office recently indicted a Hezbollah smuggling ring operating in Michigan that helped fund that terrorist organization with profits from bootlegged cigarettes, counterfeit tax stamps, phony Viagra tablets, and stolen toilet paper, according to a Federal indictment unsealed in Detroit in July 2006. A similar Hezbollah ring was prosecuted in North Carolina in 2003. Other terrorist supporters in the United States have been indicted for credit card fraud, smuggling blue jeans, and currency violations. Moreover, just as with terrorism itself, terrorism financing is global. According to the Canadian agency responsible for tracking money laundering, Canada's suspected financing for terrorism almost tripled to C$180 million (US$153 million) in 2005.

In the United States, a Federal judge found two U.S.-based Islamic charitable organizations and an individual fundraiser liable for the 1996 killing of an American in Israel by Hamas terrorists. The Islamic Association for Palestine and the Texas-based Holy Land Foundation were both found liable for funneling money to Hamas. Battling such sources of terrorist support is a universal task—and one that yields information at every turn. The need is to exploit that information. In November 2005, more than 180 experts from 55 countries met in Vienna to consider the problem. Attendees included specialists from the North Atlantic Treaty Organization, United Nations Office on Drugs and Crime, U.S. State Department, and the Organization for Security and Cooperation in Europe.

Closer to home, U.S. intelligence agencies, including those of the Department of Treasury and FBI, have been adopting innovative forms of investigation to deal with the issue. For example, the Terrorist Financing Operations

Section (TFOS) of the FBI Counterterrorism Division was formed in response to this critical need. TFOS combines traditional FBI expertise in conducting complex criminal financial investigations with advanced technologies and has built on these established mechanisms by obtaining cooperation and coordination among law enforcement, regulatory, and intelligence agencies, both domestic and foreign, to become an internationally effective terrorist financing investigative operation. The mission of TFOS has evolved into a broad strategy to identify, investigate, disrupt, and dismantle all terrorist-related financing and fundraising activities. Following the money can lead to an individual relevant to the military mission abroad.

Weapons of Mass Destruction

If it is true that we are in for a long, drawn-out struggle against terrorism, the chance of avoiding another event involving weapons of mass destruction (WMD) grows slimmer. The difficulty of obtaining or developing chemical, biological, or nuclear weapons has made their use rare, but these weapons have been used for terror purposes. Sarin, a chemical nerve agent, was used in the Tokyo subway system in 1995 by the Aum Shinrikyo cult. Anthrax bacteria were used in 2001, infecting individuals in Connecticut, New York, Florida, and the District of Columbia. Also, salmonella bacteria were used by the Rajneeshee cult in 1984 in an attempt to influence local election turnout in Oregon. Ricin, a toxin, was mailed to the White House in 2003 and Congress in 2004.

Domestically, there is a significant opportunity to control access to materials that contribute to WMD. Federal law enforcement agencies now have greater power to gather intelligence on terror groups and their members. Increased information about groups, combined with apprehension of any who have chemical or biological weapons, may create further barriers to terrorist acquisition and use of these weapons. A registration system for researchers and facilities possessing select agents has been developed by the Department of Health and Human Services, and additional restrictions regarding access to these agents have been made law.

Internationally, the picture is far murkier. Where terrorists find haven, they can seek the means of destruction they desire. It is known that terrorists have experimented with chemical and biological materials, most likely without significant success. Furthermore, most chemical and biological agents are difficult to apply with the precision that would be desirable to induce terror. However, chemical, biological, radiological, and nuclear weapons are themselves harbingers of fear, so it is almost beyond cavil that terrorists will seek and use them if possible.

Although there is repeated evidence of terrorist interest in chemical weapons or chemically enhanced explosive devices, available information suggests that this is more a reflection of jihadist aspiration than an indication of genuine capability. Nevertheless, jihadist Web forums contain manuals describing the construction of gas dispersal devices. Also, in late 2001, videos discovered in Afghanistan purported to show the testing of hydrogen cyanide gas on dogs. This category also has to take into account the possibility of a "dirty bomb." There are no truly accurate historical events that give us an idea of what the effect of a dirty bomb might be. However, there is a relevant event in which a tragic radiological accident occurred in Brazil between September 1987 and March 1988. An abandoned radiotherapy clinic was burglarized, and a capsule containing Cesium-137 chloride was opened and handled by several individuals. From this incident of common burglary, over 112,000 people were potentially exposed.

After careful monitoring, it was determined that a total of 249 people had been contaminated. Of these, 151 exhibited both internal and external contamination and 49 were admitted to hospitals, with the most seriously irradiated having doses from 100 to 800 rads (radiation absorbed dose). The contaminated patients were themselves radioactive, seriously complicating their treatment. In the end, 28 suffered radiation burns, and 3 men, 1 woman, and 1 child died. Far more problematic is the potential use of conventional explosives or other easily obtained materials to create a WMD event. Not unlike the idea of turning fuel-laden aircraft into WMDs, a conventional explosive at a chemical plant or a dam could wreak massive destruction. When household items, fertilizer, or castor beans can be turned into WMD devices, it is not governments, with all their capabilities, that are likely to detect the threat. Rather, it is local policemen, storekeepers, tourists, and ticket agents who are the eyes and ears of prevention. If terrorism is to be prevented, then any theory of transformation has to take into account all those who have a role in prevention.

Terrorist Screening Center

The Terrorist Screening Center (TSC) is a unified watch list of known or appropriately suspected terrorists that can be used by every official sworn to protect the United States— from border patrol and transportation officials to Federal agents and local police officers working their beats. "There is one watch list," TSC Director Donna Bucella told reporters during a briefing at FBI headquarters. "Our list is not a stagnant list. We add, modify, and delete every day."

The information that flows into the TSC comes from the FBI (domestic terrorist information) and the National Counter Terrorism Center (international terrorist information), which gets information from more than a dozen intelligence agencies, such as the Central Intelligence Agency and the Department of Homeland Security, under the umbrella of the Director of National Intelligence. By serving as the day-to-day, 24-hour conduit that links frontline law enforcement, and even foreign officials, to critical field intelligence on terrorists, the TSC staff can do more than maintain the database and link phone calls. Their access to a constant flow of intelligence helps them assemble a big picture view of potential threats and connect the dots for the agencies they support.

Preserving Information

Precisely because contemporary threats have no time horizon, carefully preserving information becomes an important intelligence capability. For example, what does it mean to find a telephone number in a country without telephone books? Phone numbers in other countries can be traced through law enforcement channels. Additionally, law enforcement agents have provided training to U.S. military personnel on how to exploit "pocket litter." Moreover, it is a normal function of the FBI to build up dossiers, often with fingerprints and increasingly with DNA, on every potential criminal or terrorist.

In the battle space, law enforcement officers have aided military enterprises by applying law enforcement skills to data, tangible objects, and interrogations of individuals. They have photographed, catalogued, and organized items as they would for evidentiary purposes, thereby preserving the integrity of the items for future reference. Moreover, they have applied their skills operationally, providing interpretation of information that often has been instrumental in helping the military know how and where to next apply force. Of significant importance, the FBI has developed and maintains the Investigative Data Warehouse (IDW), a centralized, Web-enabled closed system repository for intelligence and investigative data. This system allows appropriately trained and authorized personnel throughout the country to submit queries relevant to investigative and intelligence matters. Information contained in IDW comes from all agencies of government and, more importantly, from information picked up on the battlefields of Iraq and Afghanistan. This is a constantly growing database.

IDW now provides special agents, intelligence analysts, and members of Joint Terrorism Task Forces with a single access point to more than 47 sources of counterterrorism data, including information from FBI files, other government agency data, and open source news feeds, that were previously available only through separate, stove piped systems. New analytical tools are used across multiple data sources providing a more complete view of the information possessed by the Bureau. Users can presently search up to 560 million pages of international terrorism-related documents and billions of structured records, such as addresses and phone numbers, in seconds. They can also rapidly search for pictures of known terrorists and match or compare the pictures with other individuals in minutes rather than days. Coupled with sophisticated state-of-the-art search tools, the IDW enhances governmental ability to identify relationships across cases quickly and easily.

It is a simple fact of contemporary life that the current security environment presents unique and difficult issues that few of us have trained for. Even leaving aside the complexities of stabilization and reconstruction, addressing the direct threat requires the expertise and technological capabilities of law enforcement agencies, both in the conflict arena and at great distances, in order to terminate or restrict support to terrorism. Moreover, the effective utilization of law enforcement capabilities requires the cooperation of networks of not only law enforcement organizations but also military organizations across the globe.

12

The Age of Terrorism and Public Safety

The age of terrorism into which we have been flung presents new and unique challenges for law enforcement in the field. At a time when nightclubs, office buildings, buses or pizzerias are all targets for international terrorists, the police officer, uniformed or not, has become a frontline counter-terrorist agent. There are many ways to maximize success in that role. Chief among them is training, by all levels of command, for preventing mass-casualty attacks before they occur and for handling the situation if they do.

At the time of any high-profile event, the commander on "watch" needs to be trained to properly make strategic and tactical decisions, based on the needs of the district, the specific event and the units available at any given moment. When tactical decisions made in the wake of a terrorist attack are implemented in an instantaneous fashion, immediate goals are met and the system operates efficiently, with minimal losses and a quick return to normalcy for the citizens.

One city with extensive experience of terrorism's effects is Jerusalem, where I was the captain responsible for the busy center city district. To understand how a modern police force trains for and copes with terrorism, let us examine a real-life scenario from the days of severe and frequent terrorist attacks in the Israeli capital.

The Scenario

The busy Friday night in the center city of Jerusalem was rattled by an explosion in the parking lot of a large concentration of discos and pubs. It happened approximately 20 feet from a unit that I was visiting at the time. In fact, I was the first to report the sound of the explosion, relaying to dispatch what had become a sadly routine report of a suspected terrorist attack.

Under pressure to start the ball rolling - the treatment of the wounded, the clean up and investigation, and most importantly, the hunt for the perpetrators - I ordered the opening of a command center and told the dispatcher to stay on the set routine frequency, while I moved to the Emergency Operations Center (EOC) frequency. There is a limited amount of resources at a commanding officer's disposal in order to catch assailants and adequately care for the scene itself, including coordinating specific routes and avenues of approach for the incoming units that are ultimately needed for securing the scene.

Events that night unfolded according to standard procedure. Additional emergency services, ranging from firefighters, EMS and police, were dispatched to the targeted location. The roadblocks were closed, and I updated the sergeant on duty as to what was happening. He stayed on the routine band, working with dispatch, as I worked solely on the EOC channel. In addition to the regular emergency calls, the sergeant was to ensure that the units not at the scene of the explosion were on heightened alert for any additional threats or secondary attacks that may follow in our locale. I transferred the units coming in to my scene to the EOC channel and delegated a specific task to each unit.

In the event of such a terrorist incident, securing the scene is a priority. The potential for a secondary device or attack is extremely high, as proven in the very recent past. Each incoming unit was tasked with shutting off the scene of the explosion, clearing a path for emergency vehicles and, more importantly, scanning the vicinity for potential secondary threats.

Taking into account an eyewitness report of someone fleeing the scene of the attack, the direction the suspect ran, and the proximity to the predominantly Arab areas of Jerusalem, I was able to coordinate incoming units to cover specific high probability paths the felon might attempt to take. As it turned out, an incoming unit met the fleeing suspect head on and was able to arrest him.

Lessons

When responding to an incident of terrorism, there tends to be different aspects that need immediate attention. In addition to securing the scene of the explosion, police multitasking will include:

- the manhunt for accomplices or perpetrators;
- the search for additional devices targeting the responding emergency personnel; and
- the securing of other sensitive locations that may be targeted in a series of attacks.

Preplanning for any large event is imperative, but even more so if the large, sudden event is a terrorist attack. To prevent further loss of life in the aftermath of a terrorist attack, all commanders and all units must know what to do, and how and when to do it.

Training

In Jerusalem, the patrol units are so well-trained in responding to terrorist incidents that they perform the sweep, the patrol and the ultimate suicide bomber confrontation in such a natural fashion that it appears almost routine. The police officers carrying out these operations are 21-year-old cops who proactively patrol the streets, picking out suspicious behaviors, individuals, packages or vehicles that may be involved in terrorist activity, in addition to acting as a familiar reactive force. This dual role - as an emergency response team that every agency is familiar with and as an active counter-terror unit - requires of the patrol officers extreme self-discipline and unit cohesion.

When any emergency dispatch call may in fact be a potential suicide bomber en route to his or her target, the importance of well-trained security personnel is self-evident. The soft targets of the public transportation routes, restaurants, sidewalk cafes and entertainment districts require that even the two-man patrol unit be able to transform itself into a fighting machine when confronted with a terrorist incident.

Daily Training

To successfully ensure that the patrol units will properly perform in such a stressful situation, the officers must be drilled on a daily basis. Through drilling and briefings on the current threats, tactics and responses, the patrol unit will instinctively respond in such a fashion as to ensure their own safety and the safety of the civilians.

Integrated Training

There should be complete integration of hands-on training and drills with classroom-style lectures and briefings, including case studies relevant to the potential threats within the jurisdiction. The hands-on training should utilize walk-through table-top scenarios, as well as live drills and exercises.

Multilevel Training

Training scenarios, whether table-top or real-life, need to be drilled at the level of the lone patrol up to the level of an entire unit. Furthermore, commanding officers should be drilled by their supervisors along with their subordinates. The benefits of such an approach are abundant: the commander can improve at a personal level, as well as learn to better identify training points for him to focus on among his personnel. As the commanding officer needs to be at the scene of an actual terrorist attack as soon as possible, managing the incident, he also needs to be an integral part of the training and drilling for such an event.

Reflective Training

All training scenarios and all real incidents need to be followed by an after-action debriefing among the commanders and personnel who took part. Lessons learned from such an event should be forwarded to all relevant parties. Such debriefings and reporting contributes to a scenario-based review of agency policies and procedures further up the command chain, with specific focus on minimizing additional casualties while enforcing the law and making the response mechanism more efficient.

When policy or procedural changes are made, the training needs to adequately incorporate them, as they will be reflected in possible scenarios confronting security personnel. The agency may have excellent procedures and policies in effect; however, when the officers are unfamiliar with the integration of the policy or procedure, it will fail.

Pitfalls

The best policies and procedures will fail when security personnel succumb to the ever-deadly laziness. The terrorist enemy is out at all hours of the day, learning and studying the agencies; while the typical patrol commander or sergeant is making the rounds only to large incidents or for periodic checks throughout the shift, as a result of being overly tasked. Therefore, all emergency services personnel must understand that the adversary is looking for a weakness in the system, and this weakness may very well be the "human factor": the officer that takes a nap, drinks a cup of coffee, or worse, abandons his post.

Commanders must be aware of such vulnerabilities, and adapt their inspections and supervise their personnel adequately and at all times of their shifts. Finally, to be effective, any type of training must include drills that periodically test both the commissioned and non-commissioned officers, as well as any emergency services that are to respond jointly with law enforcement.

As a commander or someone in a supervisory position, it is imperative to ensure that your personnel are properly trained and educated to respond to terrorist scenarios, so as to minimize operational complications, misunderstandings, lack of communications, or injury to civilians and emergency personnel, as well as to maximize response efforts. Constant attention to training assures the optimal functioning of the commander himself, as well as each and every one of his unit subordinates.

Building Success on Professionalism

A saying that is commonly expressed in Australian Aboriginal culture goes some- thing like, "To plan for our future, we must first understand the past". As the AFP enters 2003, we are engaged in a number of major activities that draw heavily on policing experience of the past while still presenting problems never before experienced. The obvious example is the current investigation into the bombings in Bali last October. Terrorism as a form of political violence has unfortunately found its way into our part of the world, but it has not found us totally unprepared.

Over the past decade, the AFP has been deliberately redesigning itself in anticipation of the fact that modern crime is not predictable. At a moments notice, an organisation that polices crime needs to be flexible enough to react quickly and creatively and with a sense of purpose.

Nothing could sum up the AFP's reaction to the Bali bombings more succinctly. While the crime took place outside the AFP's jurisdiction, it was a crime against our people and our friends. Such were our professional links with the Indonesian National Police that we were able to confidently offer assistance and merge into the INP investigation with the mini- mum of fuss. Relationships like this are not created overnight and are a result of years of inter-agency contact that builds trust and mutual respect between professional law enforcement operatives.

Building a professional history between agencies is what makes such cooperative endeavours possible and this is what makes a professional law enforcement body. The AFP has the privilege of being the face of Australian policing to the world, it is the face of federal law enforcement throughout Australia and it is the face our police in suburban Canberra. At each level of policing the most important tool an officer has to work with is the relationships created through daily contact with those he or she is empowered to protect. And the most critical aspect of each level is that a history of trust and respect needs to be created in order to make the job work.

The *Platypus* shows how this history of trust has been developed and put into practice in various ways. Overall, the articles relate to how dealing with crime requires a multifaceted approach. Through research, revision, and interaction with the community and allied agencies, levels of cooperation and trust are developed which in the end make the task of law enforcement that much more effective. In the article "Closing the Circle – the AFP's Capacity to Fight Terrorism," which I delivered as a speech to a mostly commercial and business audience, I have outlined how, when viewed as a criminal act and not solely a political act, the established criminal investigation methodologies can become an effective tool in heading off terrorist incidents or an effective way to bring the perpetrators to justice.

The momentum to establish the AFP was created in 1978 with the explosion of a bomb at the Sydney Hilton Hotel during a Commonwealth Heads of Government Meeting. The explosion killed two council workers and eventually a police officer died from injuries inflicted by the bomb. Terrorism was no longer something that happened on the other side of the world and reviews were put in place to enable Australia to deal with the development.

Fortunately, while those incidents are not common in Australia, the preparedness to be able to deal with them has been growing continually since that time. The reaction of Australian agencies to the bombing in Bali is testimony as to the working relationships that have developed between state and federal agencies. These relationships made it possible to deliver appropriate people and services to the task in a minimum amount of time. At the individual level, I am aware of many instances where relatively junior federal agents cut a swathe through potential red tape by using their own initiative and recognise that all agencies involved abandoned many set procedures because the nature of the incident demanded it.

This type of response is made possible because "the AFP's longstanding relationship with law enforcement agencies across our region has been the corner- stone of much of our success". Quietly and deliberately working away in the back- ground since the Sydney Hilton bombing has been the Australian Bomb Data Centre. Its job of recording and collating copious amounts of bomb-incident data over the past quarter century is applied and made use of regularly in a variety of ways through its relationships with similar agencies around the world. This accumulated knowledge and skill has easily proved its worth during the investigations in Bali and the article *A Coming of Age – the Australian Bomb Data Centre* gives a good account of the ABDC's role in fighting terrorism.

Terror of a different kind arrived in the south-western suburbs of Canberra on Saturday 18 January in the form of a fire front of a size and ferocity never seen before in any Australian city. "The Day the Thin Blue Line took on a Wall of Red" is an article reprinted from the *Canberra Times* and provides accounts of individual AFP officers on the day of fires. It is a stark endorsement of the positive relationships that exist between our police in Canberra and the ACT community. With a strict mission of preserving life, the officers involved had to deal with emotionally charged residents under intolerable stress, in incredibly dangerous conditions. The fact that so many citizens had trust in the police was undoubtedly a contributing factor in minimising the loss of life.

Like all other incidents that occur in policing, there will be lessons to be learned from Bali and from the Canberra fires. Policing is an ongoing procedure of action and review. This is a process illustrated by the remaining articles in this edition which in their own way express how law enforcement procedures, whether they are directed against international terrorism, transnational crime, or crime in the neighbourhood, can only be successful when they are built on professionalism that springs from trust and cooperation.

Finally, the power to police is derived from the community whether it be local, national or international. As an organisation, therefore, we must represent the community we serve. In those areas where we don't, such as religious minorities, we need to reach out even further in order to reflect and represent the values of the whole community and not just bits and pieces of it — or the bits we like to do that takes commitment and fair-mindedness.

The terrorist threat is being materially and normatively shaped by national and global institutions of law and order: Spain & beyond Spanish political elites and law enforcement have come to understand, according to Conde and Gonzalez, that 'terrorism is not a conjunctural phenomenon but a structural one, and as a result, it cannot be confronted militarily (as in the US) or with exceptional and extraordinary norms (as in the UK), but through ordinary legislation in compliance of the rule of law'. As a result, Spain's law enforcement and security-intelligence services have found in the legal principles that underpin Spanish counter-terrorism practices a successful tool to counter the internal terrorist threat as well as international terrorism. This makes the Spanish experience with terrorism a unique case study in the Western world.

Simultaneously, the international homogenization and regularization of norms are shaping not only the terrorist threat and how it is to be countered, but also security in a broader sense. The present article will explore how *the terrorist threat is being materially and normatively shaped by national and global institutions of law and order.* The first part will discuss the evolution of Spanish counter-terrorism practices in an effort to explain Spain's unique case in shaping terrorism as a threat; the second part will explain how the Spanish counter-terrorism model evolved alongside democratic accountability and civil liberties concerns; and a third part will contextualize global normative and material developments shaping the terrorist threat in Spain and the way Spain enforces not only its counter-terrorism practices, but also its overall security.

From a realist perspective it is assumed that 'laws, simply stated, precede and define criminality', but the reality is that it is the material conditions of life that do, for legal relations as well as forms of state could not be understood by themselves, nor explained by the so called general progress of the human mind'. Nonetheless, '[t]he homogenization [and regularization] of criminal norms throughout international society [is] a historical process driven primarily by the criminalisations of dominant states ... and their efforts to export their own criminal justice preferences to other states'. At the same time, however, it is also a historical process driven by self-interested individuals or corporate actors (public and private) whose interests for political or economic advancement merges with a perceived necessity to securitize national and international society. These views will be further explained in detail. A conclusion will summarize key points from the discussion.

The Spanish counter-terrorism model

Max Weber argued that 'states lay claim to the legitimate monopoly over the use of violence'. Spanish law enforcement and security-intelligence services argue they are compelled to practice security in a proactive way as Spain has had a long experience with terrorism. In the traditional conceptualization of the term terrorism in Spain falls under two categories; Homegrown since the 1960s; and Islamist terrorism since 2004. For MacKinnon, 'Homegrown' Spanish terrorism embraces the activities of both ideologues and separatists. Anarchist and fascist terrorists inflicted widespread casualties on the Spanish public during the late 1970s, 1980s, and into the 1990s as they sought to impose their respective visions of government on the Spanish people. But MacKinnon's affirmation is inaccurate for Anarchist terrorism has been relevant in Spanish history but certainly not during this period of time where it would seem quite difficult to point out any low intensity terrorist activity based on Anarchist ideology.

It seems MacKinnon fundamentally misunderstands the ideological differences between leftist violent groups, for it seems he considers the left-wing GRAPO (*Grupos de Resistencia Antifascista Primero de Octubre*) an Anarchist terrorist organization that operated during this period of time, when in fact, GRAPO had Maoist origins and later Marxist-Leninist leanings. According to Jaime-Jimenez, four distinct phases may be appreciated with regard to democratic Spain's fight against terrorism characterized by:

1. Chaotic counter-terrorism guidance and inefficiency between 1976-1980;
2. General coordination of counter-terrorism organizations between 1980-1983;
3. Reorganization of strategic operations under the Interior Ministry between 1983-1988, also characterized by the Antiterrorist Law of 1984; and
4. Dispersal of ETA prisoners between 1989-1996.

The period of most intense terrorist turmoil in Spain occurred throughout the Euskadi Ta Askatasuna (ETA) terrorist organization's birth and throughout the democratic transition period. On the other hand, although casualties in the 11 March 2004 attacks in Madrid were attributed in first instance to ETA and subsequently to the Moroccan Islamic Combatant Group (MICG) or even to an off-shoot organization of the MICG, Salafiya Jihadiya, the final ruling for the trial of the 11-M attacks concluded in 2007 the initial hypothesis was incorrect. The Court based its ruling on the fact that, although Hassan el-Haski, one of the indicted terrorists, was a leading figure within MICG, this instance did not substantively and necessarily prove a chain-of-command structure existed linking MICG to the 11-M attacks, and thence released him from the charges of inducing to commit terrorist activities while indicting others.

Nonetheless, it was widely conceived that '[t]he March bombings were ostensibly part of a global *jihad* and possibly directed at Spanish support for the war in Iraq'. In spite of this emerging threat, Spain has retained counter-terrorism policies that were designed to combat the homegrown terrorism of the 1970s and 1980s [and also 1990s], even as they wage a new fight against Islamist terrorism. Spanish political elites and law enforcement have come to understand, according to Conde and Gonzalez, that 'terrorism is not a conjunctural phenomenon but a structural one, and as a result, it cannot be confronted militarily (as in the US) or with exceptional and extraordinary norms (as in the UK), but through ordinary legislation in compliance of the rule of law'.

As a result, Spain's security-intelligence services have found in the criminalization of terrorism a successful tool to counter the homegrown as well as the international terrorist threat. The democratic Spanish counter-terrorism model originates in January 1977 when, in an attempt to move away from Francoist repressive practices, the National Court *Audiencia Nacional* is created in Madrid to deal with serious crime and terrorist offences. As Alonso and Reinares note, '[t]his implied a fundamental jurisdictional change, since terrorist crimes would be dealt with, from that moment on, by ordinary judges instead of military courts as was previously the case'. This occurred because, [d]uring the democratic transition and the years of democratic consolidation, the emerging political elites had to remove those practices and reform those agencies, introducing new ones in accordance with the rule of law and the principles of an open society.

But due to the intrinsic characteristics of the political change experienced, many of these reforms took place rather slowly, to the extent that indiscriminate repression by police forces when presumably performing operations against terrorism happened while the existing legal framework was being replaced. All this resulted in the counterproductive application of some legislative and coercive measures against terrorism. This circumstance was duly exploited by the separatist heterogeneous group *Herri Batasuna* (HB: People's Unity). Both Reinares and Jaime-Jimenez concluded '[t]his disloyal opposition [group] based its main collective arguments on the fact that the 1978 Spanish constitution does not recognize the right to national self-determination, thus capitalizing on the difficulties which arose during the implementation of the autonomy arrangements'. While not an insignificant claim, it has to be contextualized at a time when a segment of Basque

Country youth became reactionary towards the democratic institutions being created as a result of the trauma of the Francoist experience, thus empathizing with ETA violence. Between 1978-1980 terrorist violence peaked and the Spanish government decided to reform a dysfunctional internal security structure especially to meet ETA's challenge, though it may be argued this reform originated previously in 1977 with the creation of the Ministry of Defense and the intelligence service *Centro Superior de Información de la Defensa* (CESID) in 1977.

As Antonio Diaz explains, 'CESID arose from the fusion of the Central Service of Documentation (SECED), an entity involved in internal espionage, and part of the military High Command, the upper echelons of the armed forces'. CESID was essentially a military intelligence organization organically dependent on the Ministry of Defense but from a functional standpoint dependent on the Presidency, to which the Director of the CESID reported. Nonetheless, in terms of internal security CESID worked in counter-intelligence and counter-terrorism along with the different policing forces: (1) *Policía Nacional* (National Police); (2) *Guardia Civil* (Civil Guard); and (3) *Ertzaintza* (Basque Country Regional Police) each of which developed their own intelligence units. In 1979 following the escalation of ETA violence a sizeable number of special security teams from the different internal security apparatuses, including the Special Operations Group (GEOs) from the National Police and the Rural Antiterrorist Groups (RAG) from the Civil Guard (largely cradled under foreign experts' advice) were sent to carry out a terrorist area assessment on ETA capabilities in the Basque Country. The imprint these 'special' groups left upon early Spanish counter-terrorism efforts and practices was regrettable and counterproductive.

In this regard, Reinares and Jaime-Jimenez lamented that pseudo-fascist or antidemocratic tendencies ruled groupthink attitudes not only between commanding officers, but also amongst subordinates, and clearly the attitude of the former inhibited or encouraged the actions of the later. This in turn caused frequent insubordination cases along with empathy towards terrorist activities perpetrated by fascist leaning groups; hardly the type of people capable of defending the democratic covenant.

Fortunately, 'the democratic government of Spain was always cautious enough not to involve the armed forces in internal security issues, contrary to the experience in Northern Ireland [NI]'. Yet the memory over Francoist military involvement in internal security was still vivid. It was not until the 1980s that GEOs from the National Police and *Ertzaintza* were deployed in anti-terrorist matters. In this respect, '[c]oercion performed by national police and justice was resilient thanks to the adherence to law and order'. At the same time the CESID was also involved in the fight placing moles, conducting wire-tapings, etc. Despite the difference with the NI case, it can also be said these groups experienced transformational policing phases akin to those transforming the practices of security services in NI, which included three phases in the cycle of policing—the *militarization* phase, the *normalization* phase and the *counter-insurgency* phase, identified by Ni Aolain during the period of the 'Troubles'.

Admittedly, it would certainly be difficult for this scheme to be applied in the Spanish context with the same linear fashion as in the NI case. For example, the *militarization* phase may be of limited consideration since, as mentioned previously, Spain was fortunate not to involve the military in internal security matters and '[i]n a sense, [*militarization*] of the police represents the point at which the criminal justice model fades into state terrorism'. Nonetheless, the paramilitary connotation of the GARs and the GEOs may still lend some, albeit limited, credence to this categorization within the Spanish context for, after all, *militarization* 'represents [also] the immediate reaction by the state to the outbreak of civil disturbance', which occasionally occurred within the Basque context, and for a brief period of time in 1979 an Army General was appointed Minister of the Interior. *The normalization* phase applied in the Spanish case is perhaps the most identifiable, since it was conceptualized early on that a military intervention would not be followed by a political solution. Hence, in order to normalize the conditions of life in the Basque Country, restoring or reorganizing the civil institutions of law and order was critical.

This may have been achieved by applying the *Audiencia Nacional* process and by delegating increasing responsibilities to the *Ertzaintza* Unfortunately, *normalization* may have coexisted with *counter-insurgency* policing as an institutionalized practice, though not by any measure in a systematically legally sanctioned form as occurred in NI, where even the British Special Air Services (SAS) were deployed. Arguably so, during the early years of the democratic transition period, *counter-insurgency* activities were conducted under the auspices of the Basque-Spanish Battalion *Batallón Vasco Español* (BVE) or the Triple A against ETA, inspired by Israeli and German intelligence services. It appears these practices resurfaced in the following years.

In 1980 the establishment of the Counter-terrorist Unified Command *Mando Único para la Lucha Contraterrorista* (MULC) attempted to frame the fight against ETA within the rule of law causing the dispersal of right-wing affiliated groups. Simultaneously, the Interior Ministry fomented the reinsertion of ex-activist thereby seeking reintegration and the continuous normalization of the societal order. This policy bared fruits in due course when many activists from ETA (pm), the organization's politico-military wing gradually abandoned armed struggle. In 1983, under Interior Minister Jose Barrionuevo the Special Zone North Plan *Plan Especial Zona Norte* geared towards isolating ETA within Basque society is developed. Unfortunately, that same year the Antiterrorism Liberation Groups *Grupos Antiterroristas de Liberación* (GAL) shamefully emerged as a group composed of security functionaries and [mainly French] mercenaries sanctioning extra-judicial assassinations of alleged ETA terrorists, even within French territory, which resulted in the killing of 27 people between October 1983 and July 1987 before the group was terminated.

Eventually, the Guardia Civil would be entrusted with the lion's share in the fight against ETA in detriment of the Central Intelligence Brigade *Brigada Central de Información* (BCI), the Police's elite counter-terrorism unit attached to the General Intelligence Commissariat *Comisaria General de la Información* (CGI), by virtue of its successes attributed to its more disciplined command structure. Simultaneously, the need to positively socialize the Guardia Civil perception within society at large may have also geared the ruling government of the *Partido Socialista Obrero Español* (PSOE) towards this decision. At this juncture, Spain had codified constitutional protections of the rights to freedom from (1) prolonged preventive detention (a maximum of 72 hours with the possibility of extension up to five to thirteen days under the discretion of the Defense Minister and previous judicial review) (2) freedom from warrant less searches and (3) access to defense counsel, among other rights. Further, in 1988 a land-mark anti-violence accord *Pacto de Ajuaria Enea* is reached.

This agreement incorporated the Basque moderate nationalists into a broad consensus on internal security matters and subsequently influenced the central government's policy in a number of measures, such as the definitive abolition of special anti-terrorist legislation that same year (though some provisions were incorporated into the criminal code, or the implementation of new penitentiary initiatives in 1989, also facilitating a progressive but significant increase in police efficiency ...). Later in 1992, then Interior Minister Jose Luis Corcuera pushed through parliament legislation dubbed *ley de la patada en la puerta* (i.e., the kick to the door law). Such law authorized police and security services to search and seize property within a private domicile on suspicion that a crime was being committed, without previous judicial warrant of any type.

In 1993 the Constitutional Court *Tribunal Constitutional* ruled against this provision. Further, the *Pactos de la Moncloa,* Chapters IV-V of the Spanish Constitution of 1978 and subsequent legislations leading to the so called Anti-terrorism Law of 1995 underpin these counter-terrorism tools. The 1995 Anti-terrorism Law regulating terrorist crimes particularly, a.571-a.580 within Chapter V of the Spanish Penal Code is of most relevance even when slightly amended in 2001. These articles regulate what constitutes a terrorist crime and how it is to be prosecuted. Article a.571 defines terrorists as, those who belong or act on behalf of, or collaborate with armed groups, organizations or terrorist groups, whose objective is the subversion of the constitutional order, or attempt to gravely alter public peace, commit crimes and havoc or burnings typified in a. 346 and a. 351, respectively, will be punished with 15-20 years prison sentence without prejudice of the crime attributed to them should it incur in injury to life, physical integrity or health of people.

In 1998, Interior Minister Jose Barrionuevo and also Secretary of State for Security, Rafael Vera, were indicted as a result of being involved in the dirty war against ETA conducted by the GAL. Top official's involvement in extra-judicial activities reflected internecine battles within Spanish security higher-offices, particularly Interior Ministry and Defense Ministry to show success in the fight against Basque terrorism and gain influence within the Spanish security community in an attempt to gain control of the Spanish intelligence apparatus, which would place them in a position of privilege. The counter argument might be that France was highly uncooperative with Spanish authorities in the fight against Basque terrorism, even when the Basque separatist movement also claimed three of France's southeastern provinces as part of a Basque Homeland. France allowed Basque terrorists freedom of movement in the border region following its *Sanctuary Doctrine*.

As a result, GAL extrajudicial counterterrorist activities 'may have been partly justified as a result of the role Francoist security services performed throughout the 1960s shielding [members of] *the OAS* [*Organisation de l'Armee Secrete*]', associated with right wing politician Jean Jacques Susini, after they had committed terrorist acts in France. The GAL in fact, had adopted exactly the same *OAS* modus operandi. Notwithstanding, as early as 1986 Franco-Spanish cooperation did exist and proved critical in the disarticulation of ETA's leadership in France, which in turn unearthed vital financing information relating to extortions and the so called 'revolutionary tax' by which ETA partly financed itself. This instance may call into question whether GAL extrajudicial activities hindered or aided Spanish policing efforts to seek greater French cooperation. But what became evident was that at best, if some state security officials did not aid GAL directly they tacitly approved of its actions.

What was clear was that developments spelled some of the dangers that arose then as a result of the excessive autonomy irresponsible security managers possessed in the context of slow developing checks and balances to counter their mandates. As a result claims over counterterrorism abuses increased leading Basque families to file numerous claims against the Spanish government. One of the claims presented by the families of those indicted by the *Audiencia Nacional* is that alleged terrorists and their families incur in financial costs as a result of being subpoenaed to Madrid. Prisoners are jailed outside the Basque country since 1989.

While families claim human rights violations, Spanish counter-terrorism authorities argue it is a vital tool in both the break-up of command structure and in the reintegration of prisoners into society. But 'to some extent the progressive and deep weakening of ETA has made the dispersal of ETA prisoners redundant'.

Nonetheless legislation introduced in 2002 banned the political wing of ETA, HB. In 2004 the European Court of Human Rights (ECHR) ruled against a suit brought forth by the Basque government of the moderate nationalist PNV party of the Basque Country, claiming the Spanish government was violating Basque citizens' human rights under a.6, a.7, and a.11 of the ECHR. The ECHR's unanimous ruling 'concluded that an autonomous government within the state was unable to sue its own state'. The position of Spain's highest courts was that 'the banning of ETA's political wing was the protection of democracy and the safeguarding of citizens' rights in the Basque Country'. Judge Baltasar Garzon's review illustrates this position when he accused ETA and HB of pursuing a campaign of ethnic cleansing in a report in which he also argued 'that both organizations had promoted the "depuration of the census" in the Basque Country through the elimination of those citizens who would prevent a nationalist hegemony'. It is clear there was a fight between the Government of Spain and the regional government of the Basque Country to frame the policy discourse in a way that would support either the constitutional interest, on the one hand or the regional government agenda on the other, in an attempt to shape the terrorist threat.

The United Nations Special Rapporteur concluded in 2004 that torture or maltreatment of prisoners in Spain is not a systematic practice. He also observed that the system made torture possible, particularly in incommunicado detention, and recommended the recording of the interrogation of detainees *[sic]* to prevent any infringement of their rights. However, police trade unions have frequently rejected such a practice, as the disclosure of their identities would seriously endanger their work, and also put their lives at risk.

Nonetheless, a Human Rights Watch report concurred with the Special Rapporteur with regard to the potential occurrence of torture since under the Spanish Code of Criminal Procedure *Ley de Enjuiciamiento Civil* (LEC) [t]he right of terrorist suspects to an effective defense, already undermined by the limitations on access to counsel during the incommunicado period, is further impaired by the use of secret legal proceedings. Judges may – and often do – impose secrecy, or *secreto de sumario,* on the investigation and judicial proceedings, either in whole or in part. Under *secreto de sumario,* defense attorneys do not have access to critical information regarding the charges against their clients or the evidence against them, including the full grounds for remand to pre-trial detention. This restricted access may be kept in place until the investigative phase of the legal process is almost concluded.

Over time the ETA organization has been weakened and Spanish counter-terrorism and law enforcement practices have proved to be successful. The idiosyncrasy of the Basque situation is that the ruling party in the Basque government, the PNV, acquiesces to the systematic insecurity of half of the regions' non-nationalist Basque citizens who are compelled to live under constant fear. In fact, '[a]lthough new legal measures, increasing police efficiency and growing international cooperation continue to debilitate ETA and its supporting network, around 42,000 Basque citizens live under daily threat from the terrorists and its supporting gangs'. This is a unique situation in democratic Europe 'where systemic violations of human rights still occur … [and paradoxically] … victims are mainly, and almost exclusively, non nationalist Basque citizens'. These facts point to a deliberate sanctioning of an insecurity state on behalf of the Basque government ruled by the nationalist PNV party.

Recent Spanish electoral results reflected a loss of PNV influence. Iñigo Urkullu, recently appointed PNV leader, conceded that the PNV had failed to understand and adapt to the evolution of the Basque society. The question remains as to how to continue making counter-terrorism successful while eradicating this feeling of insecurity within the Basque region? The Spanish counter-terrorism model is notable insofar as it represents an example of legitimate policing activities conducted by a democratic and sovereign nation state within its internal boundaries under the rule of law as a response to a situation affecting its citizens' material conditions of life. No system is perfect and government overreaching is still not only possible, but feasible constitutionally. However, '[t]he analysis shows that the Spanish model evinces greater facial respect for checks and balances [than other models], inasmuch as it explicitly provides a role for the three branches of government in the design and execution of counterterrorism policy'.

Democratic accountability and civil liberties

Two new phases in the fight against terrorism may be identifiable in addition to the previous four discussed above: (5) Consolidation of adherence to policing practices within the rule of law between 1996-2002 with greater responsibilities for regional polices *Ertzaintza* and *Mossos d'Esquadra* (in Cataluña); and (6) Reorganization of intelligence gathering structures and capabilities across the State Security Forces *Fuerzas y Cuerpos de Seguridad del Estado* (FCSE) characterized by (a) the creation of an Executive Committee of the Unified Command of the FCSE, *Centro Ejecutivo del Mando Unificado* (CEMU) of the FCSE; *Terrorismo* (POLT) between 2001-2006. Developing events throughout these periods would unearth the legal mechanisms that underpin the Spanish counter-terrorism model while raising some concerns with regard to democratic accountability and civil liberties.

When the *Partido Popular* (PP) party arrived to power in 1996 sound reform of security and counter-terrorism activities was expected to strictly conform to the rule of law. Spanish state security agencies began to accommodate to mechanisms within the rule of law to be applied in their law enforcement practices. But in 1998, even at the outset of supervisory reform, the journal *El Mundo* published that the CESID had continued its extrajudicial counter-terrorist practices, eavesdropping this time throughout HB party offices; it became an embarrassment for the PP government. More so after General Galindo, a prominent antiterrorism figure from the *Guardia Civil* was indicted. Yet this hiccup was not followed by a stream of resignations as in 1996. The eavesdropping was labeled a 'mistake' from inherited past practices.

While not denying knowledge of the eavesdropping, both ex-President Felipe Gonzalez and ex-Defense Minister Narcis Serra, declared that CESID informs about results, not about means'. This response was reminiscent of ambivalent responses from informed state security forces with regard to the GAL affair. At the same, time this occurrence postponed reform of the CESID until 2002 when it was rebranded National Intelligence Center *Centro Nacional de Inteligencia* (CNI). The GAL extrajudicial counter-terrorism experience and the political eavesdropping embarrassment revealed critical flaws in supervision and accountability practices not only within the intelligence service at large, but also within the legal due process which inhibited violations of civil liberties. In this regard, should any individual be a party to any judicial proceeding where the intelligence service may be involved, he or she lacks any defense recourse.

Not even the Spanish Ombudsman *Defensor del Pueblo,* who in other countries may seek to review an intelligence service's conduct as pertains to a citizen's claim may exercise such supervisory role. To all effects a proceeding labeled as a national security item under the Official Secrets Act will be off-limits for proper democratic review. Arguably, this may still be a cause for concern today. The actual existence of the pre-Constitution Law of Official Secrets *Ley de Secretos Oficiales* (LSO) of 1968, though subsequently modified in 1978, is still considered a contentious element within the Spanish democratic system of checks and balances, including freedom of the press. To illustrate this sentiment senator Martin-Retortillo, from the Progressive Independent Socialists, declared that the law of 1968 that is now modified '*served* [then as it would now] to silence the press, and not the professional functionaries, since these already conformed to norms sanctioning release of secrets'.

And yet, paradoxically, it was a breach of the LSO that unearthed the dirty counter-terrorist war the GAL unleashed against ETA members and financed with discretionary *fondos reservados,* reserve funds appropriated for the necessary expenses for the security and the defense of the state assigned to the security, defense and intelligence structures, including the CESID. Once discharged from service in 1991, Coronel Juan Alberto Perofe, ex-Chief of the Special Means Operations Group *Agrupación Operativa de Medios Especiales* (AOME) within the CESID, conceals over 1,200 classified documents, some of which find their way to the journal *El Mundo,* which publishes some of these causing public outrage leading to the collapse of the PSOE government in the 1996 elections. The documents ostensibly proved the CESID had been eavesdropping on civil society elites. These events nearly paralyzed the CESID which entered in a deeper operational crisis than that suffered in 1981 when it was acknowledged some of its members participated in the failed 1981 *coup d'état.*

Control of the intelligence services, an important counter-terrorist element, is *suppos*ed to be ensured through four different mechanisms (1) Executive Control; (2) Parliamentary Control; (3) Budgetary Control; and (3) Judicial Control.

But in order to meet the objectives of the discussion herein, as far as the Spanish intelligence service is concerned, the focus will be placed on parliamentary and judicial controls since these two supervisory mechanisms would gain preeminence in the attempt to reveal the missing clues within the 11-M Commission investigation that followed the 11 March 2004 terrorist attacks on the Madrid public transport system that wrecked havoc causing over 191 deaths and over 1,400 injured. In the same order of work, it might have caused a conflict of interest with the judicial investigation and final ruling of the 11-M Trial resolved in 2007.

Past experience, overwhelmingly proved overall poor supervision of the CESID had been a recurring trend, mainly because the CESID lacked a clear defined set of objectives under which a legal case for defining accountability may have been made. Supervision at the parliamentary level was also poor as a result of both legal and bureaucratic obstacles, which led to the creation of the parliamentary Official Secrets Commission *Comision de Secretos Oficiales* (CSO) in 1995, formed by Congress deputies. Yet to all effects, access to classified information by the CSO remained weak and limited since the LSO was conceived to protect national security interests, and the criminal and military codes impose serious sanctions on the publication of official secrets irrespective of who causes revelations.

As far as judicial control, the criminal prosecution of functionaries and others involved in GAL extrajudicial counter-terrorist activities proved judicial controls may work. Nonetheless, this may only occur once classified information is ready and available, a circumstance subject to governmental scrutiny. In the GAL case, it should not be forgoften that without Coronel Perofe's betrayal, perhaps knowledge of the GAL experience may have never been revealed. This circumstance could have allowed for the extended corruption of the CESID and the rule of law in Spain. With regard to the CESID eavesdropping of civil society elites the *Audiencia Nacional* requested necessary documentation to undertake its investigation. But as Diaz Fernandez pointed out, the CESID 'refused to release [documents] on the grounds that it constituted classified information. The request ended up in the council of ministers that also refused to declassify it; yet again, events confirmed how governmental control over such documentation tended to be absolute, thus turning judges into a very necessary counterbalance, although not always with the desired results'.

Contrary to popular belief the 2002 and the 2006 reforms of the Spanish intelligence service did not arise as a result of the abrupt impact of Islamist militant terrorism in the international stage in 2001, but as a natural evolution in the quest to improve its overall efficiency and its operational capability. Thus, the 2002 Reform essentially transformed the CESID into the National Intelligence Center *Centro Nacional de Inteligencia* (CNI) adding some internal structures to foster greater flexibility, efficiency and budgetary transparency. However, terrorism or organized crime information gathered by either the National Police or the Guardia Civil 'fall outside the system of supervision, except for matters that may be dealt with by the Interior Committee of Congress'.

As far as judicial supervision of its activities the 2002 reform forces the CNI to: (1) seek prior judicial approval of search and seizure activities, including communications, by a magistrate from the Supreme Court *Tribunal Supremo* (TS) appointed for this task; (2) Issuance of such requests must be formalized in writing by the Director of the CNI and must specify: (a) the required measures; (b) the circumstances in which the request is grounded; and (c) the objectives that motivate it and the reasons supporting the adoption of such measures; it must also include details of the affected person or persons, if known, and the location at which they are to be put in place; (d) these measures cannot last for longer than 24 hours in cases of entering premises and three months in the case of interception of communications sent by post, telegraph, telephone or by any other medium. Both periods may be extended for times of equal duration whenever necessary (3) the magistrate shall, within a period of 72 hours that cannot be extended, concede or refuse the requested authorization; this deadline may be reduced to 24 hours whenever justified on the grounds of urgency by the CNI, notwithstanding which the request must contain all of the information mentioned above. The content of these measures adopted by the magistrate shall be classified as secret; and (4) the CNI will destroy immediately all and any communication material pertaining to the aforementioned authorization for search and seizure.

However, the reforms still enabled the CNI with a great degree of discretion. Both the 11-M Commission investigation and the *Audiencia Nacional* in charge for prosecuting the 11-M attacks acknowledged frustration over their inability to determine (1) which information was pertinent to their efforts and (2) how to access such information. While some documents were declassified by the Council of Ministers, others were made available to the CSO, which subsequently 'turned debates into political slanging matches'.

These instances of course are hardly transcendent to an innocent individual who could fall prey to proceedings within the scope of both the LSO as well as the LEC. The inability on behalf of both the 11-M Commission and especially the judiciary to perform appropriate review is reminiscent once more of questionably democratic, highly politicized, practices of the past that may result in the corruption of the entire democratic apparatus of checks and balances. Such corruptive behaviors sat precedent soon after the 11-M attacks as the PP party declassified CNI documents with the sole objective of proving it had acted responsibly. This instance implied a breach of Government Law *Ley de Gobierno* which sent chills throughout CNI cadres.

As international events unfolded, Spanish security services were reaffirmed in the need to retain the intelligence apparatus within a monocephalic structure, without dividing it into internal and external intelligence apparatuses such as the British model. MacKinnon's past categorization between homegrown and foreign-grown terrorism was being reassessed. The 2006 Reform amended previous legislation finally formalizing the organic structure of the CNI. The most important characteristics were (1) the creation of three technical departments with new directors and (2) confirmation that the CNI would remain organically dependent on the Defense Ministry while reporting directly to the Presidency.

These final touch ups came as a result of the need to ensure operational effectiveness and put behind supervisory problems of the past with the added supervisory control of the CSO, composed from parliamentarians from each of the different political parties. Yet, effective supervision of the CNI continues to be questionable particularly after CNI Director, Alberto Saiz, refused to declassify documents revealing a CNI officer had sold classified material to a Russian intelligence service. In order to better supervise the CNI as well as to maximize its efficiency and that of the *Audiencia Nacional* in counter-terrorism matters, an intensive discovery process, under the guidance of the almost omniscient anti-terrorist magistrates, akin to that in France, may bring positive results, since the 'tight integration with intelligence allows the judicial system to act more effectively'.

Counter-terrorism beyond Spain

International cooperation has also played a part in supporting Spanish counter-terrorism efforts and therefore in the shaping and countering of the terrorist threat. The conservative Aznar government battled in the EU for the homogenization and regularization of a European Arrest Warrant (EAW). A timid agreement was reached in 1999, though it was not until 2004 that the EAW regime was fully in force and helped bring to justice ETA terrorists as France, particularly, buried the hatchet with ghosts from the past that hindered Franco-Spanish cooperation. Furthermore, the Financial Action Task Force (FATF), first created by the G-7 to curb money laundering from drug-trafficking and later expanded to curb the financing of terrorist activities, enabled Spain to cut the international financing of ETA. This task was furthered by the creation of the Terrorist Activities Supervisory Commission *Comisión de Vigilancia de Actividades de Financiación del Terrorismo* (CVAFT) under the Interior Ministry, in 2003. Evidently, Spanish counter-terrorism efforts would have been fruitless had the US Department of State not included ETA as a terrorist organization for the first time in 1997.

As it may be deduced, before the advent of *hyper-terrorism*, a pattern of international cooperation in criminalizing terrorist activities was embedded in Spanish counter- terrorism practices. Unfortunately, success against ETA terrorism may have caused Spanish counter-terrorism authorities to overlook the evolution of Islamist militancy within Spain proper. While this hypothesis may be true at the policy level, it does not hold much standing within expert circles. In fact, Mariano Rayon, Chief of Central Command for Foreign Intelligence at the National Police *Unidad Central de Información Exterior de la Policía* (UCI) informed Government authorities in November 2003 that Spain was in al-Qaeda's radar.

In the same line of advice, Reinares also affirmed in 2003 that 'al-Qaeda has used Spain as a base possibly transforming its citizens and leaders in targets of global terrorism'. The what 'ifs' may pile up given hindsight reflections with regard to policymakers being in-sync or out-of-sync with the level of perceived threat shared by some security intelligence officials and field experts. And yet, surprise attacks remain by definition unavoidable.

With a solid understanding of how the terrorist threat has been shaped in Spain and particularly in the Basque Country, both materially and normatively, we can extrapolate why counter-terrorism policies and practices have been facially unaltered within Spain in the wake of the international terrorist threat posed by militant Islamists. There is one major point of concern. While Spanish counter-terrorism was traditionally aimed at preventing and responding to an internal and localized threat making a clear distinction between the roles and functions of internal security-intelligence agencies and the military, the full blown homogenization and regularization of global counter-terrorism policies and practices as mandated by United Nations Security Council Resolutions (UNSCR) and the European Union 2005 Counter-terrorism Strategy (EU CTS), under the guidance of a Counter-terrorism *Czar*, particularly, raises questions over the feasibility and desirability of the application of these within Spain as internal and external aspects of security become blurred.

The Lisbon amendments to the Treaty of the EU (TEU) further continued that trend emphasizing the continuous interlocking of Common Foreign and Security Policy (CFSP) and Police and Judicial Cooperation in Criminal Matters (PJCCM) competences. This means an opportunity, as well as a risk, to frame and shape perceptions of security exists at the international level which may come to redefine power relations between and amongst democratic polities so as to serve a particular interest; and measures adopted by the EU Group of Personalities in 2006 point in this direction. It is assumed that functional integration of peoples, organizations, capitals and goods follows globalization trends. 'As crime problems become more global, so the logic of this functional narrative goes, so do the responses to these problems'.

With this premise in mind intelligence and security services world-wide argued appropriate counter-terrorism legislation had to be swiftly passed granting them extraordinary powers to face the challenge of domestic as well as international terrorism that came forth as a result of the radicalization and politicization of Muslims world-wide which vividly materialized in 2001 and the following years. Considering the threat to Western states had been unprecedented in its magnitude in the post-Cold War period, such was the feeling with regard to the need for the tightening up of security. While citizens of many democratic countries debated over the need for new legislation, they also balanced their concerns over the degree of invasiveness associated with provisions in these new legislations in which their civil liberties were being sidelined for the securitization of society.

These dynamics have granted political elites and security-intelligence managers' broad powers enabling them to frame and shape not only the terrorist threat, but also security and insecurity at the national, transnational and international levels. How is this connection relevant and what does it actually entail with regard to the maintenance of both security and insecurity? In 2004 Spain creates the National Antiterrorism Coordination Center *Centro Nacional de Coordinación Antiterrorista* (CNCA) to coordinate intelligence work between the National Police, the Civil Guard and the existing intelligence service CNI, as well as increasing the number of agents in both agencies dedicated to intelligence-gathering on international terrorism. However, information gathered by each service may only be seen and operated by those attaches from each service working within the CNCA. The CNCA is modeled after the British Joint Terrorism Analysis Centre (JTAC).

The CNCA coordinates efforts with JTAC and similar foreign anti-terrorism units such as the *Contra-Terrorism Infobox* (CTI) in the Netherlands; the Common Anti-terror Center *Gemeinsames Terrorismusabwehrzentrum* (GTAZ) in Germany; and the French Anti-terrorism Coordination Center *Unité de Coordination de la Lutte Anti-Terroriste* (UCLAT). However, Ludo Block points out that 'without having direct access to the information of the participating bodies [other counter-terrorism units' intelligence] and largely dependant on face-to-face meetings, UCLAT's coordinating role [for example] remains suboptimal'.

Similarly, the possibility of internal security services vying for turf is a concern that results from these trends. In the UK, for example, the Secret Intelligence Service (MI6) moved competencies into the area of terrorism, 'which was not received with a great deal of enthusiasm by the Metropolitan Police Special Branch; thereafter, MI5, concerned itself with organized crime, again not to the satisfaction of the police services'. In this regard, Stewart Baker's warning that '[c]ombining domestic and foreign intelligence functions creates the possibility that domestic law enforcement will be infected by the secrecy, deception and ruthlessness that international espionage requires', should not be taken lightly. The Spanish FCSE including the CNCA could face similar turf battling constraints. Nevertheless, these instances prove important structural advances have been made to adjust internal as well as external coordination and cooperation between both Spanish FCSE and international security structures to better combat terrorism.

Similarly, some noticeable structural changes have also occurred abroad. In France, for example, two of its intelligence organizations, the Directorate of Territorial

Security *Direction de la Surveillance du Territoire* (DST) and the Central Directorate of General Information *Renseignements Généraux* (RG) have merged into one agency, the Central Directorate for Domestic Intelligence *Direction Centrale du Renseignement Intérieur* (DCRI) to better fight terrorism. While this may be consistent with the increasing need to avoid the overlapping of functions, maximize resources and ensure efficiency, questions over the possibility of the infringement of civil liberties arise particularly as a result of the revelation that 'a controversial "Big Sister" database in which the intelligence services will store details on millions of citizens, including their health, social life or sexual orientation' [has been created].

The database, called EDVINGE, is mandated by decree to collect information on anyone aged 13 or above who is 'likely to breach public order'. This initiative in France follows on the steps of German counter-terrorism *technologization* methods. In the 1980s, [l]arge amounts of statistical data were scanned into computers in the effort of identifying overlapping clusters of suspicious traits in particular population segments. For example, the police used the files of utility companies to identify customers who paid their bills in cash or through third parties. This group was narrowed down further by running data checks on lists of residents and automobile registrations as well as receipts of social security and child care payments.

The people that remained in this "drag-net" were potential suspects. German counter-terrorism methods have since followed this trend and although early German counter-terrorism practice may be understood in that particular historical context, these practices are called into question in Germany today irrespective of their potential benefit in the fight against terrorism. This has been the security-policy discourse since approval of the invasive 2002 Antiterrorism Law, and since 2006 with the introduction of a new antiterrorism database linking Germany's law enforcement, intelligence and border agencies. However, in order to assuage critics, the Act on Joint Databases establishes that, [t]he order opening a data file shall be approved by the Federal Ministry of the Interior, the Federal Chancellery, the Federal Ministry of Defense, the Federal Ministry of Finance and the supreme Land authorities responsible for the participating Land authorities.

The Federal Commissioner for Data Protection and Freedom of Information shall be consulted before the order opening a data file is adopted. In Italy, by virtue of security intelligence reform, following a string of eavesdropping scandals and collusion with Central Intelligence Agency (CIA) extraordinary renditions involving the Military Intelligence and Security Service *Servizio per le Informazioni e la Sicurezza Militare* (SISMI), Italy produces two internal security agencies and an external agency: (1) the Internal Security Intelligence Agency *Agenzia Informazioni e Sicurezza Interna* (AISI) headed by a General, ex-number two in the *Carabinieri*, the Italian paramilitary police; (2) the Department for Intelligence Security *Dipartimento delle Informazioni per la Sicurezza* (DIS), which supplanted the Executive Committee for Intelligence and Security Services *Comitato Esecutivo per i Servizi di Informazione e Sicurezza* (CESIS) with a mainly coordinating role, now headed by an ex-police chief; and (3) the *Agenzia Informazioni e Sicurezza Esterna* (AISE) replacing SISMI. It was extremely important for Italy to produce appropriate oversight and supervision to avoid its services' activities to violate civil liberties.

Although the Prime Minister is under direct control of the new 'security information system', law 03/08/2007, No. 124 includes some checks and balances since '[t]he intelligence services are forbidden from employing or commissioning advisory or co-operation services from elected politicans [*sic*] at the European, national, regional and local level, members of governing bodies or constitutional bodies, judges, religious ministers and journalists'. However, no judge may incriminate intelligence officers for providing false evidence or entering an individual's private property. That belonging to political parties, unions, and journals is off-limits. Thus, while some positive security measures protecting civil liberties have been adopted, these remain lax. In fact, the adequacy of the reform was called into question when Italy moved in 2008 to criminalize illegal immigration but was finally forced to soften its measures after public scrutiny.

As far as balancing counter-terrorism, democratic accountability and civil liberties in Spain, the question is whether these foreign trends have affected Spanish counter-terrorism methods and practices. Has Spain adopted similar *databasing* initiatives thereby conforming to the way the terrorist threat is being shaped? The answer is yes. In 2006, the Antiterrorist Operations Coordination System *Sistema de Coordinacion de Operaciones Antiterroristas* (SICOA) is created. SICOA will be used by the General Intelligence Commissariat of the National Police *Comisaría General de Información del Cuerpo Nacional de Policía* (CGI) and by the Guardia Civil Intelligence Service *Servicio de Información de la Guardia Civil* (SIGC) to introduce data related to actual terrorism investigations as well as those related to it for the sake of the state security bodies' efficiency.

At the same time parameters for clear guidance under which government officials in the different diplomatic sites, foreign missions and international organizations are to coordinate between themselves and the Interior Ministry and the CNCA with regard to terrorism related issues are well defined, though commensurate legal oversight does not necessarily follow under this scheme since CNI *attaches* within the CNCA may consider classifying information subject to democratic oversight. On the supra-national scene, since EU legal mechanisms have not developed clearly yet in terms of regulating transnational operations on behalf of supra-national state policing bodies it remains to be seen under what discretion they may operate, not only with regard to securitized *databasing*, but also with regard to Joint Investigations Teams (JIT) which may operate trans-nationally as well. Spain has been the only EU country that complied fully with the EU JIT Framework Decision thereby protecting itself against others' criminal and civil liabilities if, and when, they do operate within Spanish territory.

Yet, this has to be contextualized within the Spanish LEC mechanisms (i.e., secret proceedings *secreto de sumario*) and the LSO. These integrationist trends and mechanisms may explain recent Franco-Spanish antiterrorist successes. As greater cooperation in security–intelligence matters increases so does the integration of these structures. The creation of the Joint Police Chief's Task Force (JPCTF) in 2000 and the Counter-terrorism Group (CTG) in 2001 are illustrating; 'The CTG co-operates closely with the EU, although there are no formal links – most national intelligence services are reluctant to give the EU any formal role'. Further, in 2006 the launching of the European Gendarmerie Force (EGF), headquartered in Italy and sponsored by France, Italy, The Netherlands, Portugal and Spain aims at improving crisis management capabilities in sensitive areas illustrates this trend.

According to its mandate the EGF responds to the need to rapidly conduct all the spectrum of civil security actions, either on its own or in parallel with the military intervention, by providing a multinational and effective tool. The EGF will facilitate the handling of crisis that require management by police forces, usually in a critical situation, also taking advantage from the experience already gained in the relevant peace- keeping missions. However, fear over supra-national official's lack of appropriate oversight is a concern. The oft mentioned EUROPOL scandal is a case in point. In 2001 EUROPOL headquarters in The Hague were raided by a special Dutch police team following the arrest of a French official on the accusation of forgery. As a result EUROPOL's functionality has been much debated. In fact, the existence and work of many of these supra-national security entities is not well understood by many Europeans, including Spaniards or EU immigrants whose perceptions about one another are being redefined.

When Spain joined the European Community (EC) in 1985 a major requirement for its adhesion was the implementation of an immigration policy that would be grandfathered by EC members. As a result, Spain approved the Alien Law *Ley Organica de Extranjeria* (LOE) on July 1, 1985. The result of the projection of this law throughout time has been the 'restructuring of identities in the "new" Spain, through a juxtaposition with those who have traditionally been defined as "cultural others."' The transformation of the conceptions of citizenship, among Spaniards in Andalusia, Spain's southern tier region, and 'their shifting orientation to their African immigrants with whom they shared not only class solidarity but also a long history of cultural amalgamation has created an aura of animosity that contradicts the 'substantial rhetoric about immigrants' rights and integration, 101 as related to both the LOE and the EU CTS requirements for border security for the realization of an area of freedom, security and justice. FRONTEX agents will be tasked to approve or deny entry-exit to the EU based on information systems mechanisms within the Schengen area agreement which will be connected to a larger technology of information systems network, potentially connected to EURODAC, if approved, and to ATLAS and TECS. 'The so called Passenger Name Record (PNR) agreement with the US, whereby data on passengers travelling to the US are transferred to that country; and the "Returns Directive", setting out minimum standards for the expulsion of non-EU citizens from the EU [will also form part of the drive to concentrate *technologization*]'. These tendencies have also had a negative impact on Spain's treatment of illegal immigrants which is cause for concern. At the center piece intelligence services are coordinating such efforts. The fact that data exchange is subject to national law 'afford cooperating authorities a comparatively broad degree of discretion in terms of the data they [, security-intelligence services, decide to] share'.

Fears over terrorists blinding immigration officials resulted in Parliament changing direction in Spain. Since 2003, a terrorist suspect may be held incommunicado for a maximum of thirteen days, whereas suspects accused of other crimes now face a maximum of five days of in communication. In addition while the LEC, under the Spanish Penal Code, 'establishes that all persons arrested must be brought before a competent judge within seventy-two hours of the arrest, those detained on suspicion of membership or collaboration with an armed group (including terrorist organizations) may be held for an additional forty eight hours. This means that terrorism suspects may be under police custody for five days before being seen by a judge'.

These securitization dynamics are relevant as security-intelligence officials across the EU claim the EU CTS will be effective. However, as Parkes suggests, [t]he logic of 'effectiveness' in security cooperation has entailed both an extension of executive power in policy and a reinforcement of executive autonomy in policy-making. The disinclination of those ministers and officials charged with providing security to submit to robust parliamentary input and human rights protection may, therefore, have more to do with their desire to extend their autonomy *vis-à-vis* other actors and less with a desire to engage in effective cooperation.

In Spain these warnings should be reinforced by the acknowledged severe overload of the Spanish justice system (SJS) as a whole. Currently the SJS is under funded and understaffed, lacking appropriate technology systems akin to those in other modern democracies that impair its functioning efficiently and expediently. Arguably, these deficiencies may have forced the release of a GRAPO terrorist who was apprehended with French cooperation for the assassination of a Spanish police officer in 2000. As a result of the increased pattern in the international *technologization* of security, it cannot be affirmed that Spain's model has been 'unaltered' in the aftermath of *hyper-terrorism.* The terrorist threat is therefore being materially and normatively shaped and framed to suit the interests of actors interested in 'policing at a distance'.

This stance is reinforced by the fact that while suffering ETA terrorism for decades, Spanish state security authorities created the CNCA only after 11-M. It is as if Spanish FCSE efficacy in rounding up an al-Qaeda cell in November 2001 is forgotten. The reinforcement of security managers' autonomy will have implications not only for the internal security of Spain and the whole of the EU but also for the internal security of the EU neighborhood countries from which both illegal immigrants and the foreign 'others' arrive since EU security managers will be in a position to manage the security and shape the insecurity of foreign countries as well.

Ever since the UN responded to the terrorist threat with UNSCR 1373, which created the UN Counter Terrorism Committee (CTC) under Chapter VII of the UN Charter, in the aftermath of 9/11, the international community has been witnessing the international homogenization and regularization of norms countering the terrorist threat. The CTC is composed of appointed UNSC members and is 'mandated to review measures taken by states to prevent and punish acts of terrorism'. In 2002 and in 2003 respectively the US and the EU presented their Security Strategies (SS). The EU SS though surprising to many observers, bares much resemblance with the US SS, dubbed

'Preemptive Security Strategy'. As it may be observed from examples mentioned previously, '[a] closer examination of European technologies of counter-terror reveals that Europe or at least the European Union, vigorously appropriates and develops preemptive security practice'.

The EU CTS aims to 'combat terrorism globally while respecting human rights and make Europe safer, allowing its citizens to live in an area of freedom, security and justice'. However, its strategic commitments to Prevent, Protect, Pursue and Respond have the potential to create a supra-national police state under the surveillance of both public and private actors tasked with *databasing* information of 'potential' terrorist threats. 'Defending the Fortress' has now become common phraseology referring to the EU. These trends may be seen as undermining the conventional notion of sovereignty of the nation state. As Bigo concludes, [the central question relevant to defining security is thus; WHO is vested with, or who is delegated, the symbolic powers to designate what the threats are? It must be qualified by paying attention to who is in the position of enunciation and the positions of authority of the enunciators themselves, keeping in mind their personal, political and institutional interests within the field.

The reality is that within the EU, actors that advise or enforce securitization practices date as far as the International Criminal Police Commission, better known as Interpol, the Club de Berne or TREVI in 1976, and other organizations founded on international police-intelligence cooperation. As McGinley and Parkes have noted the final, analysis suggests that EU home affairs cooperation was initiated less as a measured response to the emergence of common European problems than is often assumed and more due to a search for autonomy on the part of national security officials. Officials trounced their domestic opponents by shifting policy-making to the European level and taking advantage of a more amenable institutional environment.

What have occurred indeed, have been the acceleration and the institutionalization of these mechanisms of crime prevention. Considering security-intelligence organizations across the EU have a vested interest in managing coercion and insecurity in order to advance their corporate interests, concern over the necessity of the implementation of such legislation is not completely unfounded as adoption and regularization of this legislation and its practice may be seen as a strategy of power and control that ultimately creates a form of racism which is being deployed spatially. At least this is what is now being perceived recently from the Spanish case as immigrants are increasingly being prevented entrance to and deported from Spain, traditionally an immigrant-friendly country.

So if there were some control mechanisms in place to fight terrorism proactively in Spain, why the drive to *technologize* and police at a distance? Why is this policy and practice necessary? Whatever the response as Bigo points out, '[t]he expansion of a transnational way of policing insecurity through the interlocking of internal security agencies and the subordination of both military and police to "intelligence" services needs to be seriously assessed and cannot be accepted as the only answer to a question framed as global terror'. National intelligence agencies and the different Europol National Units have legally binding international contractual obligations with regard to the *databasing* of 'critical information sharing'. NATO, for example, imposes on member states the appointment of a competent authority to manage classified information.

In the case of Spain, this competent authority rests with the Director General of the CNI, whose number two, Elena Sanchez Blanco, affirmed that while there is a need to create and expand a culture of intelligence within Spain to improve society's transparent perception of it, no country has the ability to protect itself on its own in the post 11-S and 11-M world. As a result, new technology to modernize the

CNI and enhance its performance is needed. Here lies the security-civil liberties discourse's current dilemma.

The EU CTS might break current checks and balances set by the Spanish Parliament, Courts and Executive to control their security organizations, de facto providing security- intelligence manager's excessive leverage to present an agenda potentially inconsistent with real security needs or interests. The fact that shortly after both 11-S and 11-M Spanish state security forces rounded up the alleged suspects very quickly, questions the depth with which this trend should come to pass. The merging of internal and external aspects of security may break the order of work these organizations have come to familiarize with in a democracy, under the *aegis* of the respect for the rule of law, potentially involving the military in internal political affairs and the internal security organizations in external security which traditionally has not been their competence.

Clearly, the global drive for securitization as a result of the homogenization and regularization of international norms has sidelined concerns over their effectiveness and desirability *vis-à-vis* civil liberties. As Dana Eyre and Mark Schumann once put it, 'technology is never just technology every machine has a socially constructed meaning and a socially oriented objective', and this must be understood in order to explain how and why the terrorist threat is being shaped.

In Spain, the transition to democracy saw the transformation of law enforcement and security-intelligence practices because of the need to remove excessive autonomy from security managers with self-interested agendas at the same time that it attempted to safeguard civil liberties and the rule of law as they were being created. This might be in jeopardy today. In particular, the EU CTS is placing broad powers on security-intelligence managers who are shaping how national and EU security legislation, and particularly that related to terrorism, should be law enforced, therefore shaping not only the terrorist threat, but also security in broader terms. It is evident from the information presented herein these dynamics will need to be carefully scrutinized in order to guarantee civil liberties both in Spain as well as in the whole of the EU and beyond in the near future.

13

Nation-Building and Terrorist Safe Havens

When conventional wisdom and empirical reality part ways, as they periodically do in matters of state, the result is policy which can produce paradoxical outcomes at an astronomical cost. That is precisely what is happening in the international community's approach to nation-building. Current nation-building practices may inadvertently yield exactly the kind of states – weak, ineffectual "quasi-states" – within which terrorist networks thrive, producing the very sanctuaries for terrorism which the US and its allies are seeking to eliminate.

Unintended consequences are hardly a surprise in the messy and chaotic context of collapsed states like Somalia and Afghanistan. But in this instance the problem is also the result of a partial misdiagnosis of the relationship between terrorism and failed states – a product of conventional wisdom led astray by a seemingly self-evident set of assumptions about the kinds of operating environment terrorist networks need. That misdiagnosis, combined with chronically sub- optimal execution of nation-building – one driven by the compromises inherent in multilateralism, financial foot-dragging, sub-contracting to the UN, risk aversion, and a preference for quick fixes – is yielding half-way measures rather than a comprehensive, strategic, and effective long-term response. When it comes to the pursuit of nation-building in the name of combating terrorism, half-way measures are not merely in-adequate – they are actively counterproductive.

Nation-building in the 1990s

"Nation-building" – the generally pejorative term used to describe efforts to revive and rebuild governance, peace, stability, and rule of law in places running chronic deficits in those commodities – is enjoying a renaissance of sorts. In the early 1990s the issue served as ground zero for a nasty and partisan foreign policy debate in the US when both the Bush Sr. and Clinton administrations encountered the post-Cold War phenomenon of failed states. Advocates of nation-building justified their position as one of enlightened self-interest, arguing that the anarchy of collapsed states threatened American and global interests.

Ken Menkhaus is Associate Professor of Political Science at Davidson College. He is currently working on a study of protected conflict in the Horn of Africa on a research grant from the US Institute of Peace in a stable world order. Detractors viewed nation-building as misguided social engineering that diverted attention and money to small and remote countries of marginal relevance to vital American interests, bogged the US and UN down in Third World quagmires, and eroded the combat readiness of the American military. Worse, these critics argued, nation-building in some instances placed the armed forces in harm's way for what amounted to social work. The 1993 debacle in Somalia appeared to vindicate this position decisively. The disaster in Mogadishu gave nation-building such a bad name that the expression simply went out of parlance for a time, except as an epithet occasionally hurled at liberal internationalists. It also destroyed any appetite American politicians had for humanitarian intervention, an aversion which includes the now embarrassing refusal to respond to the 1994 genocide in Rwanda.

But lost in the smoke and heat of angry debates over America's policy to ward failed states was a loose, passive consensus which emerged more by default than design and which spanned across Republican and Democratic administrations. That consensus was built on several propositions: first, regardless of whether or not collapsed states are a threat to American interests, it is politically necessary to support (or at least appear to support) efforts to address them; second, the US lacks the political will to sustain a long-term commitment to intervention and nation-building in collapsed states and is usually not the appropriate actor for such interventions; third, a direct US role in collapsed states should be limited to initial phases of armed interventions and only when significant American interests are at stake; and, fourth, longer-term, messy, and high-risk tasks of nation-building are best sub-contracted out – usually to the United Nations.

The result is a now familiar pattern. In collapsed states and complex emergencies where the US has strong security or political interests (such as northern Iraq, Somalia, Haiti, Kosovo, Afghanistan), the crisis culminates in a US-led, UN-sanctioned armed intervention. Occasionally a US ally with stronger interests in the crisis area plays the role of initial intervener (France in Rwanda, Australia in East Timor). Thereafter, a rapid handover occurs to a UN operation which enables the US and friends to partially or fully withdraw forces. The UN successor mission includes peacekeeping troops and a collection of UN civilian departments which are tasked with different aspects of nation-building – everything from reforming the judicial and police sectors to overseeing elections to reviving the economy. The UN mission is sometimes joined (and occasionally overshadowed) by multilateral organizations such as the World Bank, the Organization of European Cooperation and Development, or the Organization of American States. Hundreds of non-governmental organizations and a dozen or so UN specialized development agencies (UNICEF,

UNDP, UNHCR, etc.) create a crowded playing field for nation-building, competing over donor funds for thou sands of unconnected projects promoting a dizzying array of goals: rule of law, judicial and police reform, demobilization, peace-building, good governance, decentralization, capacity-building, civil society empowerment, gender and minority rights, youth outreach, education, economic recovery, and more. This collection of aid programs is never referred to by donors and implementing agencies as "nation-building" – the term carries far too much political baggage. Instead, agencies from the World Bank to UNDP are savvy enough to refer to this line of work as "post-conflict reconstruction." But what is happening from Kosovo to Sierra Leone and, most recently, Iraq, is nation-building dressed up in more palatable development jargon.

The denouement to this ritual also follows a familiar pattern. Mounting frustrations and setbacks plague efforts to promote nation-building. Armed conflicts may reemerge, and criminality soars. Donor interest in the country plummets; budgets drop accordingly. Top international specialists in "post-conflict" development jump to the next front-page crisis, leaving a second-string team of variable quality overseeing projects. Whether these problems eventually culminate in a complete withdrawal from the country (Somalia, Haiti, Angola) or continuation of nation-building efforts in a state of suspended animation (Kosovo), or a hasty declaration of "mission accomplished" despite serious unresolved crises (Cambodia), the final result can rarely be termed a success. When post- conflict development is given only lukewarm financial or political support from major donor states, the intervention can look to some like a charade, with external actors seen as "going through the motions" on a mission no one believes will succeed but which everyone needs to be perceived as supporting.

The sub-contracting out of nation-building tasks to the UN and other agencies has held numerous advantages for the US. First and foremost, it shifts the risk of failure onto another political actor. This allows American political leadership to claim credit for the initially successful portion of the intervention (the part with all the quick and easy photo-op victories – protection of humanitarian relief deliveries, cessation of hostilities, refugee repatriation) while handing the UN the unenviable and high-risk task of long-term post-conflict reconstruction. The UN and its specialized agencies would complain if failure came at some cost to them, but happily for multilateral development organizations they are able to sustain an extraordinarily high rate of failure in "governance" and other post-conflict programs with virtually no repercussions. But America's preference for sub-contracting its way out of nation-building duty comes with a price – namely, an even higher rate of failure.

As Marina Ottaway recently argued, in peace operations "US participation is important because the country is the most powerful member of the international community. Otherwise, the United States sends the message that it doesn't care what happens next – and in so doing, it undermines fragile new governments and encourages the emergence of feuding factions and warlords." The high failure rate of nation-building ventures in the interregnum period from 1989 to 11 September 2001 was for the most part acceptable in Washington, for the simple reason that, with few exceptions, the countries in question appeared to pose little if any threat to vital American interests. Even crisis-ridden Haiti, which attracted a US-led, multi-billion dollar international intervention in 1994 and which has the potential to create considerable headaches for the nearby United States, was quietly abandoned by donors in 2000 out of frustration with political corruption and paralysis. What was significant about interventions in the 1990s was not just the rate at which they occurred, but also the rate at which the US and the West walked away.

This dynamic was a function of the fact that the interventions themselves were driven mainly by political, not strategic, interests – by the need for administrations to "do something" about a stomach-turning humanitarian or political crisis saturating the evening news. When the stakes are political, not strategic, then the policy choices will also be driven by political rather than strategic concerns. That tends to place decision-making authority in the hands of a US president's pollsters rather than the National Security Council, and focuses priorities more on the appearance of solving a problem (until the media departs for the next crisis) than on actual success.

The Securitization of Nation-Building

It, however, appears to have changed since the al-Qaeda attacks of September 2001 and the subsequent war on terrorism. Now, failed states are viewed by American policy-makers as potential security threats of a high order. US President Bush's National Security Strategy document of September 2002 declares that "America is now threatened less by conquering states than we are by failing ones." A recent study co-produced by the Center for Strategic and International Studies and the Association of the United States Army summarizes an argument which has quickly become conventional wisdom:

One of the principal lessons of the events of September 11 is that failed states matter – not just for humanitarian reasons but for nation- al security as well. If left unattended, such states can become sanctuaries for terrorist networks with a global reach, not to mention international organized crime and drug traffickers who also exploit the dysfunctional environment. As such, failed states can pose a direct threat to the national interests of the United States and to the stability of entire regions.

Nation-building and post-conflict reconstruction have consequently been, or are in the process of becoming, "securitized" – that is, they are now justified not as worthy humanitarian, development, or commercial objectives but rather as a tool with which to promote a broader national security goal. That objective is to combat terrorism by "draining the swamp" to deprive terrorist networks of safe operating bases. Failed states are part of the swamp.

The securitization of nation-building in the aftermath of 11 September has led to a renaissance of sorts for the concept of nation-building. Now, the constituency for post-conflict reconstruction is considerably broader and includes a much larger (though not necessarily enthusiastic) chunk of the US national security establishment than before. At least for the moment, nation-building is earning a grudging place in the portfolio of realist thinking on national security. The lethargic Western responses to nation-building in Afghanistan and Iraq attest to the precariousness of this commitment, which at this point in time appears to be a mile wide and an inch deep.

Detractors of nation-building (generally from the conservative side of the political aisle, but increasingly from the left) still voice occasional concerns but have largely been converted or silenced. Traditional conservative objections about nation-building which not long ago enjoyed an air of hard-nosed realism now seem timid. A recent *Foreign Policy* cover page featuring the title "Nation-Building Is Not for Sissies" almost seemed a taunt aimed at those who would dare to invoke old buzzwords like "quagmire" and "mission creep" in opposition to nation-building. Hawks may still prefer strategies which emphasize aerial attacks and hunt-and-destroy missions to eliminate terrorist targets, and may privately bristle at the idea of nation-building, but are hard-pressed to present an alternative as part of the long-term strategy in the war on terrorism, especially since important elements of nation-building – such as building up local policing capacities – are now enshrined in the US National Strategy for Combating Terrorism.

Second, the securitization of nation-building has considerably increased the political and strategic importance of those small and remote countries which not long ago were considered marginal to US national interests. Presidential candidate George W. Bush campaigned on a promise to focus our foreign policy on "big countries," but like his predecessors Bill Clinton and George H. Bush, he too has found most of his attention drawn to unexpected threats from small and remote countries. In the expanded war on terrorism, the list of countries most often invoked as sites of potential threats – Afghanistan, Yemen, Somalia, Kenya, Pakistan, the Philippines – reads more like the bottom rung of the UNDP "Human Development Index" rankings.

Misdiagnosis of Collapsed States and Terrorism

The securitization of nation-building insures more sustained American and Western attention to failed states as a matter of national interest. This is a welcome development. But sustained attention is no guarantee of success if nation- building strategies are based on a misdiagnosis about the relationship between collapsed states and terrorism.

Conventional wisdom holds that collapsed states constitute a safe haven for international terrorists. The logic behind this proposition is, on the surface, entirely reasonable and compelling. Zones of state collapse appear to offer a sanctuary beyond the rule of law, where terrorists can establish bases or staging grounds with little risk of detection. Terrorists will, therefore, naturally prefer the impunity of anarchy to the risks of operating within the reach of a national security and police force.

This was the logic which propelled so many in the US government and media to short-list Somalia as a site for an expanded war on terrorism following the 11 September bombings. Somalia is not only a completely collapsed state – it is an Islamic society with a known and active radical Islamist group, *al-Ittihad al-Islamiyya* (AIAI). As such, it was self-evident that the country would be a likely place for *al-Qaeda* to flee and regroup. The claim that Somalia hosted terrorist camps was repeated so often by government officials and media pundits that it became gospel, despite the absence of credible evidence that such a threat existed in Somalia. It nearly led to direct US military action against suspected terrorist bases in Somalia, until closer investigation revealed no such targets presented themselves in the country. Subsequently, Somalia has been kept under close surveillance, but evidence of significant terrorist threats emanating from within its borders has not, to date, been compelling. The environment assumed to be most attractive as a safe haven for *al-Qaeda* was, for some reason, not.

The case of Somalia suggests that external observers may have been mistaken in our assumptions about the relationship between terrorism and collapsed states. The reality is that, at least up to now, transnational criminals and terrorists have found zones of complete state collapse to be relatively inhospitable territory out of which to operate. There are certainly exceptions – the fiefdoms of drug-lords and radicals in parts of Colombia, for instance. But in general, terrorist networks have instead found safety in weak, corrupted, quasi-states – Pakistan, Yemen, Kenya, the Philippines, Guinea, and Indonesia. Terrorist networks, like mafias, appear to flourish where states are governed badly rather than not at all.

Why are areas of state collapse such as Somalia apparently not so attractive as safe havens? First, in zones of complete state collapse, terrorist cells and bases are much more exposed to international counter-terrorist action; violations of state sovereignty by a US Special Forces mission would be less problematic (or would even go undetected) where a central government either does not exist or is unable to extend its authority to large sections of the country. Second, areas of state collapse tend to be inhospitable and dangerous, meaning few if any foreigners choose to reside there. The fewer the foreigners, the more difficult it is for a foreign terrorist to blend in unnoticed. In an environment like Somalia, a non-Somali's presence is known to all, and the agenda of that foreigner a matter of great interest to local communities. To the extent that secrecy matters to a terrorist cell – and it is safe to presume it matters a great deal – a collapsed state is not necessarily an ideal location. There, terrorists may be beyond the rule of law, but not beyond the purview of curious and suspicious locals.

Third, the lawlessness of areas of state collapse may reduce the risk of apprehension by a law enforcement agency, but it exponentially increases vulnerability to the most common crimes of chaos – kidnapping, extortion, black- mail, and assassination. The same security threats which plague international aid agencies in these areas would also afflict foreign terrorist groups. Once in place, a terrorist cell would find itself at the mercy of hosts who fully appreciate the bargaining leverage they have over the fugitives; the risk of betrayal by local interests hoping to cash in on an anti-terrorist bounty would be quite high. One American defense official concluded that in Somalia "the environment is so opportunistic . . . that any [terrorist] presence there is liable to being sold out."

Finally, external actors find zones of endemic state collapse and armed conflict a notoriously difficult environment in which to maintain neutrality. Local contacts and supporters are invariably partisans in local disputes, and the external actor – whether an aid agency or terrorist cell – can quickly become embroiled in those disputes and be seen as having "chosen sides."

The apprehension of suspected terrorist Suleiman Abdalla in Mogadishu in March 2003 is instructive on this point. Suleiman, a Yemeni national believed to have played a central role in the 1998 al-Qaeda bombing of the US Embassies in Nairobi and Dar Es Salaam, sought refuge in Mogadishu, taking on a business partnership with a Somali as co-owner of a hotel. In March 2003, he was apprehended by some combination of local, Kenyan, and American forces, and turned over to Kenyan authorities for questioning.

The fact that this foreign terrorist suspect was exposed and apprehended in Somalia despite the absence of a functional police force reinforces the argument that stateless Somalia is a treacherous and non-permissive environment for terrorists. Competing Somali rumors which subsequently flowed about the arrest – one claiming he was kidnapped and turned in by a rival sub-clan to that of his Somali business partner, the other that his business partner served him up in order to assume full ownership of the hotel – may or may not be true, but both accounts share the common motif of treachery. On the other hand, the fact that Suleiman was apparently able to live and do business in Somalia for over four years is a worrisome indicator that in some circumstances foreign terrorists are able to exploit Somalia as a safe haven. The case of Suleiman Abdalla suggests that both interpretations are probably right. In the short-term, most anyone can make arrangements to live and work in Somalia. But the longer one stays, the more one accumulates grievances with local partners, the more information leaks out about the visitor, and the more prone to extortion, threats, and betrayal the visitor becomes.

This pattern is painfully familiar to international aid agencies, which with only a few exceptions follow a predictable cycle in Somalia – initial welcome, followed by "mistakes" which create enemies, followed by mounting security problems which culminate in termination of the project, often via an inglorious evacuation. This reflects a long- standing tradition in Somalia of the commoditization of guests, who are quite rightly viewed as resources to conserve, protect, expend, exploit, and dispense with as the situation dictates. By contrast, quasi-states offer a modicum of protection. Governments, however weak, enjoy and fiercely guard juridical sovereignty, forcing the US and key anti-terrorist coalition allies into awkward and not entirely satisfactory partnerships with those governments in pursuit of terrorists. The mixed track record the US has had with the government of Yemen over investigations into the terrorist attack on the *USS Cole* is a case in point.

Anti- terrorist joint ventures with governments of quasi-states are cumbersome and often ineffective, since the capacity of such states is often very low. They can also be dangerous, since governments of quasi-states are often riddled with civil servants and military officers with divided loyalties to both the state and the cause. Information-sharing in such a setting can quickly lead to leaks, failed missions, and the danger of compromising informants. Finally, rulers in quasi-states are often exceptionally vulnerable to internal opposition and are as a result unenthusiastic about embracing anti-terrorist actions which might alienate radical groups with whom they have established a *modus vivendi*. This is an important political dynamic even in relatively strong states such as Egypt and Saudi Arabia, as the journalist Thomas Friedman has so vigorously pointed out.

The alternative – to simply violate the sovereignty of a quasi-state in pursuit of individuals or groups suspected of terrorist links – is an option, but one loaded with political complications, a fact which terrorist networks no doubt appreciate. Such an operation would create a political backlash even in a friendly but weak state (such as Kenya,

Yemen, or Pakistan), generating a windfall of angry new recruits for al-Qaeda, reinforcing the conviction in some quarters that the real threat is American/Western imperialism, and possibly jeopardizing the government in power or forcing it to take anti-American positions for the sake of political survival. A botched operation – one in which innocent locals were killed, or counter-terrorist forces taken hostage – would be enormously difficult to manage if it was conducted without the consent of the government of the quasi-state. Though it is easy to disparage the principle of state sovereignty as a legal fiction, the fact is that a military violation of a quasi-state's sovereignty in the pursuit of terrorists carries a hefty price tag.

A second reason terrorist cells prefer weak states over collapsed states is because they play host to a large foreign community – diplomats, aid workers, businesspeople, teachers, tourists, missionaries, and partners in mixed marriages, among others. That gives foreign terrorists a decisive advantage in their ability to move about and mix into the society without arousing immediate attention. In cases like Kenya and South Africa, where the citizenry is already thoroughly multi-ethnic (including African, Indian, European, and Middle Eastern descent), this advantage is magnified still further. Large, un-policed, multi-ethnic cities and slums are especially easy places to dissolve into the crowd. The large foreign presence not only provides cover but also a range of soft targets, a reality that Kenya has now endured twice in recent years – first with the 1998 bombing of the US Embassy, and more recently with the attack on Israeli tourists at Mombasa. By contrast, the zones of state collapse – southern Somalia, southern Sudan, eastern Congo, and Angola – present a paucity of enticing Western targets, unless that country's crisis happens to attract a UN peace operation.

Third, quasi-states generally feature very corrupt security and law enforcement agencies, but not such high levels of criminality that a terrorist cell is especially vulnerable to lawless behavior. Bribes to police, border guards, and airport officials allow terrorists to circumvent the law even while they enjoy a certain level of protection from it. Whether such corruption is a function of the economic desperation of underpaid policemen or the greed of rich civil servants, the effect is the same – a virtual carte blanche to operate under the radar screen of internal and external security monitors. The extraordinary denouement to the December 2002 terrorist attack in Mombasa, Kenya – in which the suspects "escaped" from police who are widely suspected of accepting a bribe in exchange – is the most damning evidence of how corruption produces a permissive environment for terrorists.

All this means that a terrorist network in a region such as East Africa would have a strong and logical preference to work out of Nairobi, Dar Es Salaam, or even Kampala rather than Somalia. And that is precisely what has occurred – the weak quasi-state is repeatedly preferred over the zone of complete state collapse as a base of operation, a lair for evading detection, and a setting for terrorist attacks. That is not to argue that the world can rest easy about terrorist exploitation of anarchic zones of collapsed states such as Somalia. Areas of state collapse clearly appear to have a niche role to play in the terrorist playbook. Available evidence suggests they are useful primarily as transit stations, through which the movement of men, money, and materiel can be arranged into neighboring states with little fear of detection. The Horn of Africa is currently awash in un-policed, cross-border smuggling of small arms, people, and goods; indeed, the top commercial activity in Somalia has for a number been transit trade of basic consumer goods from Mogadishu beach ports overland into Kenya's lucrative market.

The use of collapsed states for terrorist transit operations has the advantage of exploiting the already flourishing smuggling networks (so little suspicion is aroused, and hiring of trucks and agents is routinised) while keeping such involvement in the collapsed state short-term in duration, thereby minimizing risks. Local agents need not be members or sympathizers of a terrorist movement; for a fee, virtually any merchant or local warlord will assist in the transit of a shipment, a money transfer, or a convoy of people with no questions asked. This underscores the fact that careful monitoring and surveillance of zones of state collapse is an entirely justifiable component of the war on terrorism. But it suggests that monitoring in those areas should focus more on beach ports and cross-border smuggling than on a search for terrorist cells and training camps. It is not what is in these zones of anarchy, but what passes through them, which is of greatest immediate danger.

There is also the risk that individual terrorists, either indigenous or foreign, will, like Suleiman Abdulla, seek to safe haven in collapsed states. Indeed, the more successful counter-terrorism measures are elsewhere, the more likely individual terrorists are to turn up in places like Somalia, where they will assume a role in business or an Islamic charity in hopes of remaining undetected. Recourse to such environments is hardly a first choice, however; it is reasonable to presume that a growing presence of foreign terrorists in places like Mogadishu suggests a measure of weakness and lack of alternatives. Still, this scenario demands much closer scrutiny of and transparency on the part of business partnerships and Islamic aid agencies.

Swamps of Concern

If an important component of the Western counter-terrorism strategy is to "drain the swamp," and if collapsed states are among the "swamps of concern," then the obvious prescription is to promote vigorous state-building and post-conflict reconstruction in collapsed states. Leaving states like post-Taliban Afghanistan in a state of chaos would clearly be self-defeating. Hence, the US and its allies have pledged billions of dollars in post-conflict reconstruction to Afghanistan, a commitment which attracts the usual armada of international agencies crowding the state-building playing field wherever states have collapsed and funding is promised. By the same logic, a current Kenyan-sponsored peace initiative to resolve the Somali crisis and create a government of national unity there has attracted much more active support from the US, the European Union, and some international advocacy groups. The promise of substantial assistance for post-conflict reconstruction is being used to entice Somali leaders to agree to the revival of a central government which would presumably develop a police and security capacity to control terrorist elements within its borders.

In practice, there are a number of distinct problems with the enterprise of rebuilding functional governments in collapsed states with the expectation that they will grow into reliable partners in a war on terrorism. Firstly, many local figures in places like Afghanistan and Somalia simply do not share our agenda. Setting aside the many local authorities with little stomach for a war on terrorism or with lingering sympathies to terrorist causes, the bigger concern are the many more who are not even interested in the revival of effective government and rule of law. Many contemporary crises of collapsed government are products of warlordism and war economies, in which powerful local (and sometimes external) actors profit economically or politically from a continued state of lawlessness, armed conflict, and state collapse.

The conflict constituencies – often includes the very individuals whom external mediators repeatedly convene to the negotiating table in hopes of brokering a peace – risks losing out on lucrative illicit business ventures were rule of law to be reintroduced. "Blood diamonds" in several of Africa's complex emergencies are the most famous but hardly the sole commodity associated with crises wherein war is an instrument of enterprise and "durable disorder" a desired outcome for parochial political or economic reasons. This sobering observation is even more worrisome when one takes account of the fact that these same conflict constituencies exist and operate in some rather strategic quasi-states. In Kenya, for instance, efforts to improve the state's capacity to crack down on endemic lawlessness are stymied in part because important sections of the Kenyan police are themselves complicit in criminal behavior ranging from corruption to extortion to murder.

Likewise, efforts to mediate peace in some of Kenya's extraordinarily violent pastoral clashes – conflicts which have rendered much of the northern portion of the country beyond the rule of law and hence a zone of concern in the war on terrorism – fail not because these clashes are captive to timeless tribal hatreds but because Kenyan elites at the highest levels have profited from and orchestrate these bloody, commercialized cattle raids. In these situations, nation-building projects which aim to produce rule of law and a robust police and security capacity to enforce the law will either encounter active resistance and sabotage by powerful political actors, or will be quietly subverted by local authorities who will gladly go through the motions required by externally-funded capacity-building programs, but with no intention of allowing them to become effective. This game of charades is distressingly familiar to aid workers and diplomats who have worked in post-conflict settings from Haiti to Sierra Leone.

The Projectization of Nation-Building

Post-conflict reconstruction is also handicapped by the fact that the present system of implementation for nation-building in collapsed states is broken, so much so that it almost appears purposefully designed to produce unwanted results. The long string of failed or frustrated nation-building ventures the international community has attempted in the past 15 years should in and of itself be ample evidence on this score.

In policy discussions, nation-building as an enterprise tends to be discussed in the abstract. Very few of the policymakers and pundits pronouncing judgement on the matter have any direct field experience in post-conflict reconstruction, and even the informed public would be hard-pressed to explain how we actually "do" nation-building. It is simply assumed that the tools, expertise, and system are all in place to build capacity, good governance, and public security. This assumption is reinforced by the often inflated reporting and rhetoric of those agencies which deliver those "products" to post-conflict societies.

The reality is that the operationalisation of nation-building on the ground is alarmingly weak. Strategies of post-conflict reconstruction are, to put it charitably, a work in progress. The main actors in funding and delivering post-conflict reconstruction assistance – the US Agency for International Development, the World Bank, the UN Development Program, the UK's Department for International Development, and dozens of non-profit organizations and think- tanks – have been scrambling to devise effective approaches to capacity-building and good governance projects, but little consensus exists among them. Most of the flood of recent literature on effective peace-building and post-reconstruction aid are either collections of self-evident bromides or are "lessons learned" exercises aimed at sifting through the debris of a decade of failure. More coherent strategies may eventually emerge from these efforts, but for the moment strategy on the ground is *ad hoc*.

Delivery of post-conflict reconstruction is even weaker than strategy. Nation-building in practice in settings like Afghanistan, Kosovo, and Somalia is little more than a cacophony of hundreds of projects large and small. This "project" orientation to nation-building is a direct import from conventional development assistance, and the template is fundamentally flawed. Multiple donor agencies allocate funds to a virtual army of UN specialized agencies and international NGOs to execute projects within a broader post-conflict reconstruction pro- gram. Those agencies jostle at the feeding trough for position in high-visibility sectors and regions. Agencies then often sub-contract out to local organizations to do the actual project implementation – training workshops for police, demobilization projects, media training, teacher training, training of trainers, and so on. Where peacekeeping forces are present, foreign military units with no experience in development work often participate in this process as well, both in direct training and joint exercises with local military forces and in participation in civil society projects such as bridge, road, and school repairs.

Efforts are made to coordinate these efforts – indeed, interagency coordination meetings become an almost full-time occupation for exhausted aid officials. But coordination in such settings is akin to herding cats. The projectisation of nation-building insures that the delivery of post-conflict reconstruction is chaotic and as balkanized as the post-conflict societies for which the aid is intended. Nation-building at the operational level has been thoroughly captured by the quarreling and competitive agencies which collectively comprise the development industry. This is on aggregate very bad news for nation-building. Those agencies were initially reluctant to tread in the unfamiliar and often dangerous (or at least uncomfortable) settings of collapsed states. But once it became clear in the mid-1990s that post-conflict reconstruction was where the bulk of aid funding was being targeted, the fleet of mainly North American and European NGOs and their UN agency rivals were quick to position themselves as specialists in capacity-building, peace-building, and good governance, though few could legitimately make such a claim.

Their success in marketing themselves as nation-building sub-contractors insured that all of their shortcomings as development agencies were transferred to the nation-building enterprise. These short- comings include variable and generally low levels of expertise in post-conflict reconstruction; low institutional memory and high personnel turnover; internal reward systems for winning project contracts, not achieving successful results; a strong aversion to cooperation and coordination with rival agencies, which occasionally erupts into open turf battles; preoccupation with internal bureaucratic infighting, budgets, and procedural matters; lack of flexibility and quick-response capacity; a tendency to recruit top local staff at much higher pay than local government can offer, thereby creating a brain-drain which erodes capacity in the name of building it; variable but chronic problems of accountability and transparency; a focus on meeting narrow, superficial, and measurable project outputs rather than the broader and more sustainable objectives of capacity-building; and a very short-term vision and commitment.

The last point is critical. A short-term mentality is antithetical to a long- term process such as nation-building. Yet projects are inherently short-term in nature. Project funding is year-to-year (and often delayed), project proposals are usually premised on impact and completion within a few years, and international project personnel tend to move onward and upward within a year or two. Nothing about a project approach to post-conflict reconstruction lends itself to long-term commitment and vision. The projectisation of nation-building thus builds a serious flaw into the enterprise.

The public relations units of these UN specialised agencies and international NGOs will rush to refute this portrait of post-conflict reconstruction, arguing that their organization is not like the others. Some are correct. There are a number of first-rate, thoughtful, and committed organizations working to promote aspects of nation-building. But those agencies operate in a sea of mediocrity, opportunism, and indifference. For the moment, the sub-contracting out of nation-building to UN agencies and international NGOs, and the project template which these agencies operate on, virtually insures that post-conflict reconstruction efforts will fall well short of objectives, even in those rare occurrences when external funding is timely and adequate.

The Security Paradox of Nation-Building

Perhaps the most critical problem of all in nation-building is temporal. The task of rebuilding the capacity of a collapsed state to govern and police effectively is enormous, and even in the best of situations can require a decade or two of sustained assistance. Most assessments of the prospects of nation-building worry that the United States is unable to commit to such long time-frames, that political pressures for quick fixes, exit strategies, and zero casualty interventions will overwhelm efforts to stay the course in collapsed states. This is not a misplaced concern, but there is an even greater temporal obstacle – the problem of transition from collapsed state to fully functional government.

The long stretch of time which passes between state collapse and effectively rebuilt government constitutes a dangerous transitional stage, a period when the government on the receiving end of nation-building efforts is weak, vulnerable, but sovereign -- in other words, a quasi-state. Hence the security paradox of nation-building: the very success of post-conflict reconstruction in a collapsed state will produce a temporary political situation in which terrorist networks appear to thrive. Paradoxes associated with transitional phases in development are not new. Samuel Huntington argued over three decades ago that while both traditional and modern polities are stable, political instability is endemic in countries in transition from traditional to modern society.

Likewise, economists have long been aware of the paradoxes of transition in economic development, noting, for instance, the tendency for gaps in income to actually widen as an economy develops before closing again around a larger middle class in a developed economy. If this same transitional dynamic is true in nation-building and public security, then we can expect that current sites of nation-building initiatives will likely become more, not less, dangerous as terrorist safe havens in the short-term. This outcome is possible even if post-conflict reconstruction initiatives are strategically coherent, vigorous, seamlessly coordinated, and flawlessly executed. But it is almost a certainty if current nation-building systems and practices are left in place, delivering the half-way measures which can do no better than produce quasi-states.

Policy Implications

At the heart of the security dilemma of nation-building lays two propositions, both of which are disquietingly true. The first proposition, voiced by advocates of nation-building, correctly identifies collapsed states as a major security threat in the war on terrorism. The second proposition, offered by critics of nation-building, correctly argues that nation-building as currently conceived is a fool's errand.

There are several potential policy responses to this dilemma. One is to quietly abandon the nation-building enterprise and accept that the war on terrorism will be reactive, not preventive, executed as a protected military and counter-terrorist operation against threats which thrive in swamps we have opted not to try to drain. There are obvious costs and shortcomings with this approach, but it has attractive virtues too. It has the simplicity of a duck hunt, and because it calls for responses for which the US is well-equipped, it is entirely plausible that this approach will win favor if and when frustration levels with nation-building hit critical mass. A recent comment by US Senator Joseph Biden hints at this possibility. "Some of these guys [defense officials] don't go for nation-building," he observed. "They think it's cheaper to just go back in and empty the swamp again if you have to."

It is also plausible that nation-building practices will continue with only incremental reforms, despite the fact that they are clearly failing. Nation-building as it is currently pursued has attracted a substantial collection of interest groups eager to advance the cause and quick to attack proposed changes in policy. More importantly, current nation-building practices fulfill the important political objective of demonstrating that we are "doing something" while blame for failure can continue to be conveniently placed on locals and third parties. Nation-building as an elaborate game of charades comes at a cost, however, in that it cedes the playing field to terrorists.

A third option is to fix the broken system of nation-building. This approach accepts the threat assessment that collapsed states are unacceptable security risks, but not the hand-wringing position that nation-building is doomed to fail. Overhauling post-conflict reconstruction so that it stands a much better chance of success would be neither easy nor politically popular. The subcontracting of management of post-conflict reconstruction to the UN would have to be rethought; the US and its allies would need to assume much more direct over- sight and control of nation-building programs in collapsed states if nation-building is ever to acquire the necessary level of strategic coherence and competence. Second, the "project" approach to nation-building would also require serious reconsideration, with an eye toward devising more systematic and truly coordinated efforts that may involve direct execution by the US government.

Third, much closer attention must be paid to the development of strategies of post-conflict reconstruction which actually work in practice. There are organizations working on innovative and long-term approaches to this challenge, but their critical voice is often drowned out. Finally, in some areas of state collapse the US and a "coalition of the willing" may need to assume more direct involvement in security and policing functions during the long transition from collapse to effective governance, to insure that the transitional period of nation-building is not exploited by terrorists.

Some of these reforms would push the US and its allies into an acutely uncomfortable policy discussion – namely, the politics of trusteeship. Trusteeship-type solutions to the paradox of nation-building and global security enjoy almost no constituency. The term itself is stained with the sins of its distant cousin colonialism. Many voices from the Third World object strongly to any erosion of state sovereignty under any pretext, and would view the proposal to establish a trusteeship over a collapsed state as a neocolonial Trojan horse. The astronomical costs and risks which the US and its allies would have to shoulder in a trusteeship would generate strong opposition to the policy from within the US public and government as well. For these reasons, trusteeship has been a virtually taboo subject to date. But the topic may soon be unavoidable. Post-war Iraq is the latest and most controversial example of quasi-trusteeship arrangements being assumed by the US. In Iraq, however, the direct American administration is portrayed as a strictly short-term and transitional arrangement until such time as an interim Iraqi authority can be stood up. The kinds of quasi-trusteeship this analysis suggest may soon be inevitable would be longer-term and more indirect in nature – a security umbrella arrangement under which local law enforcement and governance capacities can gradually be built and strengthened without having to take on the impossible burden of monitoring and asserting terrorist activity within its borders before it has the capacity to do so.

For as unpleasant as trusteeship is, there appears to be no other way to effectively monitor and combat terrorism during the long transition from collapsed state to functional government. The key question – one which merits sustained discussion and debate – is whether a new form of trusteeship can be forged, a progressive rather than neocolonial trusteeship which would constitute an opportunity for, rather than an imposition on, nations in receivership. Such a trusteeship would have to combine the external security oversight required of a war on terrorism while at the same time providing sustained political space for progressive, democratic, and capable new national governments developed by and for local populations.

14

Fighting Terrorism through Data Integration

Crime knows no boundaries. The constellation of clues and evidence related to criminal activity is often spread across disconnected databases and paper files in thousands of local, state and federal agencies across the nation. If this disparate data was fully integrated and subjected to state of the art analysis tools, law enforcement agencies would be much more effective in both preventing crime and solving open cases. In many cases criminals who have been stopped by the police are freed when local law enforcement data searches miss important information that is stored outside of their own systems.

An integrated data system would enhance the ability of law enforcement to identify suspects quickly. Accurate identification is the key to successful investigations. Whether a person is arrested or is released for a crime that occurred in another jurisdiction is frequently based on the ability of the police to confirm the subject's identity. It is the person's identity that links the person to an arrest warrant. Warrants are stored in databases on the local, state and federal level. In addition, terrorist watch lists and investigative alerts are also computerized and stored in different databases. Most of these databases are not integrated and therefore the information contained within them is not shared.

Since the greatest majority of arrests occur during vehicle stops, an effective system requires timely information. The widespread use by police departments of in-car computers connected by wireless networks now make the sharing of information between agencies at all levels possible.

Artificial intelligence programs could be used to search databases, detect patterns and to link suspects and evidence, leading to a more sophisticated and efficient criminal information system. Law enforcement agencies could then prioritize their resources to focus on areas identified as high risk. This is especially important in the pursuit of terrorists, so that their preparations for attack can be disrupted before they result in destructive actions.

To proactively address both traditional criminal activity and the more recent threat of terrorism, technology must be put into place that creates a seamless data grid that can be queried in real time as needed by authorized agencies. In this article, we will look at a number of current initiatives focusing on the integration of criminal justice data. Today, law enforcement agencies are generally aware of only the crimes that occur in their jurisdiction or in their domain of authority. Information about crimes that take place in other areas is often gleaned through media coverage or through after-the-fact criminal exchange meetings between different agencies. This occurs even if two agencies have adjoining jurisdictions or associated authority.

The terrorist attacks on September 11th have graphically exposed the risk of our current stovepipe data structure. If we had an integrated data system in place, the isolated data points of suspicious activity at flight schools might have been recorded and analyzed, and reports of the risk of terrorist hijacking might have alerted law enforcement in time to prevent the tragic events.

Since 9/11, the federal government has been aggressively working to link the databases of its many agencies and to improve information sharing between federal, state and local agencies. However, it is quite likely that information exists in far-flung databases that could avert the next terrorist attempt. Given that major existing threat, a system needs to be in place to correlate, connect and integrate the disconnected pieces of data that currently reside in separate data sources.

National Criminal Databases

Currently, national databases such as the National Crime Information Center (NCIC) are in place to archive and provide access to data concerning fugitive, missing and wanted persons and vehicles, criminal histories and stolen property. Criminal information is sometimes shared by entering the data into separate databases as is done in the investigation of violent crimes using the Violent Criminal Apprehension Program (VICAP). VICAP is a nationwide data information center designed to collect, collate and analyze crimes of violence - specifically murder. The F.B.I. provides the VICAP database software to state and local law enforcement agencies, free of charge. The program has been embraced by many large and small agencies nationwide.

Unfortunately, no national database exists for sharing information among criminal justice agencies concerning criminal activity and information contained within law enforcement incident reports. Historically, this has occurred for several reasons.

1. There has been resistance to sharing information between agencies. In many communities the fact that crimes are being committed is concealed from the public as much as possible. No community wants to be perceived as being an unsafe place to live or work. If information about crime is shared between agencies it is feared that the information would become known to the public.

2. Computerized records management software designed for law enforcement is a relatively new phenomenon. This technology has only become widely used in the last 20 years. Most law enforcement agencies have records management software but there are many small agencies that continue to use paper reports.
3. Record management systems are typically developed in house or purchased from a vendor. Some public safety vendors have written software programs that allow multiple police agencies to link their databases as long as each agency is using the same vendor's system. Efforts are now underway to find a uniform way to connect legacy systems that utilize vendors' proprietary systems.

National Initiatives

Several large-scale efforts are developing criminal justice integration standards. The successful integration of data is highly dependent upon the development and adoption of accepted standards. Among these are the following:

- **The GLOBAL Initiative**

The International Association of Chiefs of Police (IACP) has recognized that the ever-increasing interstate and transnational nature of crime is a serious issue to the country and has urged the Administration and Congress to support efforts such as the GLOBAL Justice Information Sharing Initiative for improving the integration and compatibility of local, state, federal and international criminal justice information systems.

GLOBAL is a consortium of 32 local, state, federal and international justice organizations that are working on sharing information using a common XML standard. Member organizations participate in GLOBAL out of shared responsibility and a shared belief that, together, they can bring about positive change in interorganisational communication and data sharing that will span the spectrum of law enforcement, judicial, correctional and related bodies. GLOBAL released the first operational version of their XML Data Model (GJXDM) in February 2004.

As part of this effort, the Global Advisory Council (GAC) was established to advise the nation's highest-ranking law enforcement officer, the U.S. Attorney General, on public safety matters. GAC aids its member organizations and the people they serve through a series of important initiatives such as: the facilitation of the GLOBAL working groups; the development of technology standards, such as the GLOBAL Justice XML Data Model; the creation of white papers on data sharing issues, such as the National Criminal Intelligence Sharing Plan; and the dissemination of information via the GLOBAL Website.

GLOBAL aims to develop and implement standards-based electronic information exchange capability, providing the justice community with timely, accurate, complete and accessible information in a secure and trusted environment. The value of a GLOBAL Justice Information Sharing Initiative capability is that it benefits all operational justice officials.

The efforts of the Global Justice Information Sharing Initiative (Global) Advisory Committee (GAC) have directly impacted the work of more than 1.2 million justice professionals. The organization's mission positions GLOBAL to impact citizens of the U.S., Canada, and beyond. GLOBAL'S mission - the efficient sharing of data among justice entities - is at the very heart of modern public safety and law enforcement.

- **SEARCH**

SEARCH, The National Consortium for Justice Information and Statistics, is a nonprofit membership organization created by and for the states. SEARCH is dedicated to improving the criminal justice system and the quality of justice through better information management, the effective application of information and identification technology, and responsible law and policy.

Since 1969, SEARCH's primary objective has been to identify and help solve the information management problems of state and local justice agencies confronted with the need to exchange information with other local agencies, state agencies, and agencies in other states or with the federal government.

SEARCH is governed by a membership group comprised of one gubernatorial appointee from each of the 50 states, the District of Columbia, Puerto Rico and the U.S. Virgin Islands, as well as eight at-large appointees selected by SEARCH's chair. Members are primarily state-level justice officials responsible for operational decisions and policymaking concerning the management of criminal justice information, particularly criminal history information.

A staff of professionals works from SEARCH headquarters in Sacramento, California, to implement solutions identified by the membership group. Through its staff and with the direction of the membership, SEARCH provides justice agencies with diverse products, services and resources through three program areas: systems and technology, law and policy, and research and statistics.

Funding for SEARCH activities is provided by annual fees from member states for the operation of the consortium and board of directors' grants from various U.S. Justice Agencies, state grants and federal, state and local contracts.

The Justice Information Exchange Model (JIEM) is a product of SEARCH. Its components include a conceptual framework, research and planning methodology and the JIEM Modeling Tool, a Web-based software application that enables users to document and analyze justice information exchanges. JIEM is the model that is preferred by NASCIO (National Association of States Chief Information Officers) for inter-state integration of justice systems by the states.

JIEM incorporates the use of the Global Justice XML Data Model (GJXDM). GJXDM has been created to facilitate a common set of XML definitions to be used by all levels of justice professionals to share information.

The Law Enforcement Information Technology Standards Council (LEITSC)

LEITSC is a joint effort of the International Association of Chiefs of Police, the National Sheriffs' Association, The National Organization of Black Law Enforcement Executives and the Police Research Forum to develop information standards specific to the law enforcement community. LEITSC utilizes integration practitioners, industry representatives and justice standards representatives to review and evaluate existing information standards, specifically designed to meet functional and technical XML standards.

Working cooperative with the National Center for State Courts (NCSC), the Corrections Technology Association (CTA) and the American Probation and Parole Association's Standards Committee (APPA) and others, LEITSC is researching and compiling data needed to develop and prepare recommended standards.

There are a number of other national integration efforts. The Office of Law Enforcement Standards' (OLES) Public Safety Communications Standards program is developing standards for voice, data, image and video transfer. OLES work closely with GLOBAL. Project coordination is by the Office of Justice Planning (OJP) and the Bureau of Justice Assistance (BJA).

The Organization for the Advancement of Structured Information Standards (OASIS) announced in January 2004 that the Legal XML Lawful Intercept (LI-XML) Committee was formed to help meet agencies' information sharing needs.

XML is being used by NLETS (National Law Enforcement Telecommunication System). This initiative is supported by the American Association of Motor Vehicle Administrators (AAMVA). AAMVA is a voluntary body of all state and provincial officials in the U.S. and Canada that administer and enforce motor vehicle law.

The Industry Working Group (IWG) and the Integrated Justice Information Systems (IJIS) Institute represent over 200 private companies that specialized in criminal justice technology. Its members participate in the standards development effort at the national level through its participation on subcommittees of the Global Justice Information Sharing Initiative and by directly assisting jurisdictions in CJIS integration.

Intelligence Data Sharing

Sharing of information about individuals or groups that are involved in criminal activities is very limited. In fact, a survey conducted by the Major Cities Chiefs Association revealed these problems:

- Lack of communication and information sharing - specifically, lack of a centralized analysis and dissemination function, either at the state or federal level, lack of intelligence from federal agencies and state statutory requirements that present hurdles to sharing information.
- Technology issues - specifically, lack of equipment to facilitate a national intelligence data system, lack of interconnectibility of law enforcement and other databases (e.g., immigration services), limited fiscal resources, lack of technological infrastructure throughout the state and lack of uniformity between computer systems.

- Lack of intelligence standards and policies - specifically, lack of common standards for collection, retention and dissemination of intelligence data; a need for increased local training on legal standards for collection, storage and purging of data; access to classified data; and lack of standards for determining when to disseminate intelligence to federal agencies.
- Lack of intelligence analysis - specifically, lack of compatible analytical software and lack of analytical support, personnel, equipment and training.
- Poor working relationships - specifically, unwillingness of law enforcement agencies to provide information due to parochial interests and a culture within the federal system that does not foster sharing of information or trust between agencies.

Federal Initiatives

Federal authorities are also taking steps to address criminal justice integration. Following is a summary of initiatives in progress.

United States Department of Justice

In February 2004, the U. S. Attorney General created the Justice Intelligence Coordinating Council to coordinate intelligence sharing among Justice Department components. The federal government designated the six regional information sharing centers systems (RISS) to share information with state and local law enforcement. RISS was linked to Law Enforcement Online (LEO), the FBI's information sharing system, to form RISS/LEO.

The system is being used to provide security information to be distributed quickly to all RISS and LEO users through a new Internet-based alert system. A new project called ATIX-RISS anti-terrorism information exchange recently began testing in several states running across the RISS/LEO system. This plan grew out of the recommendations of the Global Justice Information Sharing Advisory Committee (GAC).

United States Department of Homeland Security (DHS)

Since the Department of Homeland Security's inception in early 2003 it has been developing and implementing a national security communications net. The DHS communication net is designed to provide threat analysis and intelligence information between the component agencies of the DHS and to state and local agencies. The net has three components, JRIES (Joint Regional Information Exchange System), HSDN (Homeland Security Data Network) and HSIN (Homeland Security Information Network).

JRIES is a secure network and a suite of applications currently operating at the sensitive but unclassified (SBU) level. Participants currently include approximately 100 organizations, including federal agencies, states, municipalities and other local government entities with a significant law enforcement user base. All participating entities have a certified counterterrorism mission. Approximately 1,000 users currently have access to the system. JRIES's collaboration tools are used for threat analysis and provide real-time links to the DHS operation center.

HSDN is a private secure network for the sharing of information between the 22 agencies of the Department of Homeland Security. HSIN is the primary network for sending alerts and sharing information in emergency situation between DHS and all states, 50 major urban areas and five territories.

In October 2004, Secretary of Homeland Security Tom Ridge launched the Office of Interoperability and Compatibility along with the release of tools designed to help state and local public safety practitioners improve communications interoperability. The Office of Interoperability and Compatibility (OIC), part of the Science and Technology directorate, will oversee the wide range of public safety interoperability programs and efforts currently spread across Homeland Security. These programs address critical interoperability issues relating to public safety and emergency response, including communications, equipment, training and other areas as needs are identified.

State Initiatives

In 1997 the Commonwealth of Pennsylvania created a secure virtual system online environment for the sharing of criminal justice information among participating agencies. As of September 28, 2004 JNET is connecting:

- More than 15,000 total users
- 54 participating counties
- 39 state agencies
- 17 federal agencies
- More than 220 municipal police departments
- More than 200 state police divisions
- More than 500 district justice offices

The JNET office is involved in two national information-sharing efforts with the National Governors Association (NGA). The first effort is being sponsored by Governor Mike Leavitt of Utah and involves developing a national framework for homeland security information sharing. This model is being endorsed and sponsored by the National Office of Homeland Security. The JNET model and governance structure will be used as a framework for this initiative.

The second effort entitled, "The Middle Atlantic Justice Information Sharing Initiative," was initiated, hosted and sponsored by the JNET office. Representatives from seven surrounding states, the National Office of Homeland

Security, Office of Justice Programs, National Governors Association, SEARCH and the National Criminal Justice Association are collaborating on an effort to share information amongst participating states as a pilot for a national integrated justice system. The JNET model and governance structure will be used as a framework for this initiative.

Regional Initiatives

The most successful regional effort for sharing criminal justice information is the San Diego region's Automated Regional Justice System (ARJIS). ARJIS is a complex criminal justice enterprise network utilized by 50 local, state and federal agencies in the San Diego region. ARJIS is chartered with supporting a regional Web-based enterprise network that utilizes technical and operational standards to build interfaces to all criminal justice systems in the region. The ARJISNet secure intranet contains data on the region's crime cases, arrests, citations, field interviews, traffic accidents, fraudulent documents, photographs, gang information and stolen property.

ARJISNet integrates more than 2,500 workstations and printers throughout the 4,265 square miles of San Diego County. There are more than 10,000 registered and authorized users generating over 35,000 transactions daily. ARJIS is also utilized for tactical analysis, investigations, statistical information and crime analysis. Officers and investigators can additionally request electronic notification when information is obtained by another agency or officer concerning an individual, location or vehicle. The critical success factor for ARJIS is the "single point of entry" to query all regional justice data. ARJIS is current-ly collaborating with the National Institute of Justice (NIJ) to build new Web based technologies to continue the support of the criminal justice community.

Barriers to Successful Integration of Criminal Justice Data

Not all initiatives for information sharing have proven to be successful due to legal and political concerns over privacy rights. One example is the Multistate Anti-Terrorism Information Exchange System (MATRIX). Shortly after the Sept. 11, 2001, terrorist attacks, the Florida Department of Law Enforcement (FDLE) decided to improve the way they shared information. Working with an industry vendor they developed the Multistate Anti-Terrorism Information Exchange (Matrix) system.

Matrix started as a way for law enforcement officials in Florida, Georgia, New York, Oregon and Pennsylvania to share data, but a handful of other states also were attracted to the project. By mid-2003 it had grown to encompass 13 states, accounting for about 50 percent of the U.S. population. Using the Factual Analysis Criminal Threat Solution, the Web-based technology core of Matrix, users can submit a query on anything relating to a possible suspect or a criminal situation and get back a slew of related information within seconds. From a technological point of view, Matrix was a success.

However, in late 2003, the American Civil Liberties Union (ACLU) started campaigning against Matrix, claiming that law enforcement agencies could mine an array of personal information contained in the databases. Stories began appearing in newspapers nationwide comparing Matrix to the Total Information Awareness program, which was conceived by officials at the Defense Advanced Research Projects Agency as a way of tracking potential terrorists in the general population. Officials had to shelve TIA after a public outcry over privacy implications.

Several participants dropped out after the ACLU's campaign gathered momentum. Utah officials backed out because of privacy concerns after the governor and other state political leaders complained that they learned of the state's involvement only through the media. Other state opted out of the program due to cost and other considerations such as control over their data.

Involvement in Matrix is now down to five states: Connecticut, Florida, Michigan, Ohio and Pennsylvania. Law enforcement officials who use Matrix are making adjustments. For example, they recently decided to move to a distributed database so that states would be able to control their own data, alleviating concerns about the security of data that is moved to a central database.

Legal restrictions on the sharing of intelligence data have slowed the progress of several initiatives. The Criminal Intelligence Systems Operating Policies of 28 Code of Federal Regulations (CFR Part 23) and state laws in some cases prohibit agencies from participating in a data warehouse that commingles criminal and intelligence data or sharing local records with the federal government.

In today's interconnected world, public safety officials at all levels of government are attempting to establish standards and protocols for sharing information about criminal activity. The importance of the ability of government to collect information, analyze that information accurately and share it appropriately has been brought to the forefront by recent terrorist activities. The failure of emergency responders to be able to communicate with each other during incidents has been identified and attempts to improve the communications systems are being pursued. The establishment of systems for sharing accurate and timely information is being put into place so that effective responses can be activated and resources deployed effectively.

Millions of dollars are being spent to enhance intelligence sharing and communications between our government's homeland security and public safety agencies.

The use of extensible markup language (XML) has been determined to be the technology of choice for many of the ongoing CJIS initiatives.

15

Regional Crime Fighting and Counter-terrorism

A Better Perspective

For most of its history, law enforcement in the United States has been a localized affair. A sort of patchwork of miniature kingdoms, each jurisdiction was responsible for itself. Even within cities themselves, individual precincts often manage crime on their turf — and they manage it alone. However, a new version of the legendary COMPSTAT system, now powered by Oracle, is improving how police fight crime. Four years ago, 9/11 underscored the ineffectiveness of the localized style of policing. The inability to share data and track crime effectively resulted in 19 terrorists' easily evading detection. More recently, Hurricane Katrina exposed the lethal consequences of inadequate communication among public safety agencies. In both instances, traditional methods of operation prevented emergency personnel from seeing the larger picture.

In recent years — and with renewed enthusiasm in recent weeks — the call for cooperation and integration among law enforcement agencies has grown louder. This movement for change may seem like a new idea born of tragic circumstances, but former New York Police Department Chief Lou Anemone has advocated such reform for more than a decade.

Silo Busters

When people think of Times Square today, it conjures up images of Disney, Starbucks and Coca-Cola. In fact, most folks would probably agree that it's a great place to take the family. Yet as recently as the early 1990s, Times Square was a breeding ground for New York City crime. In 1994, under the leadership of Police Commissioner William Bratton, Anemone and the late Deputy Police Commissioner Jack Maple created a management accountability process known as COMPSTAT, short for Computer Statistics. COMPSTAT revolutionized law enforcement by giving police a computerized system for crime analysis and mapping. Developed by the NYPD, the system now is used around the globe, helping officers share their data in an understandable and actionable way.

"If you walk into many police departments, what you're going to find are these silos where detectives don't talk to patrol officers, and patrol doesn't talk to the IT people, etc.," said Anemone. "And that goes on in other organizations as well."

Anemone is taking the message of COMPSTAT around the country and the world. He currently works with the Crime Fighters LLC, a subsidiary of Linder & Associates; a consulting group that has helped police departments implements COMPSTAT for a decade.

COMPSTAT provides a system of metrics that measure and analyze data relevant to law enforcement. Anemone and the Crime Fighters have partnered with Oracle to bring a new level of power to COMPSTAT. With integration technology from Oracle, COMPSTAT users see a more complete picture of crime activity in their jurisdictions.

"Our approach is to focus on four elements: intelligence, tactics, rapid deployment and relentless follow-up and assessment," said Anemone. "By focusing attention on those key critical areas, we bring everything together and create that sense of urgency within an organization. We've had tremendous results not only in New York City, but these other cities as well."

The numbers are staggering in New York. In 1990, the city witnessed 2,245 murders. With the implementation of COMPSTAT and the aggressive leadership of Anemone and Bratton (now chief of police in Los Angeles), the number of murders dropped to 590 in 2002 – a 75 percent decrease.

Cities such as Newark, N.J., Baltimore and New Orleans saw violent crime fall by nearly 60 percent after deploying COMPSTAT. These results are accomplished by collecting and analyzing data from different department sources and eliminating the silos that exist within agencies. "That's where Oracle integration technology fits in, in knocking down those silos – gathering and sharing that information among detectives," said Anemone. "That's the basic building blocks of this COMPSTAT approach – gathers all the information, look at the tactics being utilized in a city or department and make suggestions. And that's happened or is happening in each of the cities I've been working in."

Protect and Prevent

Oracle uses its database and business intelligence expertise to bring powerful, new information – gathering technology to law enforcement and counterterrorism efforts. COMPSTAT combined with Oracle integration technology allows public safety agencies to gather and evaluate huge volumes of disparate data, providing officers a holistic view of crime in their area. This solution also enables law enforcement agencies to securely share criminal and terrorism intelligence, map crime in real time, and take advantage of strategic analysis tools to reduce crime and prevent acts of terror.

Furthermore, Anemone said Oracle-powered COMPSTAT solutions could be deployed regionally as well as departmentally. The technology enables law enforcement agencies throughout a region to pool information so it can be measured, analyzed and mapped. Joe Bierly is a former Marine and now serves as Oracle's national director for public safety. He said law enforcement agencies often suffer from scarce resources, be it funding, personnel or IT. The solution is a business intelligence approach where decision-makers have a comprehensive picture of criminal activity, letting them deploy resources more efficiently and effectively.

"You have to know where the crime is, you have to under- stand where the crime is occurring," Bierly said. "What kind of patterns are we seeing, what kind of clusters, what kind of trends? Then managers can shift resources around to make those crimes go down."

This approach could be even more effective on a region- al scale. By pairing Oracle integration technology with COMPSTAT, police departments can tap into a much wider variety of data repositories — making traditional COMPSTAT initiatives automated and much more powerful. The Crime Fighters' aim is to bring this new and improved COMPSTAT to as many agencies as possible, creating an effective regional crime-fighting system.

With resources already limited, police departments might be reluctant to implement an analytical tool like COMPSTAT. Fortunately Oracle's business intelligence solutions leverage existing infrastructure. For a department using COMPSTAT powered by Oracle, data is automatically extracted from any number of repositories. The pieces of data are combined, analyzed and mapped so departments can more effectively and intelligently deploy their forces.

"We're saying keep what you have," said Bierly. "We're using integration technology to bring that data together in a data warehouse where you can do the reporting, the business intelligence, which gives law enforcement the key performance indicators they need to manage and reduce crime in the city. Before you can deal with robberies, you need to know where they are, how many there are, when they're occurring, who the victims are, and you have to have that data to do that."

Thwarting Terror

As hurricanes and terrorism illustrate, the federal government has a number of problems integrating its operations with state and local agencies. At the same time, however, modern challenges and dangers demand that local law enforcement react as first responders to disasters — and as frontline soldiers when it comes to terrorism COMPSTAT powered by Oracle integration technology gives local police and federal officials a better, more complete way to view terrorism.

"The intelligence, we believe, is not going to come from the federal side and get pushed down," said Bierly. "It's more likely going to come from the ground up. So it's important that the intelligence effort be local. The frontline soldiers in this battle are local cops. They have to know what to look for. They have to know how to report it. Somebody has to pull it together and analyze it. COMPSTAT provides timely and accurate intelligence that leads to effective deployment."

Fighting crime and terrorism is only successful if local agencies know what to look for. COMPSTAT and Oracle integration technology deliver a powerful tool for collecting and analyzing data. Agencies have to be willing to share data and work together not only to solve crimes, but also prevent them. "It's all about timely and accurate intelligence and how you deploy your forces," said Bierly. "You get the intelligence, and then you make a judgment. We have to deploy intelligently. These guys [terrorists] hate us. They're going to find a way to kill us. It takes discipline and a hardened approach to deal with it. You can't just sit there and wish they'd go away. They aren't going away." COMPSTAT and Oracle integration technology deliver the tools law enforcement needs to combat threats in the 21st century. An intelligent, regional approach to crime, terrorism and other disasters has clearly become a requirement for success.

16

Terrorism and Law

To interpret terrorism as a collective term is not always easy as even experts dealing with the theme are fairly uncertain about the notion. The word terror comes from Latin (terrororism = fright, fear, scare-news). Its meaning has gradually changed and nowadays it symbolizes violence, threat, fear, and horror. Compared to basic violence terror occurs in specialized techniques, brutal and ruthless ways. Terror can be both single and collective. A concise definition of terrorism is difficult because it involves a multitude of activities that are different in their circumstances, objectives, results, and techniques. In the background of terror and terrorism there have always been some intentions of taking revenge, of intimidation or of striking back inevitably coupled with a political, ideological or religious notion that serves to legitimization of violence. Thus the hidden goal of terrorism is more frequently to seize power than destruction of a selected (or randomly chosen) target.

All this is merely a specific tool whose use is not justified by the objective to be achieved. However, it can also be stated that sometimes the activities of certain terrorist groups tend to slip out of control and become auto telic – e.g. various acts aimed at freeing comrades – when the "genuine" objective loses its significance. There has always been a background organization which does organizing, coordination, and provides their logistic backup. New terrorism and terrorist acts are characterized by a use of weapons, demand for publicity (e.g. electronic media, live TV broadcast) and taking large numbers of hostages, violence, and threat. Well-organised teamwork, significant financial backup, and sophisticated conspirator are typical features of modern terrorism. The IT -boom, Internet, provide them with good opportunities of information gathering, smooth maintaining cross-border contacts, and in many cases anonymity, which complicate their disclosure. Terrorists have realized the opportunities provided by information society and have extensively exploited them for their own good. The vehicles of terrorist acts have also changed allowing the execution of attacks against anyone, anywhere, at anytime by any means.

In order to understand the relation between terrorism and law one should look back in history. The first typical terrorist act was committed against Emperor Napoleon III in France. The perpetrators took refuge in Belgium and were not extradited as according to the Belgian authorities they had committed a political crime which is not sanctioned by extradition. Nevertheless in Belgium an act was passed in 1866 stating that assassinations of foreign sovereigns and their families are not classified as political crime consequently the extradition law for common criminal acts was to be applied. This law is known by international legal history as Belgian Assassination Amendment. The next stage covers the period between two World Wars when the issue was dealt with by the International Association of Penal Law between 1927 and 1935.

The word "terrorism" was first used in a legal context at a Brussels conference in 1930. It was accepted and suggested for use in international legal acts in Paris in 1931, Madrid 1934, and in Copenhagen in 1935. However, the idea of a comprehensive international convention came up as late as 1934 at a session of the League of Nations. A committee was set up with the task of elaborating an international convention which can be applied for persecuting and sanctioning criminal acts with political motivations. The work of the committee was accomplished in November 1937 with an intergovernmental meeting where two conventions and a communiqué were approved.

It is worth mentioning that the first terrorism definition was outlined here in Paragraph 2 of Article 1: "In the present convention the term terrorist act covers criminal acts which are aimed at a state with the objective of creating terror with certain persons, group of persons, or communities" (1) Unfortunately, the convention did not come to force because three of the parties did not ratify it. The second convention, aimed at establishing and structure of an International Criminal Court did not come to force either, as the ratification documents were not put into deposit until the pre-set deadline. Nevertheless, both conventions play a very significant role in the history of combating terrorism as they indicate the fact that states regarded terrorism as a global problem and not just a national issue and tried to manage the phenomenon accordingly. In connection with international context the efforts of the UN and of the European countries are of primary importance.

The UN Charter, ratified on 24th October 1945, has concrete terrorism-related paragraphs and contains clear-cut ban on participating in or providing support to terrorism relating to the signatory states. These activities were classified as international criminal acts by the UN Codex approved in 1954 but the Cold War period made the management of the problem at international level difficult. Upon a US request the issue of terrorism was put on the agenda of the General Assembly in 1972. On the basis of a resolution of the General Assembly a committee was set up analysing the problem paying special attention to its political and ideological roofs and the possibilities in fighting terrorism. On the 50th anniversary of the UN combating terrorism was marked as one of the priorities of the organization. In spite of the various propositions and resolutions the definition of terrorism as a phenomenon and an overall international convention failed to be established.

The struggle under UN aegis, however, can be classified as successful – though no global solution has been found to the problem – as several international conventions have been worked out and approved, among others actions against acts posing a threat to international civil aviation. Hungary joined the convention signed by 44 countries in Chicago in 1947. In this field three other international conventions were agreed upon. An important landmark is the Convention on prevention and sanctioning criminal acts committed against internationally protected persons – including diplomats – approved on 11th December 1973. Another UN-brokered document is the International Convention Against the Taking of Hostages, signed on 18th December 1979 and the International Convention for the Suppression of Terrorist Bombing approved on 15th December 1977.

Besides UN framework, the Paris meeting of the G7 and Russia should also be mentioned where a 25-paragraph packet was agreed on. This was aimed at limiting and the prevention of the free movement of terrorists' sources of money and weapons and an exchange of information among the concerned countries. In order to prevent financing terrorism a tighter control was introduced over cultural, social, and charities which may operate as cover organizations. Naturally, in Europe a number of initiatives were launched by various organizations in order to manage terrorism-related problems. Europe has been providing a lot of "tempting" opportunities for terrorism. The geopolitical situation, coexistence of various cultures, and other factors affecting security induced the introduction of special ways of cooperation, which can prove effective in prevention. This forced regional cooperation dates back in

1950 when the member states of the European Council expressed their concerns about terrorism in a convention.

In the following years terrorism got the problem into focus again. In 1972 a steering committee was set up for controlling and analyzing terrorism-related legal issues. A document was elaborated by the European Committee dealing with penal issues of the Council of Europe for outlining directions of penal measures. The convention, securing judicial assistance, and mutual extradition was signed in 1977. However, the international Penal Code does not allow these measures in a number of cases. On the basis of Article K.3 of the Maastricht Treaty an agreement was signed on the establishment of Europol (European Police Agency). Besides traditional criminal investigation counter-terrorist activities and prevention also belonged to its responsibilities.

The so called La Gomera Statement is also worth mentioning, approved by the EU Council on 23rd November 1995. This document regards terrorism a threat posed to free exercising human rights, and economic and social development. Naturally, after the terrorist attacks on September 11 2001 terrorism-related issues got re-evaluated. In the following period of time several effective international conventions are expected to be created for a more efficient cooperation, intelligence, and prevention. The world has already had a lot of experience in combating terrorism. By drawing conclusions from the lessons learned a unified and efficient counter-terrorist tactics and strategy should be worked out in precise details.

Hungary and Terrorism

Thanks to its foreign policy concept the Republic of Hungary has a wide range of international relations thus various foreign personalities and facilities of political, economic, and other fields are present in our country among them a number of people who may turn top targets for different terrorist organisations. Terrorism-related persons are well aware of the fact that Hungary – due to its political openness – can be regarded as a liberal country with its tourism, alien policing and border policing systems which allows them to cross Hungary or stay in the country for various periods of time without taking any risk. This fact poses a significant security and risk factor. Fortunately, Hungary – and most of Central Europe – has remained an island of peace in the world, where political terrorism has not taken its victims.

However, this does not mean, that Hungary was free of bombings, moreover series of bombings, aimed at politicians (businesspeople, mob kingpins). The typical feature of these acts was that their executors, organizers, or coordinators do not take public responsibility for political or economic terrorist acts. In Hungary there have been terrorist act-like or terrorism-related events: - in 1973 a terrorism-related acts was committed in Nograd County. In Balassagyarmat two armed brothers took several girls hostage in the local secondary school and had various demands (money, airplane, free withdrawal). In 1987 an attack was carried out against the Columbian Embassy in Budapest on request of a Columbian drug lord.

In the early 1990's a terrorist bombing was executed against Russian Jews leaving for Israel via Hungary, on Ferihegyi road, Budapest. Series of bombings targeting Hungarian politicians (nobody took responsibility for the explosions – posing potential threat to human lives – damaging the house of Jozsef Torgyan and Jozsef Szajer). Bombings, assassinations, murders, showdowns between criminal groups, Fenyo-murder, Aranykez-street bombing and a number of other bombing showdowns and executions have an arsenal similar to that of political terrorism. However, those were primarily not acts with political or ideological motivations but armed conflicts among rival groups. Bombings carried out by mentally handicapped persons. The so called "ketchup bombing" was a remarkable case of them committed by a young man in Esztergom. Those acts, however, had no political motivations whatsoever. Young people interested in chemistry should also be mentioned here. They downloaded instructions for bomb-making from the internet but their devices exploded before time causing injuries and deaths. Although the used technology may be appropriate for terrorist acts, those young people had no terrorist links.

Domestic Regulation

As for the domestic legal regulation in my opinion the situation settled after the change of social system should be analysed in order to understand the trends in Hungarian legal thinking and the realization of and political tendencies. The report compiled by the Legal and Human Rights Committee of the Council of Europe in 1977 should be mentioned here. The report analysed the augmentation of European democratic institutions and anti-terrorist activities. It was stated that in Europe terrorist activities had increased, terror gained new forms, and its character had changed. This refers particularly to certain Central and Eastern European countries. An increase in terrorist activities was experienced with a significant financial and logistic backup in certain countries of the Council of Europe. The frameworks of the traditional police and legislative cooperation, however, are not sufficient for reducing the phenomenon.

Among other tasks the creation of an internationally acknowledged and interpreted legal codification was approved. Terrorism is different from common crime in its motivation, objectives, and essence as well. Countering terrorism requires special techniques because terrorism presents a threat not only to public safety and order but also has its negative impact on national security. In accordance with Paragraph c. Article 5 of the Act on

National Security countering terrorism is the responsibility of the National Security Agency. Thus the Intelligence Department of the National Security Agency counteracts to the activities of foreign powers, organizations, or persons, aimed at executing terrorist acts. In accordance with Act XXXIV of 1994 it is the police forces that have to take measures in case information on terrorist acts reaches police.

It is also the Act and other legal regulations that regulate the activities of the counter-terrorist units but these are limited to concrete elimination of terrorists and terrorist acts. Terror may be both individual and collective. That is why it is extremely important to define the notion relating to terrorist acts (terrorist crimes). Terrorist acts incorporate various types of criminal acts that are defined as a separate category in the legal system of nearly every country. This makes the competence of international legal treaties an important aspect. Terrorist acts are defined as common crimes by the Hungarian Penal Code, which can be committed by anybody – any natural person – without being a member of a terrorist organisation.

It is important to emphasize that terrorist acts have two specifications differing from other common crimes. These are: motivation (objective) and the way of perpetration. Chapter XV of the Penal Code details terrorism-related crimes in the framework of crimes targeting public order. Public order is defined as legal order and state and social order that appropriate to the norms of social coexistence by the Constitution of the Republic of Hungary and by other laws. Public security is defined by law as the general situation, the real situation of social coexistence where the life, corporal integrity, work, and properties of citizens, and civil communities are secure against unlawful attacks. Within the category of crimes against public security terrorist acts are described in Article 261 of the Penal Code as follows: "Anyone who deprives someone of their personal freedom or usurps significant material goods and makes the freedom of the person or return of the goods dependent on fulfilling their demands aimed at a state organ or social organisation." Penalizing terrorist acts by the Penal Code was necessitated by the creation of a new type of forcing and blackmailing by organized crime.

Another terrorist act defined by the Penal Code is the unlawful seizure of aircraft. Terrorist acts are complex criminal acts which pose a primary threat to the seamless operation of state administration, NGOs, which is also a basic pre-condition for public security. In relation with Penal Code it would be useful to analyse terrorist acts too. These criminal acts, taking into consideration other factors identified by the law do not fit the category of terrorist acts even though in practice their execution frequently have terrorist act features. These can be: kidnapping, defined in Paragraph 175 of the Penal Code; crimes causing public danger defined in Paragraph 259 of the Penal Code; disturbing the operation of public utility companies defined in Paragraph 260 of the Penal Code; abuse with explosive materials and devices defined in Paragraph 263 of the Penal Code; and homicide or aggravated assaults (genocide, destruction, etc.)

Future Trends

It is inevitable to conduct a proper analysis of the legal regulation outlined in the present study, in connection with prospective solutions. Naturally, what I mean is the elaboration and introduction of international legal norms that can prove an efficient tool in combating terrorism. In early September 2001 all the necessary measures underpinning and summarizing future trends in combating organized crime and terrorism were approved by the government. A unified definition of the notion of terrorism may prove a significant step and in connection with it the opportunity of direct handover of persons from one country to another. The frame resolution may or will have its impact on the legal regulation of the signatory states.

The actual international agreements obviously cannot form a base for further legislation. Thus it is imperative to rethink the current regulation including valid and suggested proposals submitted by the Government to the Hungarian National Assembly in early September. Besides fighting terrorism the frame resolution also deals with preventing money-laundering which is a financial basis for terrorism? The Act eliminates all the previous opportunities providing background support to terrorism. The Hungarian Government joined the declaration of European states and governments and fully supports the increase of efficiency of international anti-terrorist activities. A European inter ministerial committee was established to coordinate measures for executing these tasks on the basis of an action plan.

The new state of affairs of Penal Codes on terrorism should be elaborated and approved within this framework. The following crimes can be identified as terrorist acts: homicide, assault, crimes against traffic security, crimes causing public danger, disturbing the operation of public utilities, seizure of aerial vehicles, abuse with explosive materials and devices, abuse of firearms and ammunition, abuse of radioactive materials, the threat with public danger, environmental degradation, nature damage, theft, robbery, blackmail, and sabotage. It is an important point that a threat with any of the listed crimes is regarded by the framework-resolution as a terrorist act if it is aimed either at intimidating population or at destroying/changing the economic, political, social structure of a state.

One of the important factors of terrorism definition is: a structured organization consisting of more than two persons created for organizing, coordinating and committing terrorist acts. The "Legal Cooperation" Chapter of the operational plan outlines the acceleration of the elaboration of a new law on international criminal cooperation between investigation agencies and on mutual assistance. In accordance with Paragraph 4 of Government Decree of 8th September this activity is the responsibility of the Minister of the Interior until June 2002. It should not be forgotten that Penal Law and its tools can only support state power. In fact the self-protection capabilities of communities and states depend on how mechanisms other than Penal Law work in prevention and intelligence.

Missions of Law Enforcement Agencies

National Security Agency

The National Security Services are listed by Act CXXV of 1995, defining their responsibilities and the system of Parliamentary control over them. In accordance with a bipolar structure of national security organization the Act outlines their division into civil and military security services. The National Security Special Service is a background institution of those organizations that are authorized to use special means and techniques of gathering secret information. The primary missions of the National Security Agency are regulated by Article 5 of Act CXXV of 1995. In the field of anti-terrorist activities the National Security Agency discloses and prevents threats coming from a changed security policy environment and fully complies with the commitments of Hungary, generated by NATO membership.

The National Security Agency continuously monitors and assesses events and on the basis of these activities supplies the decision-making organs with the necessary information. An active exchange of information is also conducted with other national security services, domestic law enforcement agencies and its foreign counterparts. The Agency has detailed plans for accomplishing its tasks. Gathering terrorism-related information, disclosing and preventing terrorist acts – regardless of the perpetrators' religion, nationality, native language, and ethnic origins –

are classified as the responsibilities of the National Security Agency. BORDER GUARD the counter-terrorist activities of the Border Guard are regulated primarily by Act XXXII of 1997 On Border Guard and Border Policing, and by international conventions and agreements. In accordance with Article 2 of the Border Guard Act the protection and defence of the state border are the responsibility of the armed forces. Border Guard is an organization with dual designation and a special legal state, which accomplishes the defence of the country in accordance with the Law on the Armed Forces and border policing on the basis of Border Guard Act and other related laws and statutes. In anti-terrorist activities information and data exchange is conducted on the basis of agreement on collaboration between the Government of the Republic of Hungary and the Government of the Republic of Slovakia.

This information includes: - data on planned and executed terrorist acts, on perpetrators, on the techniques of acts, and on the means; - on terrorist groupings – and their members – that organize, execute or have executed their acts on the territory of the other country, damaging its interests and creating havoc. Data exchange on counter-terrorist activities. In accordance with this agreement each border traffic outpost has prepared its own plan for preventing terrorism and other violent acts. This plan includes joint actions and at the same time comprises a part of the Regulations of the border traffic centers. The Operative Division of the Border Guard Directorate together with the organs in its subordination cooperates in eliminating terrorist acts.

Board of Customs and Excise

The fundamental tasks of the Board of Customs and Excise are defined by the Excise Act, the Fiscal Act, and the Act on Penal Procedures. The Board of Customs and Excise is an authority of national competence that conducts its legal activity under the supervision of the Minister of Finance. As a financial administrative organ the Board of Customs and Excise conducts state administration functions, collects state revenues, and with the use of law enforcement techniques performs alien policing, criminal investigation, and public security tasks. The organization is defined as a law enforcement agency by Article 94 of the Police Act XXXIV of 1994. Law enforcement plays an increasingly significant role in the activities of Board of Customs and Excise due to the current level of public security and the necessity of taking measures in public places. During its law enforcement missions the Board of Customs and Excise acts in close collaboration with various law enforcement agencies in order to prevent or disclose any breach of law.

Disaster Relief

The National Disaster Relief General Directorate of the Ministry of the Interior monitors criminal acts triggering fire, or situation of potential fire/explosion. Its field of responsibility also includes monitoring and forwarding data to other law enforcement agencies on criminal acts committed during or in relation with events controlled by Disaster Relief (especially disasters and evacuations). In order to prevent terrorist acts Disaster Relief works in close cooperation with other agencies. It has no particular responsibilities in this field although new terrorism is ready to deploy nuclear, biological, or chemical weapons for achieving its objectives thus preparedness for environmental disasters is an increasing imperative (reservoirs of potable water, pipelines, etc.).

Penal Authorities

The National Headquarters of Penal Authorities has taken steps for preventing terrorists and members of terrorist organisations from entering or crossing the territory of the country. The personnel of penal institutions is also tasked with preventing terrorists and members of terrorist organisations from entering the establishments, with taking immediate precautionary measures and with forwarding the obtained information on such events. Steps to be taken about persons in prison and having committed terrorist acts are regulated separately. For a unified execution of tasks a joint order (2/2000 – 23 August) was issued on the execution of joint instruction 6/2001.

Coordination Centre for Fighting Organised Crime

(Not a law enforcement agency but an independent national central office with nationwide competency). The Centre is subordinated to the Government and coordinates the activities and collaboration of state authorities (10 agencies) responsible for the investigation of criminal acts defined in Act CXXVI of 2000. The primary goal is an enhanced efficiency in law enforcement, a more efficient cooperation of law enforcement state organs, discovering and disclosing redundancies in investigative activities. Among other issues information and data related to terrorist crimes are managed by the Centre.

Police Prevention

One of the basic provisions of Police Act is police crime prevention activity conducted in the frameworks of national organisations. Crime prevention units operate at National Police Headquarters and regional organs. Naturally, these crime prevention organisations have tasks in preventing criminal acts aimed at public order and acts penalized by Criminal Law. The cited Act allows police authorities at regional and local levels to create so called public order and crime prevention committees in order to increase security level of population. Public order and crime prevention committees operate in various working groups – taking into consideration all local specialties – e.g. town security, ethnic and minority protection, child and juvenile protection, etc. Because of its character, crime prevention is based on project tasks. The terrorist attacks of September 11, 2001 shocked Hungarian public and the citizens' need for security became re-assessed.

This is natural, as terrorism may affect wider strata of population. It is not unimportant that according to analyses perpetrators of terrorist acts live ordinary, peaceful life among the population. Nevertheless there are a lot of minor signs indicating irregularities about a person or group. In the frameworks of crime prevention projects population will have to be prepared for filtering out potential terrorists and their accomplices. One of its possible ways can be providing the population with information by the police through these channels. A general requirement is to bring police activity closer to the population, which can be accomplished in this aspect even better. Naturally, this activity requires a serious cooperation with a number of representatives of society. The structure mentioned above may be appropriate for enlarging the front of war on terrorism and crime in general. A "secure world" may be created by an efficient prevention only on the basis of scientific achievements.

The Police Forces of the Republic of Hungary as a law enforcement agency in cooperation with other state authorities and civil organisations combat terrorism and all types of terrorism-related crimes targeting the Republic of Hungary, its citizens, or foreign citizens and organisations legally staying and operating in our country. Previously for preventing terrorist threat determined by regional and global processes and for a seamless cooperation among law enforcement agencies the establishment of a Counter-terrorist Coordination Committee was ordered by decree 19/1992 of the Head of National Police HQ. The composition of the Counter-terrorist Coordination Committee is precisely regulated by this decree.

The Counter-terrorist Coordination Committee takes measures in the field of assistance, advisory activities, and propositions too. Point g of Paragraph 3 in Article 69 of the Police Act (XXXIV of 1994) defines and emphasizes secret information gathering related to terrorism or terrorism-related criminal acts. Article 68/5 of the above mentioned Police Act states: "a disclosure of a terrorist act is a police responsibility if the reporting came to the police or the police received information on it". Article 5 of Act CXXV of 1995 on the National Security Services highlights this activity as a direct task. In several cases the relation of persons and groups carrying out or preparing terrorist acts has been proved.

Therefore police need an organisation tasked with fighting terrorism and extremism, mainly on the basis of operative intelligence. Police forces of European nations have an operative counter-terrorist prevention unit that is tasked with the prevention of and intelligence on terrorism-related criminal acts. To date the Republic of Hungary has bilateral agreements or treaties on counter terrorist cooperation with 32 countries, regulated by government decrees. In accordance with this a counter-terrorist and international crime Department was established within the Organised Crime Directorate at Criminal General Directorate of the National Police HQ. Its tasks are, among others, assessment of domestic terrorist acts, summarizing the related disclosure and creating databases. Another important task is to secure information-flow between law enforcement agencies and secret services. The cooperation with National Security Agency is of particular importance. Besides, collaboration should be established with all organisations, authorities, institutions, and citizens, which can contribute to the security of the population.

The Mission of the Centre for International Criminal Cooperation

The operative duties of the Hungarian Police are covered through Organised Crime Directorate and the Centre for

International Criminal Cooperation. In its scope the Centre covers warrant issues and commitments related to Interpol and Europol membership. The Centre is a very important institution, through which the prospective counter-terrorist service will be able to forward information and data to or request these from Interpol and Europol. Articles of a partnership were signed by the Hungarian police with the Europol with our taking full membership commitments.

Counter-terrorist Service

The order of deployment of the Counter-terrorist Service of Readiness Police Special Services Command is regulated by National Police HQ decree 7/2001 (V.21). The Counter-terrorist Service is incorporated within the Readiness Police. Its personnel have special training in order to efficiently act against perpetrators of terrorist acts or terrorism-related common crimes. The service is tasked with the physical prevention of these types of crimes. The Service has special equipment, training, devices, and techniques enabling it to carry out the above mentioned tasks. The Service has no scope in intelligence and disclosure as its primary task is to capture perpetrators of committed crimes (terrorist acts) or criminals preparing to commit a crime. Crimes in the exclusive scope of the Service are as follows:

- Terrorist acts;
- Seizure of aircraft;
- Kidnapping;
- Dealing with armed and dangerous persons in a serious threat-situation. For increasing the security of the population the Service is an extremely important factor as it participates in open shows and events where it publicly demonstrates its commitment and readiness to capture perpetrators of serious crimes. The PR Directorate of the National Police HQ is tasked – among others – with representing the Service and its activities in the traditional and electronic media for preventive

purposes. If a country has a counter-terrorist unit consisting of professionally prepared police officers and is equipped appropriately, it can deter would-be perpetrators of terrorist acts.

NPHQ Airport Security Service

This organisation is tasked with the prevention of illegal and criminal acts endangering international and domestic civil aviation operates in subordination to the Public Order General Directorate. Within its scope in the field of preventing terrorist acts the top priorities are: passengers' security checks; parcel/luggage security checks; tightened security; extraordinary security measures and restrictions; cooperation with other law enforcement agencies. The county and local police authorities cooperate in collecting and forwarding to superiors all terrorism-related information. Previously county commissioners used to have intervention subdivisions with the scope of capturing or neutralizing perpetrators of terrorist acts.

Opportunities in the Field of International Police Cooperation

In combating terrorism international police organisations have a number of tasks that require a high-level coordination of the organisations. My analysis focuses on the responsibilities and opportunities of the European police organisations only.

INTERPOL

Interpol is one of the oldest international police organisations that have been providing effective assistance with fighting cross border crime. It is a primarily administrative body, which is in close cooperation with Europol although there is a difference in their origins, legislative frameworks and responsibilities. The purpose of Interpol is to provide a support and assistance to every criminal police – within the frameworks of Articles II and III of Interpol Charter and of the effective rules and regulations of countries under the aegis of Declaration of Human Rights – and to establish and develop institutions capable of prevention and reduction of common crime. The 70th General Assembly of Interpol was held after the September 11 terrorist attacks in Budapest between 24-28 September 2001.

The General Assembly stated that terrorism presents a serious threat to the international community as terrorism grew global and took an increasing number of victims. Exploiting the Internet and opportunities in IT -crime terrorist groups organise and plan their criminal acts on the World Wide Net. Fire arms and conventional explosive materials have remained to be their means of terrorism but the mass destruction capabilities of chemical, biological, and nuclear materials should not be excluded either. The Subdirectorate of Terrorism and Public Security was established as a response to growing terrorist threat, continuous illegal trade in arms and explosive materials actions at anti-globalisation events and extremist environmentalist groups. The task of the new unit is to provide up-to-date professional knowledge, practice, and investigation support in the field of the above mentioned areas. In the past years Interpol was involved in the following projects:

- 3M project (Men, Money, and Materials)

The first part of this project focused on the analysis of financial and support systems of GIA Islamic Army. In March 2001 a working group was set up to analyse financing methods of North African terrorist groups.

Weapons of mass destruction

This program is in progress and focuses primarily on radioactive materials and chemical and biological weapons. The International Agency of Atom Energy is also involved, organizing professional courses and training programs. A reference material is being prepared by the Agency for the police and border guard forces.

Security of Civil Aviation

Interpol has a database gathered systematically on the security of civil aviation. The organisation has established a close working relation with a lot of international civil aviation organisations.

Interpol Weapons and Explosive Tracking System

This is another project in progress aimed at creating global database on firearms and explosive materials. Its database: stolen firearms (global), bombs and explosives, firearm and ammunition reference; operational summary reports in connection with weapons and explosive related crimes and analyses on them. Some plans of the Subdirectorate for the future: to provide a simpler approach to the IWETS database and support investigative authorities; data-collection on anti-capitalist and anti-globalisation groups and their activities, establishing a monitoring and information system on them; study on Central Asian terrorism The aim is to disclose religious orthodoxies and their increasing role in the countries of Central Asia.

EUROPOL

The increase of criminal acts necessitated enhanced international police cooperation in Europe. In the spirit of the Roman Treaty a joint database was created by the so called TREVI (Terrorism, Radicalism, Extremism, Violence International) countries, followed by an agreement on establishing a European criminal unit against international drug trafficking and organized crime. In 1991 a Council of Europe resolution was made on Europol followed by the Europol-convention on the establishment of the European Police Office. Hungary committed itself for an institutional cooperation with Europol in the pre-succession negotiations. Hungary also joined the Union institutions established for police cooperation and fighting organized crime and thus legislative actions are to be done in accordance with EU-conform rules.

The Tasks of Europol

To assist and rapid exchange of information in connection with terrorism. This field of activity includes collecting, analyzing, and evaluating operative (secret) information as well. The Europol database contains data of perpetrators of crimes and information that may help with identifying these persons. Also in this database there is information on potential perpetrators falling in the responsibility of Europol and all types of means and information assisting with intelligence and prevention. Terrorist acts committed against persons, money laundering, related to any criminal acts and other crimes also fall into the responsibility of Europol. The cooperation between Europol and Interpol is focused on organized crime and drug trafficking, white collar crimes, public safety, terrorism, man-smuggling and trafficking, and fugitives. This collaboration is aimed at introducing projects that can efficiently enhance prevention and intelligence in the above fields.

On the basis of the cooperation agreement approved at the above mentioned 70th Interpol General Assembly in Budapest both Europol and Interpol intended to introduce several specific projects in the field of public security and terrorism. The Police Forces of Hungary take part in this cooperation as those of a full member state. A working group – police Working Group on terrorism – was created by the EU member states and also Switzerland and Norway, to coordinate operative counterterrorist services of European criminal police forces. Its objective is to enhance the information flow on terrorist groups, suspects, criminal acts committed or planned by them. This organisation is independent from Interpol or Europol but in case of necessity it will cooperate with either of them. The key to the efficiency of the organisation is that data and information on terrorist acts and terrorist suspects are to be managed in accordance with the bilateral and multilateral agreements between the police forces of the PWGT member states, outlined in the statutes. It is primarily police cooperation that is carried out by the organisation as intelligence gathered by civil or military secret services is not the responsibility of the above organisation.

The "Nature" of Terrorism

The nature of terrorism has been analysed from various aspects and by many experts. Let me bring an example from the world of fables expressing truth that we have been questing for all our lives without realising that it has always been in front of us. Tales and stories help with understanding basic truths so they may help us with understanding the nature of terrorism too. The conclusion of my contribution is a fable with a title: "The Scorpion and the Frog".

One day a scorpion arrived at the bank of a river he wanted to cross, but there was no bridge. He asked a frog nearby that was sitting nearby if he would take him across the river on his back. The frog refused and said "I will not, because you will sting me." The scorpion replied "It would be foolish for me to sting you because then we would both drown." The frog saw the logic in the scorpion's words, and agreed to carry the scorpion across. But when they got about halfway across the river the scorpion stung the frog, the frog asked "Why did you sting me now we will both die." The scorpion replied, "Because it is my nature." They then both died.

Terrorism Profile – EU

The EU has been remarkably active on anti-terror policy. Each legislature in each European Union Member State has introduced legislation to respond to terrorist attacks in 2001 but also to subsequent attacks across Europe. The list of changes in each country is long; here we mention merely a few. The French introduced blanket communications surveillance, and the power to expel extremists, and is now proposing to increase video surveillance in public areas, and to monitor suspects' travel. Germany's opposition party proposed a power of two-year preventive arrest, while the German government has been banning anti-semitic organisations.

Greece rushed to approve new anti-terror rules before the 2004 Olympics due to pressure from the EU to implement measures for a pan-European arrest warrant, extradite Greek nationals, freeze of accounts, and introduce biometric passports. Italy has conducted immigration crackdowns, required ID cards in cyber cafés, instituted deportation powers, and called for more CCTV surveillance. In the Netherlands identity requirements were introduced, the Government proposed to regulate the movement of suspects and require regular reporting to the police, and considered a blasphemy law. Spain outlawed some political parties, and proposed to register all clergy members, places of worship and monitor all sermons.

While Member States have been busy, a significant source of policy is the European Union itself. The European Union's processes for the establishment of policy and legislation are at a critical phase and are continually dogged by claims of a lack of democratic accountability. There are currently three separate powers in the EU. Under the current system, the Council of the European Union ('the Council') consists of the ministers and government representatives of the Member States. It has a rotating Presidency, each for six-month periods, currently resting with the UK and to be followed by Austria. The European Commission also proposes and implements legislation, and is independent of Member States by design. Finally, the European Parliament sometimes approves and is consulted on legislation, though it can not initiate legislation.

The EU has created a great deal of legislation that Member States must then transpose into national law. For instance, in June 2002 the Framework Decision on combating terrorism came into force, compelling all Member States to comply by December 31, 2002. The Framework Decision offers a definition of terrorist offences, terrorist groups, offences relating to terrorist activities, and penalties. At the same time the European Parliament also approved a European Arrest warrant framework decision with little debate. Both these documents raised concerns amongst civil liberties organisations on how they would affect the right to protest but little debate occurred on either policy.

There is a conflict of laws between many of the surveillance policies emerging from the EU and the existing privacy protection regimes. Building on the right to privacy contained in the European Convention on Human Rights the EU established a Directive on privacy and data protection in 1995. Both these regimes are supposed to limit the breadth and scope of surveillance. The reality is that the existing privacy regimes have not limited the breadth and scope of the policies placed before the legislative bodies at the EU. Some policies are remarkably similar to those in the U.S. while some go even further. A significant proportion of the current policy activity is now taking place under The Hague Programme.

The Hague Programme

In November 2004 the European Council announced The Hague Programme for *Freedom, Justice and Security*. This programme is the EU's strategy for enhancing security over a five-year period, by enhancing co-operation in justice and home affairs. It was created behind closed doors and was released to the public only right before it was approved by the Council. While the preceding programme, the Tampere Programme from 1999 had as its core value the respect for the rule of law, this was removed in the Hague Programme in favour of an emphasis on 'cross border problems' such as illegal migration, terrorism and organised crime. The programme's stated objectives thus include the regulation of migration flows, control of the external borders of the Union, the fight against organised cross-border crime, repression of the threat of terrorism, realisation of the potential of cross-border police agencies, the increase of co-operation in criminal and civil matters.

With the intention of turning the programme's broad principles into 'concrete action', in May 2005 the European Commission launched its 5 year Action Plan for Freedom, Justice and Security. It contained detailed proposals for EU action on terrorism, migration management, visa policies, asylum, privacy and security, the fight against organised crime, and criminal justice.

Some of the more problematic powers include the increase of international data sharing while lacking adequate controls such as dual criminality and adherence to national law, and increased monitoring of communications and financial transactions. Though not all the initiatives at the EU fall within it but the same will play a decisive force in the future. The larger spectrum of activities on anti-terror policy is addressed below.

Monitoring Travel and Movement

Like the U.S., the EU is actively enhancing surveillance of travel and at borders. While it initially responded with alarm to the requests from the U.S. for passenger data it turned about and began considering access to the same data. Similarly, the EU is beginning to collect biometrics as well.

Logging of Movement: Passenger Records

The U.S. law on transportation security included a demand for access to passenger name records (PNR) from foreign carriers. This data would be used to analyse the names and details of all arrivals and departures from the U.S. At first the EU opposed the transfer of this data from EU carriers' reservation databases to the U.S. Department of Homeland Security on grounds that the transfers would be in breach of EU privacy protections that prevented the further processing of this data without adequate safeguards. This led to intense negotiations between the European Commission and the Department of Homeland Security.

As time went on, the European Commission grew concerned that it could not continue its opposition to the U.S. plans for access to passenger data. Apart from the threatened sanctions, it emerged during the negotiations that the European Commission wished to create a policy similar to the U.S. policy it was opposing. In fact, the Commission grew reluctant to refuse to the U.S. government access to the data on these very grounds. When negotiating with the U.S. to limit access to 'sensitive information' such as religious faith (as ascertained by the dietary choice, e.g. Halal or Kosher), the head of the EU's Directorate General for Internal Market, Commissioner Bolkestein informed the European Parliament that the EU must be careful in what it refused to the U.S.:

The EU cannot refuse to its ally in the fight against terrorism an arrangement that Member States would be free to make themselves." Pressure was rising from EU Member States, and from other sections of the European Commission. The final Communication from the Commission later stated that the agreement "with the US appears to be a sound basis for taking forward work on an EU approach (...). The list of data elements also seems broad enough to accommodate law enforcement needs in the EU. Nothing in the arrangements agreed with the US therefore seems to prejudice the development of an appropriate EU policy."

In fact the Commission began calling for a resolution to the U.S. transfer problem by creating a centralised system where all PNR for all EU carriers could be sent first to a central database and then sent onwards to the U.S. Not only would this be beneficial in terms of cost and efficiency, and then Vice President of the Commission Loyola De Palacio claimed that the centralised approach would save money for airlines and the EU as it would also assist in "adopting a community policy in the field of data processing with a view to control immigration".

The Justice and Home Affairs Commissioner went a step further. "As a matter of fact, I can even see that a centralized structure inside European Union will be able to provide the necessary guarantees on the liability aspects, the accuracy of the data on the security of transmitted data, the technological means and the filters that Vice-President De Palacio has just mentioned to you, on the supervision by adequate control mechanisms, above all the role of the giant supervisory board and for offering added value to similar initiatives conducted at national levels within the European Union."

The agreement with the U.S. was thus seen as a precursor to a European policy on access to PNR. The EU policy, however, would not be restricted to combating serious crimes and terrorism, but could be used for any law enforcement purpose, including immigration. In September 2005 the UK Presidency of the Council proposed further use of PNR as a response to the London-terror attacks, leading to an 'intelligence-led approach to border control'. As a result the UK Presidency of the EU proposed the long-term retention of this data by border security agencies.

Registration of Movement

A key mission of the EU is to ensure the free flow of people across borders. The EU thus plays a role in the assurances and procedures established to manage border traffic. A significant portion of this activity began with the

Schengen Agreement in 1985, and has since then continued with the establishment of new practices and systems.

The Schengen Information System (SIS) went live in 1995 and was seen as compensation mechanisms for the removal of internal borders between France, Germany, Luxembourg, and the Netherlands. It permits Member States to obtain information regarding certain categories of persons and property. Member States contribute by adding data on people wanted for arrest, people to be placed under surveillance or subject to specific checks; people to be refused entry at external borders; and lost or stolen items. By 2003 it had files on 877,655 people, a further 386,403 aliases.

Access to data on the SIS is limited to border authorities and police and customs checks. According to reports, EU officials acknowledged in 2003 that there are 125,000 access terminals. Since then access has been extended to security and intelligence services. Europol, the European Law Enforcement Organisation, had expressed an interest to gain access to the database to perform analysis involving relationships between relevant variables, comparing ethnic and demographic trends, and for statistical data. This form of access was denied. As the EU grew a newer system was proposed: SIS II. Additional changes were introduced at this stage to allow for the storage, transfer and querying of biometric data such as photographs and fingerprints. SIS II is set to go live by 2006.

Registration of Foreigners

In response to the terrorist attacks in the U.S. in 2001, the EU decided to implement a Visa Information System (VIS). VIS would hold personal information on every visa applicant to an EU member state including their nationality at birth, grounds for refusal, and links to other applications. It will be a central database that is complemented by national systems that together link border checkpoints of each country. It is designed to manage biometric data, i.e. photographs and fingerprints. By 2007 it will be processing 20 million visa applications annually, which would result in 70 million fingerprints to be stored for five-year periods.

The Article 29 Working Party, a committee of privacy regulators from all the EU member states have raised a number of concerns regarding the proposed measures within VIS, in particular the collection of fingerprint data. The Working Party is concerned that the fingerprints could be used for other purposes, and could also lead to stolen identities. As such the Working Party recommends that biometric data should not be stored in the central database unless absolutely necessary. Rather the Working Party recommends that the biometrics be kept only on a microchip on the visa itself. The Working party was particularly concerned with the centralisation of biometrics because the access to the VIS was ad-hoc and wide.

Since the London bombings in July 2005 the momentum has grown for additional databases and tracking mechanisms. The UK Presidency of the EU has been calling for a broadening of the access privileges to VIS, permitting law enforcement agencies across the EU to access all data held there. The Presidency is also calling for similar access to the SIS II. The UK Presidency of the EU is also calling for an entry-and-exit registration programme to keep track of those who have entered but not yet left. The use of biometrics is under consideration within a feasibility study due in December 2006.

Meanwhile the United Kingdom is proposing an E-Borders programme that will integrate travel records with biometric scans. Her Majesty's Government already has access to passenger data for customs and immigration purposes and to combat terrorism; but now the Government is seeking to regularise the use of this data, compel the collection of biometrics of all visitors, residents, and citizens, and to use this data to, according to the

Government, "support general police and criminal justice functions."

Registration of Citizens

The collection of biometrics in the EU is not being limited to visa-applicants and other foreigners however. In its interpretation of the ICAO standard on secure passports the European Council decided in 2003 to develop a shared approach on biometric identifiers for documents for third country nationals, European Union citizens' passports and EU information systems (VIS and SIS II). In February 2004 the European Commission stated its intention to follow through by requiring all EU travel documents to include the biometric of a facial image, and thus to follow the Americans. Member States were permitted to go further by implementing fingerprints as well.

Months later the Council forced a change in the strategy that both face and fingerprints be made mandatory for passports. The European Parliament opposed the inclusion of fingerprints and rejected the creation of a central database of EU passports and travel documents. The Council ignored their opposition and called for facial images to be included within 18 months and fingerprints within 36 months. In February 2005 the European Commission announced the schedule and details for the Council's plan.

So far, EU documentation points to the inclusion of only two fingerprints on a chip on the passport protected with a security mechanism called 'Extended Access Control'. This means that the data on the chip relating to fingerprint images can only be read by authorised entities. The specifications of these security mechanisms remain unclear and are not discussed openly. Meanwhile the UK Presidency, which began in June 2005, has promised to standardize identity card systems across the EU so that they also include fingerprints. The UK Presidency argues:

"To turn our backs on proven biometric technology, to ignore the use made of fingerprints, iris and digital photos by both government and the private sector would be to reject the twenty-first century." The UK Presidency also calls for the verification of identity against a centralised database, even as the UK Parliament continues to debate whether or not to approve the implementation of biometric ID cards in Britain.

Data Mining and Profiling

In the debate over access to SIS and SIS II, there was some consideration of giving Europol vast access to the databases so that statistical analysis could be done through trawling the data. Though this was rejected on SIS, it is still being considered under SIS II. Despite its strong data protection and privacy legal regime, the European Union has also been considering computer-assisted profiling. Its purpose:

"Is to facilitate targeted searches for would-be terrorists (...). It is closely connected to the German initiative on computer-aided preventive searches carried out by individual Member States on the basis of coordinated offender profiles (Europe-wide electronic profile searches). Such searches are essential to the success of security service operations. (...)

On the basis of this profile each Member State searches the relevant national data bases (e.g. registers of residents, registers of foreigners, universities etc.) subject to the provisions of national law, for persons who need to be vetted more closely by the security authorities. The more detailed the offender profile, the smaller the group of persons covered by the search."

The policy calls for increased data-sharing between EU member states and with Europol. In cooperation with Europol, the police would identify specific areas where the development of targeted terrorist profiles may assist the identification of terrorists.

"Developing terrorist profiles means putting together a set of physical, psychological or behavioural variables, which have been identified, as typical of persons involved in terrorist activities and which may have some predictive value in that respect. It may therefore be necessary to develop the profiles in such a way that individual profiles cover a well-defined and specialised category of persons who fulfill a particular function within a closely defined area of terrorism. It will also be necessary to update the profiles as often as necessary so that they always give a correct picture of the particular characteristics of the category of persons in question."

The EU identifies a number of 'elements' for these terrorist profiles, including nationality, travel document, method and means of travel, age, sex, physical distinguishing features (e.g. battle scars), education, choice of cover identity, use of techniques to prevent discovery or counter questioning, places of stay, methods of communication, place of birth psycho-sociological features, family situation, expertise in advanced technologies, skills at using non-conventional weapons, attendance at training courses in paramilitary, flying and other specialist techniques. They would then search through national databases hoping to identify equivalent elements in order to then presumably pinpoint terrorists.

This policy generated concern from the EU Network of Independent Experts in Fundamental Rights (CFR-CDF). In its first report from May 2003, the network argued:

"The development of terrorist profiles on basis the characteristics such as nationality, age education, birthplace, psycho-sociological characteristics, or family situation - all these elements appear in the recommendation on developing terrorist profiles - in order to identify terrorists before the execution of terrorist acts and cooperation with the immigration services and the police to prevent or reveal the presence of terrorists on the territory of Member States, presents a major risk of discrimination. The development of these profiles for operational purposes can only be accepted in the presence of a fair, statistically significant demonstration of the relations between these characteristics and the risk of terrorism, a demonstration that has not been made at this time."

In July 2003, the UK Government announced its participation in a pilot group comprising experts from a number of EU Member States to get this project off the ground. Little has been reported on this matter since 2004.

Surveillance of Transactions

European institutions have long recognised the value of communications data and its relationship with free expression and the right to a private life. The committee of all the privacy regulators from the EU member states once stated that traffic data was deserving of special attention.

"A feature of telecommunications networks and of the Internet in particular is their potential to generate a huge quantity of transactional data (the data generated in order to ensure the correct connections). The possibilities for interactive use of the networks (a defining characteristic of many Internet services) increases the amount of transactional data yet further. When consulting an on-line newspaper, the user 'interacts' by choosing the pages he wishes to read. These choices create a 'click stream' of transactional data. By contrast more traditional news and information services are consumed much more passively (television for example), with interactivity being limited to the off-line world of newspaper shops and libraries. Although transactional data may in some jurisdictions receive a degree of protection under rules protecting the confidentiality of correspondence, the massive growth in the amount of such data is nevertheless a cause of legitimate concern."

Contrary to the jurisprudence in the U.S., traffic data is protected under the jurisprudence on human rights law from the European Court of Human Rights. Previously the Court acknowledged in *Klass v. Germany* that because a law permitting interception of mail created a "menace of surveillance" for all users of the postal service, and because that menace struck at freedom of communication, the law therefore constituted an interference with the right to respect for private life. The *Klass* court also believed that traffic data was sensitive, and this was verified in *Amann v. Switzerland* when the Court ruled it was illegal for State security services to keep a record indicating that the applicant was a contact of the Soviet Embassy, after intercepting a telephone call from the Embassy to the applicant. The *Amann* court specifically noted that storage of the information on an index card alone was sufficient to constitute interference in private life and that the subsequent use of the stored information had no bearing on that finding.

While the ECHR acknowledges that traffic data deserves protection, unlike in the U.S., the inverse actually happens in practice. After the Courts failed to protect the privacy of traffic data, the U.S., Congress developed a statutory right to privacy to prevent traffic data from arbitrary access and proposed that traffic data is collected when authorised by a court when the data is relevant to a specific investigation. The Patriot Act extended this (albeit weak) protection to modern communications systems. Meanwhile European governments are insisting on implementing mass surveillance of communications traffic data with as little oversight as possible.

Retention of Communications Traffic Data

Perhaps the most controversial policy being proposed in Europe is the retention of communications traffic data.

One of the earliest forms of this proposal came from the UK Government in 2000, proposing that all communications service providers, i.e. telephone companies, mobile companies, internet service providers, and internet hosting providers, retain traffic data generated by their systems for period of 7 years so as to ensure that the data is available for law enforcement agencies. The Government worried that the data may be deleted because of privacy rules and business practices. This specific policy proposal never moved forward after outcries from civil liberties organisations and industry representatives.

After September 11 a number of European Member States moved to implement the policy of traffic data retention into national law. Some now have such regimes in place though the regimes are fragmented in their coverage: some only include mobile phone and landline communications data; others are comprehensive and include internet data. Some require retention periods of a few months, others for four years. Since 2003 the Council of the European Union has been working towards a harmonizing measure to ensure that all Member States have a retention policy. By the time the UK Presidency began in June 2005, the Council was wavering between 1 and 4 years for retention, with disagreements on the types of data to be retained, and possibly compelling the collection of data that communications providers did not actually collect. Regimes regulating access to the data was left to national law however. The European Parliament rejected the Council's retention proposal.

After the London bombings in July the UK Presidency of the EU convened emergency meetings on combating terrorism. Data retention was on the top of the agendas. When presenting the path forward for the UK's Presidency of the EU, it called for Parliament to approve retention, identity documents, use of passenger data, and increased use of CCTV cameras. In September 2005 the European

Commission entered the fray and declared that the Council had no role to play in data retention and instead announced its own policy on retention. The Commission's proposed Directive originally limited the retention period for mobile and telephone calls to one year and internet data for six months.

Access to this data was to be restricted to terrorism and serious criminal investigations. In October 2005 the Council declared that it would call on the Parliament to approve the Commission Directive provided that the Commission Directive would meet some basic standards set out by the Council. This included a retention period of up to 2 years, while permitting even greater periods if passed by national law. If the Parliament failed to approve the measure in time, the Council announced it would reintroduce its own proposal. According to the Danish Justice Minister:

"Are we most afraid of the European Parliament or of terrorism? We must reach a decision in December. If the European Parliament cannot help, then MEPs are not adult enough to take part in the discussion."

At the time of writing this report, the final outcome on this political situation remained uncertain. Increased pressure was being placed on the Parliament to ensure that the proposals contained now safeguards in the form of authorisation requirements (e.g. judicial authorisation) and preventing any discussion of limiting the situations in which the powers can be applied (e.g. terrorism vs. general investigations).

While the Justice Ministers from Member States speak with such strong terms at the level of the EU, their actions at home do not reflect their words. Although some national parliaments have approved data retention, they are far from the majority. Even the United Kingdom Parliament has not introduced a law that requires telecommunications service providers to retain traffic data; rather such a regime is merely voluntary and for a varying period of time (up to one year). Very few countries have a mandatory regime, and of those that do, they have yet to enforce the law, or to apply the policy to all telecommunications. For instance, Ireland has retention for three years, but only for telephone and mobile phone data, not for internet transactions. Ministers are pushing the European Union to adopt a policy that their own Parliaments have failed to approve.

It is certain that if the EU agrees on a policy on retention then all Member States will have to implement a national policy. For instance, the Irish Justice Minister admitted in his own Parliament that he was awaiting the 'EU cavalry' to come to his aid and when it had failed to do so because of a lack of agreement amongst Member States, he was compelled to introduce a law on retention under a late amendment to terrorism legislation. Yet the Irish Government and the Minister is insisting that the European Parliament push through a retention policy with a greater ambit than Ireland's own law claiming that otherwise the EU is infringing upon the sovereignty of Ireland.

Access to Communications Transactions

Unlike in the U.S. very little of the debate in the EU on data retention and communications privacy has looked at free expression. The potential chilling effect on communications and access to information would be remarkable if individuals knew that their transactions would be kept for an extended period of time. Yet if it is merely retained for the purpose of national security and combating terrorism then many would deem this acceptable, much as section 215 of the Patriot Act requires relevance to a terrorism investigation and a judicial authorisation.

Apart from the fact that the U.S. has not instituted data retention, more importantly the U.S. restricts access to traffic data by requiring court orders; and only in terrorism investigations in this requirement watered down somewhat. In Europe traffic data will be used for all investigations and will not necessarily require judicial authorisation. In some European countries, for instance, traffic data is authorised by senior police officers, with greater ease and broader applications than the controversial NSLs in the U.S.

One of the greater differentiators between the Council and the Commission proposals on data retention is that the Council plans leave regulations on access to be decided by national law. The Commission intended that the data would only be accessed for use in terrorism and serious criminal investigations. In this domain the European Commission has no jurisdiction, however, as it is up to the Governments of the Member States and their Council of the EU to decide on access due to the legal structure of the EU. This leads to a situation where the European Commission and the European Parliament may approve data retention for the purpose of terrorism even though the data will be accessed under countless circumstances because the Council has refused to limit the use of traffic data to combating terrorism. Put more simply: a law passed to combat terror will be used any way that the Government sees fit.

The UK Presidency of the EU is particularly attentive to this approach because the UK is a case in point. In the UK's Anti-Terrorism Crime and Security Act 2001, the UK's response to the September 11 attacks, Parliament approved voluntary data retention by communications service providers for the purpose of preserving national security and combating serious crime. But access to this data is instead regulated by the Regulation of Investigatory Powers Act 2000 which permits wide access to traffic data held by communications service providers. Prior to the RIP Act the police would expect voluntary compliance from communications service providers when they were asked for traffic data; the RIP Act made the disclosure of this data mandatory, even as it failed to require judicial authorisation. ACTSA vastly increased the amount of data stored in the first place.

When the public caught on to the fact that the law was passed to combat terror could be used to combat crime, a furor arose. The UK Government then opened a national consultation to review and revise this situation. The rules remained relatively unchanged. Under a statutory instrument established in 2003, now sixty-one different types of agencies and departments can access various types of retained transaction data. Local councils, environmental agencies, and health inspectorates may access data without any form of judicial authorisation. It is highly unlikely that even after ignoring the national consultative process and opposition that the UK Government will entertain any additional safeguards and restraints on the access powers because of any changes in EU law.

On top of making the data accessible for all investigations, the EU is working on ensuring that data is shared between Member States' police forces under the 'principle of availability': this principle expands data-sharing by requiring that if data is accessible to the French police in France under French law then the French have the right to demand the British Police to seek the data from a British service provider, even if there is no similar power under British law. This will ensure that the weakest safeguards in the EU will apply across Europe.

17

Terrorism and Legal Policy in India

The authority and legitimacy of modern nation states has come under a severe challenge as a result of rising trends in terrorism. Confronted with one of the most brutal forms of violence, a suitable or adequate response to terrorism is still to be framed, even as a proper context of evaluation and a sufficient understanding of its causation and methodology remain elusive. The uniqueness of terrorism lies in its complex inner dimensions, its continuous and rapid adaptations, and its wide variations across different theatres. Significantly, the transformation of terrorism over the past twenty years has been startling, with rising anxiety over its burgeoning lethality.

Traditionally, terrorism was considered to be a coercive tactic, sometimes adopted as part of a larger guerrilla strategy, in that actions created threats of worse to come if political demands were not met, and these demands tended to be geared to ending foreign occupation or to securing the objectives of a secessionist movement. The rise of modern terrorism, however, has been far more complex, tied to diverse ideological and political goals, and often astounding in the scale of violence and the ambitions of its practitioners. The weapons used in the modern terrorist attacks have grown deadlier and far more accurate than the archaic guns and daggers of the early revolutionary terrorist and as terrorist groups make increasingly persistent efforts to acquire radiological, biological and chemical weapons of mass destruction, the future outlook becomes more ominous. The situation is compounded further by the availability of enormous financial resources and new communications equipment that has immensely empowered both the terrorist 'foot soldier' and his masters.

The power of the media has also dawned on violent players, as is evident in the more symbolic ways in which acts of violence are executed or their targets selected. Yonah Alexander notes that terrorists have used the media to, first, enhance the effectiveness of their violence by creating an emotional state of extreme fear in target groups, and thereby ultimately alter their behaviour and dispositions, or bring about a general or particular change in the structure of government or society; and, second, to draw forcibly and instantaneously, the attention of the whole world to themselves in the expectation that these audiences will be prepared to act or, in some cases, to refrain from acting, in a manner that will promote the cause they presumably represent. Terrorism, then, like advertising, increases the effectiveness of its messages by focussing on spectacular incidents and by keeping particular issues alive through repetition. This is a far cry from the age when 'anarchists' met behind close doors, relying on mouth-to-ear communication to mobilize support for the 'cause', to project their secret and forbidden ideologies, and for the effective execution of their missions.

The recent spurt in terrorist incidents across the world, especially the 9/11 attacks, and the growing recognition of a burgeoning danger have prompted a number of countries to pass anti-terror laws to meet new contingencies. The spurt in anti-terror legislation appears to reflect a measure of surprise among governments around the world at the magnitude and character of the new wave of terrorist activities. A natural corollary to this legislation and to new curbs that some of this legislation places on what are believed to be integral rights and freedoms, is the question: Do we really need new anti-terror laws to check this menace? At least some cynics have suggested that, far from being a necessary part of an effective and efficient response to terrorism, such legislation actually represents a knee-jerk and substantially misdirected reaction to the more dramatic incidents of terrorism.

There are always questions of morality when new laws are enacted, especially when these relate to basic human rights and freedoms. Roscoe Pound clarifies the need for new laws in a very succinct way in terms of two 'needs' that determine philosophical thinking on the subject:

On the one hand, the paramount social interest in the general security, which as an interest in peace and order dictated the very beginnings of law, has led men to seek some fixed basis of a certain ordering of human action which should restrain magisterial as well as individual willfulness and assure a firm and stable social order. On the other hand, the pressure of less immediate social interests, and the need of reconciling them with the exigencies of the general security and of making new compromises because of continual changes in society have called for readjustment at least of the social order. They have called continually for overhauling of legal precepts and for refitting them to unexpected situations.

Nevertheless, reservations have always existed regarding the exercise of the power to refit laws to unexpected situations; such reservations are roofed in considerations of morality, the fear of criticism, and the fear of high-handedness. Nevertheless, the exercise of power is often a necessary imperative of history. As Fukuyama puts it, much as people would like to believe that ideas live or die as a result of their inner moral rectitude, power matters a great deal. German fascism didn't collapse because of its internal moral contradictions, it died because Germany was bombed to rubble and occupied by Allied armies.

Much of the reluctance in accepting the need for special anti-terrorism legislation is based on the fallacy of equating 'terrorism' with other forms of violence, and the consequent argument that the prevailing or 'ordinary' laws that have been enacted to deal with the latter are sufficient to take care of the former. Thus, Walter Laqueur describes how it was widely believed that terrorism was a response to injustice and that the terrorists were people driven to desperate actions by intolerable conditions, be it poverty, hopelessness, or political or social oppression. Following this reasoning, the only way to remove or at least to reduce terrorism is to tackle its sources, to deal with the grievances and frustrations of the terrorists, rather than simply trying to suppress terrorism by brute force.

This reasoning is, however, substantially flawed and ignores the unique social, political and ideological factors that contribute to, and are exploited by, the processes of terrorist mobilization. There is, further, little empirical evidence of a direct linkage between specific socio-economic conditions and the emergence of terrorist movements. There is, moreover, an element of defeatism in this perspective, to the extent that it insists that the issues of violence cannot, or should not, be addressed until the last possible grievance has been resolved – a task, in any world outside the realm of pure fantasy, that would necessarily remain perpetually unfulfilled. Essentially, the core issue of terrorist violence and criminality is, here, not being addressed, and the focus has been shifted to the purported 'causes' that are believed to have led to terrorists taking up arms. Further, the very idea that terrorism grows out of legitimate social grievances and upheavals cedes, without evidence or argument, the moral high ground to the terrorist: society can never be perfect and, consequently, there will always be 'just cause' for terrorism to survive.

Worse, the terrorists are entirely exempted from all norms of morality, even as the most unrealistically exacting morality is applied to 'society' and the 'state'. It is precisely this thinking that has obstructed, stalled, diluted and constantly opposed specific anti-terrorism legislation over the years, and continues to stifle and hamper prosecutions under such laws by putting forward vague and disconcerting objections. The lack of agreement on a definition of 'terrorism' has been another major obstacle to meaningful international countermeasures and laws. Cynics have often commented that, "one man's terrorist is another man's freedom fighter," an argument at once immensely strong and entirely superficial. But this argument is based, as Ajai Sahni rightly notes ... on a contra factual expectation of unique identity. In truth, individuals have multiple identities – a man may be father and murderer; husband and rapist.

We also share a multiplicity of transient identities – we are, for example, at particular times, workers, shoppers, hosts or guests. A man, on this reasoning, may be both terrorist *and* freedom fighter. The latter identity rests on his motives – what he is fighting *for*. The former relates to the methods he adopts in this fight – the targeting, specifically, of civilians, to achieve his ends. Terrorism, thus conceived, can be adopted for one among many motives – to fight for freedom, for particular environmental policies, for a ban on abortions, for animal rights, among others – and remains terrorism as long as the method or means utilized involve the intentional targeting of civilians.

If, however, terrorism is defined strictly in terms of attacks on non-military targets, a range of attacks on military installations and soldiers' residences would escape the scope of the definition. In order to cut through the Gordian definitional knot, terrorism expert Alex P. Schmid suggested in 1992, in a report for the then United Nations (UN) Crime Branch, that it might be a good idea to take the existing consensus on what constitutes a 'war crime' as a point of departure. "If the core of war crimes – deliberate attacks on civilians, hostage taking and the killing of prisoners – is extended to peacetime, we could simply define acts of terrorism as 'peacetime equivalents of war crimes'."

Difficulties with the definition of terrorism, nevertheless, persist, many of them motivated by those who engage in, support or benefit from, activities widely perceived as such. Nevertheless, it is possible to clearly identify the essential considerations that would enter into an assessment of such acts: terrorism can, thus, generally be described as the systematic use of terror or unpredictable violence against governments, the public, or individuals, to attain a political objective. Terrorism has been used by political organizations with both rightist and leftist objectives, by nationalistic and ethnic groups, by revolutionaries, by groups pursuing particular political or ethical ends, and by the armies and secret police of governments themselves.

Counter-terrorism legislation is, moreover, entirely consistent with a jurisprudential history of special laws that have been enacted from time to time to deal with special situations, and India's record is no exception. The first preventive detention law was introduced by the British in 1793, and was aimed solely for the purpose of detaining anybody who was regarded as a threat to the British settlement in India. The East India Company in Bengal subsequently enacted the Bengal State Prisoner's Regulation, which was to have a long life as 'Regulation III of 1818'. An extra-Constitutional ordinance, opposed to all the fundamental liberties which the colonial state would later pretend to be bound by, Regulation III provided for the indefinite confinement of individuals against whom there was insufficient ground to institute any judicial proceeding. Regulation III was the most effective tool in the hands of the British to quell any political violence.

The beginning of the 20th century witnessed an increase in the revolutionary movement in India, with the birth of many underground groups pursuing the goal of independence through violent means. The period also marked the emergence of several legislations to quell the rising tide. In 1908, the government passed the Newspapers (Incitement to Offences) Act and the Explosive Substances Act and, shortly thereafter, the Indian Press Act, the Criminal Tribes Act, and the Prevention of Seditious Meetings Act. A majority of these legislations were aimed at breaking the back of the revolutionary movements by curbing meetings, printing and circulation of seditious materials and propaganda, and by detaining suspects. The Foreigners Ordinance of 1914 sought to restrict the entry and movement of foreigners in India. The Defence of India Act (1915) allowed suspects to be tried by special tribunals, whose decisions were not subject to appeal.

The Defence of India Act was to expire shortly after the end of the First World War and the British Government had to come up with a new law to counter new tendencies. Based on the recommendations of Justice Rowlatt, Chairman of the Committee appointed to curb seditious movements in India, the Rowlatt Act, also known as the Anarchical and Revolutionary Crimes Act, was passed in 1919, giving unbridled powers to the colonial Government to arrest and imprison suspects without trial and crush civil liberties. The violent movement was blunted in the 1930s by the tough regulations passed by the Government, including the Constitutional Reforms of 1935.

After attaining Independence, the violence witnessed during Partition forced the Government of Free India to pass the Punjab Disturbed Areas Act, Bihar Maintenance of Public Order Act, Bombay Public Safety Act, and Madras Suppression of Disturbance Act, aimed at curbing forces that were using religion to incite violence. The rise of the Naxalite (Left-wing extremist) movement prompted the

West Bengal government to pass the West Bengal (Prevention of Violent Activities) Act of 1970.

The last three decades have witnessed a number of legislations being enacted to tackle various specific contingencies: Jammu and Kashmir Public Safety Act (1978); Assam Preventive Detention Act (1980); National Security Act (1980, amended 1984 and 1987); Anti-Hijacking Act (1982); Armed Forces (Punjab and Chandigarh) Special Powers Act (1983); Punjab Disturbed Areas Act (1983); Chandigarh Disturbed Areas Act (1983); Suppression of Unlawful Acts Against Safety of Civil Aviation Act (1982); Terrorist Affected Areas (Special Courts) Act (1984); National Security (Second Amendment) Ordinance (1984); Terrorist and Disruptive Activities (Prevention) Act (1985, amended 1987); National Security Guard Act (1986); Criminal Courts and Security Guard Courts Rules (1987) and the Special Protection Group Act (1988).

Although these laws were enacted to meet special situations, most of them were not directed against the larger menace of terrorism. The Terrorist and Disruptive Activities (Prevention) Act (TADA), 1987, and the Prevention of Terrorism Act (POTA), 2002, are the only Acts, which can correctly be termed anti-terrorism laws. The state, through these two laws, for the first time attempted to create legislative instruments to curb terrorist activities in India, recognizing the fact that it was a special crime that needed special laws for an effective response to be created.

A clear distinction between 'ordinary crime' and terrorism is, consequently, important as is well illustrated by the Supreme Court's observations in *Hitendra Vishnu Thakur vs. State of Maharashtra* that, ...'terrorism' has not been defined under Terrorist and Disruptive Activities (Prevention) Act (TADA) nor is it possible to give a precise definition of 'terrorism' or lay down what constitutes 'terrorism'. It may be possible to describe it as use of violence when its most important result is not merely the physical and mental damage of the victim but the prolonged psychological effect it produces or has the potential of producing on the society as a whole.

There may be death, injury, or destruction of property or even deprivation of individual liberty in the process but the extent and reach of the intended terrorist activity travels beyond the effect of an ordinary crime capable of being punished under the ordinary penal law of the land and its main objective is to overawe the Government or disturb harmony of the society or 'terrorise' people and the society and not only those directly assaulted, with a view to disturb even tempo, peace and tranquility of the society and create a sense of fear and insecurity. A terrorist activity does not merely arise by causing disturbance of law and order or of public order. The fallout of the intended activity must be such that it travels beyond the capacity of the ordinary law enforcement agencies to tackle it under the ordinary penal law.

The Court added further that,

What distinguishes 'terrorism' from other forms of violence therefore appears to be the deliberate and systematic use of coercive intimidation. It is therefore essential to treat such a criminal and deal with him differently than an ordinary criminal capable of being tried by the ordinary courts under the penal law of the land.

Legality, Controversy & the Judicial Response

The ground realities in India are stark and statistics provide a grim reminder of the increasing threat that terrorism constitutes. India has lost over 56,000 lives to terrorism over the last decade in the major irregular and sub-conventional wars that have afflicted the country. A majority of these fatalities have occurred in Jammu and Kashmir (J&K) and in the Northeast alone as a result of the Pakistani proxy war in the former, and a range of separatist insurgencies in the latter. A significant number of deaths have also occurred due to Left wing extremism (referred to as Naxalism in India) and retaliatory violence in some areas of the States of Andhra Pradesh, Maharashtra, Madhya Pradesh, Orissa, Chhattisgarh, Jharkhand, Uttar Pradesh, West Bengal and Bihar.

Since Independence, free India has had to contend with a number of disparate elements and groups seeking political ascendancy through violence, or pursuing secessionist goals. The Northeast has long been a troubled area, with a heady mix of the assertion of tribal identities and a few influential leaders, secessionist movements grew in this part of the country into large scale agitations which, in many cases, transformed themselves into terrorist movements. In the 1980s and the 1990s, the secessionist movements in Punjab and J&K provided no respite to the state and its security forces. The proliferation of terrorist groups in the country has also been tremendous, indeed, unprecedented in comparison to in any other theatre of conflict in the world. In J&K alone, there are reportedly 32 terrorist groups operating independently, and occasionally in tandem. In the Northeast, some 60 terrorist outfits have been involved in terrorism related brutalities.

As compared to other countries where terrorism is ordinarily localized to a particular area or region, India has witnessed the pugmarks of terrorism across the whole country. An analysis of terrorist incidents demonstrates the sheer spread of the phenomenon. Major terrorist attacks have, for instance, been witnessed in places like, Vellithirippur, (1998) and Marudayar (1987) in Tamil Nadu; Faizabad in Uttar Pradesh (2000); Kolkata in West Bengal (2002) and Mumbai in Maharashtra (2003), to name a few. Between 1992 and 2003, at least 21,497 civilians and 7,046 security forces personnel have been killed in terrorist attacks, while 26,072 terrorists have been killed in counter-offensive.

The saddening part in this war against terrorism has been the absence of a proper legal apparatus in the country, which could provide a mechanism for the conviction and legal punishment of the terrorists arrested in counter-terrorism operations. The difficulties in taking a terrorist up to the point of conviction have been pointed out by Veeranna Aivalli, Commissioner of Security (Civil Aviation), Bureau of Civil Aviation Security, in a letter to the Law Commission of India, dated February 12, 2000, where he stated, ...there is another difficulty and that is the collection of evidence in cases where the search, seizure and arrest in areas where there is no habitation and many a time these have been by security forces. In such a case, the arrested persons' confession to the security forces leading to the recovery of arms and ammunition and explosives is the only thing, which can be brought on record. Even the security force personnel do not come forward for tendering evidence because they keep on moving from place to place for performance of their duties not only within Jammu & Kashmir (J&K) but even outside J&K and sometimes outside India. The security force personnel are reluctant to depose in any case as they feel that they are not attuned for this kind of exercise. In the last 15 years of militancy in J&K, thousands of people have been arrested, lakhs of weapons seized and millions of rounds collected and quintals of explosive material seized. These figures are real eye openers and the fact that not a single case has ended in conviction nor has there been any recording of evidence and even this itself is very disturbing.

The enactment of the two anti-terrorist laws in India, TADA and the more recent POTA, was intended to patch over this chink in the state's armour in the battle against terrorism. Regrettably, their impact has been far from what was needed. Both anti-terror laws have come under sustained and substantial criticism on different grounds. Primarily, they have been attacked as being 'draconian', oppressive, unconstitutional and against the principles of natural justice. As a result from time to time, the Indian judiciary, especially the Supreme Court has been petitioned to assess whether their various provisions are within the bounds of the Constitutional framework and the principles of natural justice. Some of the most important provisions that have come under judicial review include the following:

1.1 In 1994, the Supreme Court, in the landmark judgement of *Kartar Singh vs. State of Punjab* dealt with various provisions of the Terrorist and Disruptive Activities (Prevention) Act, 1987 and upheld the constitutional validity of the Act. From the very outset, the Court, looked into the matter in a broad perspective. Acknowledging the fact that the existing situation in the country was peculiar, the Court observed that ...deplorably, determined youths lured by hardcore criminals and underground extremists and attracted by the ideology of terrorism are indulging in committing serious crimes against humanity. In spite of the drastic actions taken and intense vigilance activated, the terrorists and the militants do not desist from triggering lawlessness if it suits their purpose.

Further, realising the severity of the situation, the Court noted: "No one can deny these stark facts and naked truth by adopting an ostrich like attitude completely ignoring the impending danger."

1.2 Apart from this danger of physical violence, there is the further complication of existing prison realities. Prisons in India are overwhelmingly populated by under trials. According to statistics compiled by the Custodial Justice Cell of the National Human Rights Commission, 225,817 of 304,893 or 74.06 per cent of the total prison population are comprised of those awaiting trial. The total jail capacity in India is for 232,412 prisoners, which makes the total prison population 31 per cent higher than capacity, clearly emphasizing the urgent need for a speedier justice mechanism.

1.3 The right to speedy trial is not incorporated in any provision of the constitution, yet it is an inherent principle of any criminal justice system. A delayed trial harms the prosecution as well as the accused. Delayed prosecution means weakened prosecution, as witnesses are hard to find and memories become hazy as time goes by; there are also increasing probabilities of witnesses turning hostile if the trial is prolonged. For the accused, the delay in the trial means no end to incarceration in one of the numerous and pitiable jails in the country.

1.4 The Supreme Court in *Kedra Pehadiya vs. State of Bihar* had observed, "It is a crying shame upon our adjudicatory system which keeps men in jail for years on end without a trial." The Court added further:

> ... no one shall be allowed to be confined in jail for more than a reasonable period of time, which we think cannot and should not exceed one year for a session trial... we fail to understand why our justice system has become so dehumanised that lawyers and judges do not feel a sense of revolt at caging people in jail for years without trial.

Justice Bhagwati in the *Hussainara Khatoon vs. Home Secretary, State of Bihar* also observed:

> No procedure which does not ensure a reasonably quick trial can be regarded as 'reasonable, fair or just' and it would be foul of Article 21. There can, therefore, be no doubt that speedy trial and by speedy trial we mean reasonably expeditious trial, is an integral part of the fundamental right to life and liberty enshrined in Article 21.

1.5 This principle of providing speedy trial was reiterated and reaffirmed in the Kartar Singh case, even as the question of enactment of new procedures for speedy trial of terrorists under TADA was challenged.

The provisions prescribing special procedures aiming at speedy disposal of cases, departing from the procedures prescribed under the ordinary procedural law are evidently for the reasons that the prevalent ordinary procedural law was found to be inadequate and not sufficiently effective to deal with the offenders indulging in terrorist and disruptive activities.

1.6 Under the TADA Act, designated courts were to be established with special powers to deal exclusively with cases relating to terrorism. Further, Section 14 of the Act laid down the procedure and powers of the designated courts, which included the speedy disposal of cases. The Act also provided for the discharge of the accused by the designated court even before the evidence stage, if a *prima facie* case was not made out by the prosecution. The Prevention of Terrorism Act (POTA) Act also provides for trial in absentia, with Clause (5) of Section 30.

Notwithstanding anything contained in the Code, but subject to the provisions of section 299 of the Code, a Special Court may, if it thinks fit and for reasons to be recorded by it, proceed with the trial in the absence of the accused or his pleader and record the evidence of any witness, subject to the right of the accused to recall the witness for cross-examination.

This provision was incorporated with the objective of enhancing speedy trial in the event of the failure of the police to apprehend the accused, which is often the case in terrorist crimes.

1.7 The incorporation of these provisions to initiate speedier trial by establishing special courts and special procedures was challenged on the grounds that terrorists were being treated differently from ordinary criminals, and that this was discriminatory. But in *Kartar Singh*, the Court rejected this position, explaining that ...the rule of differentiation is that in enacting laws differentiating between different persons or things in different circumstances which govern one set of persons or objects such laws may not necessarily be the same as those governing another set of persons or objects so that the question of unequal treatment does not really arise between persons governed by different conditions and different set of circumstances.

Further ...the persons who are to be tried for offences specified under the provisions of TADA Act are a distinct class of persons and the procedure prescribed for trying them for the aggravated and incensed nature of offences are under different classification distinguishable from ordinary criminals and procedure.

Moreover the establishment of special courts and special laws was entirely in keeping with Constitutional provisions, since Article 247 of the Constitution empowers Parliament to establish courts. Indeed, a Constitutional Amendment was passed for the creation of Special Debt Recovery Tribunals across the country under the Recovery of Debts Due to Banks and Financial Institution Act, 1993. Speeding up the debt recovery mechanism is, no doubt, an important, but far less urgent imperative than the containment of terrorism which threatens the very foundations of democracy. There is, clearly, no illegality involved in establishing special courts to tackle special situations, and terrorism certainly qualifies as such.

2.1 One of the matters of great concern for human rights activists with regard to POTA is the provision relating to the admissibility of 'confessional statements' as evidence under the Act. The National Human Rights Commission (NHRC) has expressed the view that the validation of confessions made to police officers would increase the possibility of coercion and torture in securing confessions, and would consequently be inconsistent with Article 14 (3) (f) of the International Covenant on Civil and Political Rights (ICCPR) which requires universal entitlement to the guarantee of not being compelled to testify against oneself or to confess guilt.

2.2 Earlier, Section 15 of TADA had laid down: ...a confession made by a person before a police officer not lower in rank than a Superintendent of Police and recorded by such police officer either in writing or on any mechanical device like cassettes, tapes or sound tracks from out of which sounds or images can be reproduced, shall be admissible in the trial of such person or co-accused, abettor or conspirator for an offence under this Act or rules made there under...

Clause (2) of the section laid down further that, ...the police officer shall, before recording any confession under sub-section (1), explain to the person making it that he is not bound to make a confession and that, if he does so, it may be used as evidence against him and such police officer shall not record any such confession unless upon questioning the person making it, he has reason to believe that it is being made voluntarily.

2.3 This provision was one of the main grounds of a legal and constitutional attack against TADA launched by former Law Minister Ram Jethmalani. Concerns were primarily raised on the methods that would be employed by the police to gain confessions from the accused.

2.4 However, this procedure to record confessions was streamlined by the Supreme Court in *Kartar Singh,* where six safeguards were defined, which was to be employed while recording a confession. POTA incorporated these safeguards in its Section 32, which required that,

- A police officer shall, before recording any confession made by an accused under sub-section (1) of Section 32, explain to such person in writing that he is not bound to make a confession and that if he does so; it may be used against him.
- Further, provided that, where such person prefers to remain silent, the police officer shall not compel or induce him to make any confession.

- Under clause (3) of the same section it is laid down that the confession shall be recorded in an atmosphere free from threat or inducement and shall be in the same language in which the person makes it.
- Under clause (4) the person from whom a confession has been recorded under sub-section (1), shall be produced before the Court of a Chief Metropolitan Magistrate or the Court of a Chief Judicial Magistrate along with the original statement of confession, written or recorded on mechanical or electronic device within forty-eight hours.
- Further, under clause (5), the Chief Metropolitan Magistrate or the Chief Judicial Magistrate, shall, record the statement, if any, made by the person so produced and get his signature or thumb impression and if there is any complaint of torture, such person shall be directed to be produced for medical examination before a Medical Officer not lower in rank than an Assistant Civil Surgeon and thereafter, he shall be sent to judicial custody.
- Another significant departure from TADA is that if the detainee's confession is not recorded before a magistrate within 48 hours, such confession fails to carry credence.

2.5 These substantial changes with regard to the admissibility of and safeguards relating to confessions under POTA have been appreciated by earlier critics of TADA. Ram Jethmalani, who had vigorously denounced TADA, stated, "I would have opposed POFA, but it must be said to the credit of the Government that all six safeguards suggested by the majority of the judges have been introduced." He noted that the "amazing degree of dangerous sophistication which has been achieved by ruthless terrorists certainly is a material change from the situation in which TADA operated."

2.6 Interestingly, confessional statements made by the accused are also held to be admissible as evidence under various other acts: under Section 12, Railway Protection Force Act, 1957; Section 8 and 9 of the Railway Property (Unlawful Possession) Act, 1966; Section 108 of the Customs Act, 1962; and Section 40 of the now defunct Foreign Exchange Regulation Act (FERA), 1973. In *Kartar Singh*, the Court observed that ...while a confession by an accused before a specified officer, either under the Railway Protection Force Act or Railway Property (Unlawful Possession) Act or Customs Act or FERA is made admissible, the special procedure prescribed under this Act making a confession of a person indicted under TADA Act given to a police officer admissible cannot be questioned as a misnomer because all the officials empowered to record statements under those special acts are not police officers as per the judicial pronouncements of this court.

Therefore, although the provision with regard to confessional statement may be a departure from ordinary penal laws, the safeguards provided by the new POFA considerably reduce the scope of its misuse.

3.1 The bail provisions under anti-terror laws have also been criticised for their unwarranted stringency and apparent harshness. Under POFA, bail is to be decided on a *prima facie* finding that the accused is not guilty. Section 49, Clause (6) states:

Notwithstanding anything contained in the Code, no person accused of an offence punishable under this Act shall, if in custody, be released on bail or on his own bond unless the Court gives the Public Prosecutor an opportunity of being heard.

Section 49, Clause (7) adds,

Where the Public Prosecutor opposes the application of the accused to release on bail, no person accused of an offence punishable under this Act or any rule made there under shall be released on bail until the Court is satisfied that there are grounds for believing that he is not guilty of committing such offence:

Provided that after the expiry of a period of one year from the date of detention of the accused for an offence under this Act, the provisions of sub-section (6) of this section shall apply.

Section 49, Clause (8) further adds,

The restrictions on granting of bail specified in sub-sections (6) and (7) are in addition to the restrictions under the Code or any other law for the time being in force on granting of bail.

Finally, Section 49, Clause (9) states,

Notwithstanding anything contained in sub-sections (6), (7) and (8), no bail shall be granted to a person accused of an offence punishable under this Act, if he is not an Indian citizen and has entered the country unauthorized or illegally except in very exceptional circumstances and for reasons to be recorded in writing.

3.2 These provisions are definitely different and harsher than the existing bail provisions under the Code of Criminal Procedure. On the other hand, however we are faced with the fact that under ordinary bail provisions, it has been relatively easy for terrorists to get bail and return to the killing fields to inflict greater harm. As the former Director-General of Punjab Police, K.P.S. Gill, notes :

"In the Punjab, it was virtually impossible to detain any terrorist for any length of time, irrespective of charges. Terrorists were arrested again and again for the most heinous crimes, and were let out on bail 'pending trail'. In many cases, they committed other crimes while on bail, were arrested, and then bailed out again. Since the average criminal trial takes several years, it is unsurprising that the fear of conviction was the least of the terrorists' concern. In any event, witnesses could easily be intimidated or eliminated, and there was little possibility even of eventual conviction. In all this, the judiciary distanced itself from the consequences of its actions, claiming to be bound strictly be the law to release the accused on bail, even where the accused had, in the past, jumped bail and committed other crimes."

In *Bimal Kaur vs State of Punjab*, the Punjab High Court opined that:

The persons charged with the commission of terrorist act fall in the category which is distinct from the class of persons charged with commission of offences under the penal code and the offences created by other statutes... The enforcing agencies find it difficult to lay their hands on them. Unless the police is able to secure clue as to who are the persons behind this movement, how it is organised, who are its active members and how they operate, it cannot hope to put an end to this movement and restore public order. The police can secure this knowledge only from the arrested terrorists after effective interrogation. If the real offenders apprehending arrest is able to secure anticipatory bail then the police shall virtually be denied the said opportunity.

3.4 The Forty First report of the Law Commission rightly questioned the application of bail provisions of the Code of Criminal Procedure to cases of terrorism: "Can it be said with certainty that terrorists and disruptionists, who create terrorism and disruption and inject sense of insecurity, are not likely to abscond or misuse their liberty if released on anticipatory bail?

3.5 Further, the Supreme Court in *Kartar Singh* had pointed out that the language of sub-section (8) of section 20 of TADA (which is related to 'bail') was in substance no different from the language employed in section 437(1) of the Code of Criminal Procedure, section 35 of the Foreign Exchange Regulation Act, 1976, and section 104 of the Customs Act, 1962. The Supreme Court had, accordingly, upheld the validity of Sub-section (8) of section 20 of TADA, holding that the respective provisions contained therein were not volatile of Article 21 of the Constitution, which declares that, "No man shall be deprived of his life or personal liberty except according to the procedure established by law."

3.6 Nevertheless, in order to streamline the procedure of granting bail to the accused under anti-terror laws, Justice Sujata V. Manohar in *Shaheen Welfare Association vs. Union of India & Ors,* categorised TADA detenues in four groups with regard to their entitlement to bail:

a. hardcore under trials whose release would prejudice the prosecution case and whose liberty may prove to be a menace to society in general and to the complainant and prosecution witnesses in particular;
b. other under trials whose overt acts or involvement directly attract sections 3 and/or 4 of the TADA act;
c. under trials who are roped in, not because of any activity directly attracting sections 3 and 4, but by virtue of section 120B or 147, IPC and;
d. those under trials who are found possessing incriminating articles in notified areas and are booked under section 5 of TADA.

Adopting these criteria, the Court was of the opinion that under trials falling within group (a) cannot receive liberal treatment. Cases of under trials falling in group (b) would have to be dealt with differently, in that, if they have been in prison for five years or more and their trial is not likely to be completed within the next six months, they can be released on bail unless the Court comes to the conclusion that their antecedents are such that releasing them may be harmful to the lives of the complainant, the family members of the complainant or witnesses. Cases of under trials falling in groups (c) and (d) can be dealt with leniently and they can be released if they have been in jail for three years and two years respectively.

By establishing these criteria, the Court has gone a long way in rationalizing the approach to the grant of bail in cases of terrorism, rightly distinguishing between various levels of the gravity of offence, and the threat to witnesses and society at large. This approach also underlines the fact that, while bail is definitely a matter of right, its grant must also be weighed against a possibility of greater public harm which may be afflicted by too easy and mechanical a process for grant of bail in cases of terrorism. Justice Manohar's directions in this regard, are of crucial importance in the jurisprudence governing the subject.

4.1 Further, a majority of terrorists go unpunished due to the unavailability of witnesses. As criminal prosecution hinges on witnesses and the availability of a witness to any crime is the sole test to establish the soundness of the prosecution – particularly in the Indian system, where technical and forensic evidence is usually weak, and in cases of terrorism, often worse that it would be in other cases – a provision which aims at protecting witnesses by concealing their identities is crucial, but is bound to create strong opposition among those who have a vested interest in a weak prosecution. Characteristically, in the prosecution of crimes involving bodily harm, witnesses are hard to come by, as there is always a lurking fear in their minds of the possible consequences of deposition.

4.2 Provisions for the protection of witnesses are envisaged under Section 16 (2) of TADA and Section 30 of POTA. Section 30 (2) lays down that :

A Special Court, if on an application made by a witness in any proceeding before it or by the Public Prosecutor in relation to such witness or on its own motion, is satisfied that the life of such witness is in danger, it may, for reasons to be recorded in writing, take such measures as it deems fit for keeping the identity and address of such witness secret.

Under this provision, the right of cross-examination of witnesses is not denied to the defence, but the identity and addresses of the witnesses can be withheld.

4.3 Generally in trials involving ordinary crimes, when the accused persons are known to be trouble-mongers, it is seen that witnesses are unwilling to come forward to depose against such persons fearing harassment at the hands of those accused. This proclivity is even more noticeable in cases involving organised criminal gangs. Clearly, when it comes to the trial of terrorists and disruptionists, witnesses would be far more reluctant to depose at the risk of their lives.

4.4 Doubts have, however, been cast on this provision and its jurisprudence. Whatever the reasons for non-disclosure of the identity of witnesses, it is argued, the accused persons, who are liable to severe punishments under these special laws, are placed at a disadvantage with regard to the possibility of effective cross-examination and exposing the previous conduct and character of the witnesses. In general, consequently, in order to ensure the purpose and object of the cross-examination, the argument continues, the identity, names and addresses of witnesses should be disclosed before the trial commences. However, it is reasonable that this principle should be subject to an exception where the court, in extraordinary circumstances, may in its wisdom decide to withhold the identity and addresses of witnesses, especially in cases of potential witnesses whose life may be in danger. As such, section 30 of POTA gives discretion to the court to decide whether the identity of the witnesses should be protected, creating ample scope for safeguards that would prevent any prejudice against the accused.

4.5 Given the difficulty of securing witnesses to provide concrete evidence against an accused terrorist, there is a need for greater reliance on technical evidence. Section 27 of POTA, consequently, provides that the court may, on the request of the police officer, direct the accused to give samples of hand-writing, finger-prints, foot-prints, photographs, blood, saliva, semen, hair and voice of any accused person, reasonably suspected to be involved in the commission of the offence under this Act. Human rights groups have argued that this amounts to forcing the accused to incriminate them, and thus violates Article 20, Clause 3, of the Constitution, which states, "No person accused of any offence shall be compelled to be a witness against himself."

This, however, is entirely unsustainable logic. The courts have repeatedly held that "'to be a witness' is not equivalent to 'furnishing evidence' in its widest sense". The right against self-incrimination is established only where the possibility of coercion and abuse of the human rights of the accused are involved, and does not extend to the withholding of evidence. Securing scientific evidence to prove a crime does not inflict any violence on the accused, go against any human rights and this section is not a departure against the established mode of proving the guilt of an accused under the Evidence Act, which contains provisions with regard to forensic reports and handwriting reports, which have been employed even in ordinary crimes. It has, further, been held that giving thumb-impressions or impressions of foot or palm or fingers or specimen writings or showing parts of the body by way of identification are not included in the expression 'to be a witness'.

Excluding new technologies of gathering such scientific evidence, such as DNA, blood, saliva and other such bio-profiling techniques on the grounds that these techniques have not been used before misses the spirit of the law, and cannot be considered reasonable. It is useful to note, moreover, that these techniques have all been admitted into evidence in the more advanced Western countries, including those whose concerns for the protection of human rights are no less serious than ours. Indeed, Indian jurisprudence has, in this regard, tended to lag far behind technological developments and progressive international norms.

6.1 It is certainly the case that the powers of investigating officers as well as of the police in general are significantly increased by various provisions under anti-terrorist laws. The possibility of abuse of such enhanced powers cannot be ruled out. As the Supreme Court observed in *Kartar Singh* that :

We are aware that the police are still not totally free from adopting questionable practices while interrogating accused persons, but one cannot possibly deny that the greater vigilance now exercised by the public and the Press, growing awareness of citizens about their individual rights under the law and the increasing earnestness and commitment of the senior levels of command in the police structure to put down such malpractices have all tended to reduce the prevalence of such practices in the police to a lesser degree than before.

Moreover, the possibility of abuse cannot be grounds for striking down or diluting a law. In *State of Rajasthan vs. Union of India,* the Supreme Court noted:

It must be remembered that merely because power may sometimes be abused, it is no ground for denying the existence of power. The wisdom of man has not yet been able to conceive of a government with power sufficient to answer all its legitimate needs and at the same time incapable of mischief.

Similarly, in *Collector of Customs vs. Nathella Sampathu Chetty,* the Court observed that, "the possibility of abuse of a statute otherwise valid does not impart to it any element of invalidity." In *Kesavananda Bharati vs. State of Kerala,* Justice Khanna noted :

In exercising the power of judicial review, the Courts cannot be oblivious of the practical needs of the government. The door has to be left open for trial and error. Constitutional law like other mortal contrivances has to take some chances. Opportunity must be allowed for vindicating reasonable belief by experience.

6.3 However, the possibility of malicious action by police officers has been explicitly recognized under POTA and, as a safeguard, Section 58 of the Act lays down that any police officer who exercises power corruptly or maliciously, knowing that there are no reasonable grounds for proceeding under this Act, shall be punishable with imprisonment which may extend to two years, or with fine, or with both. Further, if the special court is of the opinion that any person has been corruptly or maliciously proceeded against under this Act, the court may award such compensation as it deems fit to the person so proceeded against, and it shall be paid by the officer, person, authority or government, as may be specified in the order. This section ensures that police officers will not easily abuse their powers under the Act, and would not falsely accuse a person of committing a terrorist crime, knowing fully well that such an officer may be held personally accountable for malicious prosecution.

7.1 POTA, according to some critics, also threatens the freedom of the Press, and "the provisions in POTA for making it obligatory to reveal the source of information, the provisions making the mere act of receiving a mail, even if unsolicited, a crime, aim at taming the media." The Press has complained vociferously against Section 14 of POTA, which according to them violates Article 19(1) (a) of the Constitution of India, which guarantees the right to freedom of speech and expression, from which the freedom of the Press derives. Section 14 of POFA imposes an obligation on any individual, including journalists, to furnish information that may be useful for the purposes of the Act, that is, information that relates to possible crimes that fall under its mischief, failing which the individual shall be punishable with imprisonment for a term that may extend to three years.

7.2 Once again, these concerns are based on a misunderstanding of the character of the Press and the scope of constitutional protection. The right to freedom of speech and expression, and concomitantly the freedom of the Press, is not unfettered, and is subject to 'reasonable restrictions.' At a practical level, it is useful to note, further, that the information that journalists ordinarily possess with regard to terrorists or their activities seldom have any operational value. In almost all legitimate interactions that a journalist may have with a terrorist, operational strategies are not discussed and neither is the journalist given any idea of the hideouts or movements of the terrorist. Furthermore, the Police would incline to be extremely circumspect in their use of this clause, and would avoid trying to rub the Fourth Estate the wrong way to the greatest extent possible. Few individuals and institutions of governance have been impervious to the power of the Press in India, and even those at the highest echelons of power tend to treat the Press with a high measure of deference. The Police is not, and has seldom been, an exception to this rule.

7.3 There are, moreover, legitimate limits to the freedom of the Press. "The liberty of the Press," said Lord Mansfield, "consists in printing without any previous license, subject to the consequences of the law." Closer home, the Supreme Court in *C.G. Janardhan vs T.K.G.Nair*, stated that "The freedom of the journalist is an ordinary part of the freedom of the subject and to whatever lengths the subject in general may go, so also may the journalist, but apart from the statute law, his privilege is no other and no higher."[53]

8.1 The easy availability and movement of finances has been another major contributory element in the support of terrorism. The easy availability of funds and the concomitant free flow of these funds across international borders through ubiquitous '*hawala*' channels has enormously empowered the terrorists, made the sponsorship of terrorism easy, and its control immensely difficult. After September 11, 2001, most of the discussion about the darker side of the globalisation of financial markets turned away from its distributional effects and tendencies towards periodic instability, and began focus on the manner in which it facilitated the transfer of funds that enabled global terrorism. The new challenge of financial market globalisation was how to track and freeze the financial assets of global terrorist networks. The UN Security Council through Resolution 1373 decided that all States should prevent and suppress the financing of terrorism, as well as criminalize the willful provision or collection of funds for such acts. The funds, financial assets and economic resources of those who commit or attempt to commit terrorist acts or participate in or facilitate the commission of terrorist acts and of persons and entities acting on behalf of terrorists should also be frozen without delay.

8.2 In India there have been no attempts on the part of the lawmakers or enforcers to address the issues raised by UN Security Council, prior to POTA. Before the passing of the Act, *Hawala* crimes were prosecuted under the Foreign Exchange Management Act, 1999, which describes *Hawala* as a civil offence and imposes a maximum penalty of payment of three times the money involved.

8.3 However, under Section 6 of POTA, no person shall hold or be in possession of any proceeds of terrorism and if the property acquired is through proceeds of terrorism, under Section 7 of the Act, an officer (not below the rank of Superintendent of Police) investigating an offence committed under this Act, shall, with the prior approval in writing of the Director General of the Police of the State in which such property is situated, make an order seizing such property and where it is not practicable to seize such property, make an order of attachment directing that such property shall not be transferred. This provision is a far cry from the earlier provisions, which allowed the terrorist to bring in money into India and be let off by paying fine. Already the functioning of this provision has had considerable impact, even as countries like USA and UK have clamped down on terrorist finances by freezing their assets. In India, however, a clear functioning of this clause has not been witnessed as in many cases the funds collected for and by terrorists are often transferred and are unaccounted for, which gives an added headache to the investigation agencies, as tracing these funds often leads to a dead end. The Indian *Hawala* market is one of the largest in the world and, therefore, needs stricter laws for its eradication. It is only when funds stop flowing into the pockets of terrorists that terrorism will be contained. Section 7 and 8 of the POTA are mere infant steps towards the annihilation of the process of transfer of funds for terrorist activities.

Faulty Legislation or Faulty System

Unending debates over the working of the anti-terror laws, TADA and POTA, in judicial, political and social circles have cast aspersions on the need for such a specific law. Yet, it can hardly be denied that that terrorism is here to stay, and constitutes the greatest contemporary threat to individual and collective security. No legal instrument can be perfect, and no law can attain such a measure of flawlessness that it cannot be bent or broken, as long as the human instinct to do so survives. Inherent deficiencies in the framing of laws, moreover, are magnified manifold within the context of a criminal justice system which is in as poor a state of health as India's. It is an accepted fact that convictions for any offence, whether minor traffic violations or murder, take an extraordinary length of time. The courts are overburdened, and recent estimates indicate that there are around 3.1 million pending cases in 21 high courts and 20 million in subordinate courts in the country.

There has been negligible effort on the part of successive Governments to streamline the judicial system in the country. Attempts to create fast track courts to tackle pending cases have been largely unsuccessful. Even in areas where such courts have been established, prosecution continues to be delayed. The Recovery of Debts due to Banks and Financial Institutions Act of 1993 was one such law that established fast track courts to recover money from debtors. With nearly 44,000 cases pending in various Debt Recovery Tribunals (DRTs) involving around Rs. 380 billion, the processes and procedures of these courts have also fallen into the mould of 'normal' courts in the country.

The fault lies, not in the legislation, but in the system that implements the law. Delays are chronic, right from the stage of issuing summons to the defendant, which, in some cases, can take several months, as processes are delayed on flimsy grounds. Delays in civil cases hurt particular individuals and institutions; but the failure to expedite the prosecution of the accused in criminal cases – especially of serious criminal offences such as terrorism – is a cause of alarm, as it constitutes a threat to the life of the individual and to the security and stability of the state.

TADA was victim to this process as well, and was widely criticized because its conviction rate was less than two percent. This was, curiously, advanced as grounds for scrapping the law by its critics. The argument is certainly eccentric: rape, for instance, has among the lowest conviction rates for violent crimes in India; this, however, has rightly been the basis of strident demands for strengthening of the law, and harsher penalties. The situation is nor irreparable, and the experience with the Maharashtra Control of Organised Crime Act (MCOCA), 1999, deserves special attention in this regard. This legislation was passed by the Maharashtra Assembly in view of the growing menace of organised crime. 'Organised Crime' bears an uncanny resemblance to terrorism: neither phenomenon is confined by international borders; both organised crime and terrorism involve murder, kidnapping, arson, robbery, burglary, extortion, dealing in narcotics or dangerous drugs, intimidation and violence; finally, the support structures and sources of finance are often the same for both.

The MCOCA has been an extraordinary success in Maharashtra, with a conviction rate as high as 78 per cent in some years. Many of the provisions of MCOCA are similar to those under POTA. For example, both acts have identical provisions with respect to

i. Procedures and powers of Special Court – Section 9 of MCOCA and Section 29 of POTA;
ii. Authorisation of interception of wire, electronic or oral communication – Sections 14 and 16 of MCOCA and Section 36 to 48 of POTA;
iii. Certain confessions made to police officer to be taken into consideration – Section 18 of MCOCA and Section 32 of POTA;
iv. Protection of witnesses – Section 19 of MCOCA act and Section 30 of POTA;
v. Forfeiture and attachment of property – Section 20 of MCOCA and Sections 6, 7 and 8 of POTA.

There can be no doubt that, if a clear anti-terrorism strategy involving the police, the executive and the judiciary could be formulated and executed on a national scale, the successes of MCOCA could be replicated under POTA. Regrettably, political indulgence and high-handedness have constantly undermined the implementation of counter-terrorism laws, and have infinitely complicated the terrorism debate. Among the aspects that have most frequently come under criticism is the abuse of such laws to carry out arrests of political opponents and a wide range of activists who are not covered by the intent and purpose of such laws.

Indeed, TADA was used far more often against those who would not be covered by any definition of terrorism, than it was against terrorists. Similarly, a review of the arrests made under POTA over the first year of its operation projects the Act in poor light. According to the Union Home Ministry, the total number of those arrested and put in jail across the country under the POTA was 257. The data indicates further, that it is not in the terror wracked State of J&K that POTA has been extensively used, but in Jharkhand. This newly created State has the 'distinction' of detaining the highest number of persons under POTA, at 113, as against 104 detained in J&K. Worse, among those detained in Jharkhand were a 12-year-old child and an 81-year-old man. Others in the POTA list are Delhi with 20 detainees; Uttar Pradesh and Tamil Nadu with 10 each.

It has also been nigh impossible to work out any kind of political consensus on the implementation of anti-terrorism laws. In a shocking development on June 4, 2003, the J&K Government decided that it would not invoke POTA in the State, and those detainees who had 'no serious cases' against them would be released. J&K is the worst terrorism affected State in the country, but is not the only one to refuse to implement POTA; Governments in Manipur, Karnataka, Punjab, Assam, Tripura and Madhya Pradesh have also said that the law would not be used in their States.

This negates the very purpose for which the anti-terrorism legislation had been enacted. J&K is the major theatre of terrorist conflict in the country, and its past record of convictions of arrested terrorists under any law has been abysmal. The populist and politically motivated refusal to implement POTA can only weaken the enforcement agencies in their fight against terror.

POTA is, of course, far from perfect. The difficulty with counter-terrorism legislation in this country – indeed, with much other legislation as well – is that once it passes through Parliament, it tends to be looked upon as an immutable whole, to be accepted in full, or, like TADA, cast out in entirety for its deficiencies. There was certainly a high measure of gross abuse of TADA in certain States – but this was valid grounds for re-examination and amendment of the law, not for throwing the baby out with the bathwater. To bury legislation which provided the only effective legal instrument to bring terrorists to justice on the grounds that it was susceptible to abuse was nothing short of foolhardy. What is needed is a constant process of review of the law in action, the identification of its strengths and weaknesses, and the streamlining of processes and provisions through marginal amendments that would ensure its greater efficiency in securing the ends for which it was legislated, and limiting any existing possibilities of abuse.

Bibliography

Acquaviva, Mike. *Terrorism: Special Studies*. Bethesda, MD: University Publications of America, 1989.

Addicott, Jeffrey F. *Winning the War on Terror: Legal and Policy Lessons From the Past*. Tucson, AZ: Lawyers & Judges Publishing Company, 2003.

Ahmad, Eqbal. *Terrorism: Theirs and Ours*. Open Media Pamphlet Series. New York: Seven Stories Press, 2001.

Alexander, Dean C. *Business Confronts Terrorism: Risks and Responses*. Madison, WI: University of Wisconsin Press, 2004.

Alexander, John B. *Winning the War: Advanced Weapons, Strategies and Concepts for the Post-9/11 World*. New York: St. Martin's Press, 2003.

Alexander, Yonah. *Abu Nidal: The Splinter Festers*. Washington, DC: New World Communication, 1986.

Alexander, Yonah. *Combating Terrorism: Strategies of Ten Countries*. Ann Arbor, MI: University of Michigan Press, 2002.

Alexander, Yonah. *Control of Terrorism: International Documents*. New York: Crane Russak, 1979.

Alexander, Yonah. *Governmental Responses to Terrorism*. Hero Terrorism Series. Fairfax, VA: Hero Books, 1987.

Alexander, Yonah. *International Terrorism: National, Regional and Global Perspectives*. New York: AMS Press, 1976.

Alexander, Yonah. *Legislative Responses to Terrorism*. International Studies on Terrorism; 1. Boston, MA: M. Nijhoff, 1986.

Alexander, Yonah. *Political Terrorism and Business: The Threat and Response*. New York: Praeger, 1979.

Alexander, Yonah. *Political Terrorism and Energy: The Threat and Response*. New York: Praeger, 1982.

Alexander, Yonah. *State Sponsored Terrorism*. Washington, DC: Center for Contemporary Studies, 1986.

Alexander, Yonah. *Terrorism and the Law*. Ardsley, NY: Transnational Publishers, 2001.

Alexander, Yonah. *Terrorism: Theory and Practice*. Boulder, CO: Westview Press, 1979.

Alterman, Jon B. *How Terrorism Ends*. Washington, DC: United States Institute of Peace, 1999.

American Foreign Policy Council, *Confronting Terrorism Financing*. Lanham, MD: University Press of America, 2005.

Anderson, Mark. *Campaign Against Terror*. Videocassette (VHS). Frontline. Alexandria, VA: PBS Video, 2004.

Anderson, Sean. *Historical Dictionary of Terrorism*. 2nd ed.. Historical Dictionaries of Religions, Philosophies, and Movements, No. 4. Lanham, MD: Scarecrow Press, 2002.

Ansari, Masud. *International Terrorism: Its Causes and How to Control It*. Washington, DC: Mas-Press, 1988.

Anti-Defamation League, *ADL Paramilitary Training Statute: A Response to Extremism*. ADL Law Report. New York: ADL, 1986.

Anti-Defamation League, *ADL Paramilitary Training Statute: Implementation*. ADL Law Report, Fall 1983, Vol. 8, no. 2. New York: ADL, 1983.

Anti-Defamation League, *Extremism on the Right: A Handbook*. New York: Anti-Defamation League, 1988.

Anti-Defamation League, *Terrorism: Domestic and International Challenges*. New York: ADL, 1994.

Apikyan, Samuel. *Countering Nuclear and Radiological Terrorism*. Brussels, Belgium: Springer, 2006.

Ascher, Michael S. *Countering Agricultural Bioterrorism*. "Committee on Biological Threats to Agricultural Plants and Animals". Washington, DC: National Academies Press, 2003.

Asthana, N. C. *Terrorism, Insurgencies, and Counterinsurgency Operations*. Jaipur, India: Pointer Publishers, 2001.

Barnhart, Stephen R. *International Terrorism and Political Violence*. Victoria, B.C., Canada: Trafford, 2002.

Bassiouni, M. Cherif, ed. *International Terrorism and Political Crimes: Proceedings of the Third Conference on Terrorism and Political Crimes*. Springfield, IL: C.C. Thomas, 1974.

Das, Dilip. *Meeting the Challenges of Global Terrorism: Prevention, Control, and Recovery*. Lanham, MD: Rowman & Littlefield, 2003.

Davies, Barry. *Terrorism: Inside a World Phenomenon*. London: Virgin Books, 2003.

Dewar, Michael. *Weapons and Equipment of Counter-Terrorism*. 2nd ed. New York: Sterling, 1995.

Dobson, Christopher. *Terrorists: Their Weapons, Leaders and Tactics*. Rev. ed. New York: Facts on File, 1982.

Dobson, Christopher. *War Without End: the Terrorists, an Intelligence Dossier*. London: Harrap, 1986.

Elagab, Omer Yousif. *International Law Documents Relating to Terrorism*. London: Cavendish Press, 1995.

Evans, Alona. *Legal Aspects of International Terrorism*. Washington, DC: Lexington Books, 1978.

Gearty, Conner. *Terrorism*. London: Phoenix, 1997.

Ghosh, Tushar K. *Science and Technology of Terrorism and Counterterrorism*. New York: Dekker, 2002.

Han, Henry H., editor. *Terrorism & Political Violence: Limits & Possibilities of Legal Control*. Terrorism (Oceana Publications, inc.) ; 2nd series. New York: Oceana, 1993.

Howard, Russell D. *Defeating Terrorism: Shaping the New Security Environment*. Guilford, CT: McGraw-Hill, 2004.

Howard, Russell D. *Terrorism and Counterterrorism: Understanding the New Security Environment, Readings & Interpretations*. Guilford, CT: McGraw-Hill, 2002.

Howitt, Arnold. *Countering Terrorism: Dimensions of Preparedness*. Cambridge, MA: MIT Press, 2003.

Lutz, James M. *Global Terrorism*. New York: Routledge, 2004.

MacDonald, Donald. *Parliaments Against Terrorism*. Ottawa, Canada: Library of Parliament, 1986.

Mockaitis, Thomas R. *Grand Strategy in the War Against Terrorism*. Portland, OR: Frank Cass, 2003.

Moghaddam, Fathali. *Understanding Terrorism: Psychosocial Roots, Consequences, and Interventions*. Washington, DC: American Psychological Association, 2003.

Norton, Augustus R. *Understanding the Nuclear Terrorism Problem*. Gaithersburg, MD: International Association of Chiefs of Police, 1979.

O'Day, Alan. *Weapons of Mass Destruction and Terrorism*. The international library of essays in terrorism. Burlington, VT: Ashgate, 2005.

Ontiveros, Suzanne. *Global Terrorism: A Historical Bibliography*. Santa Barbara, CA: ABC-CLIO, 1986.

Onwudiwe, Ihekwoaba D. *Globalization of Terrorism*. Burlington, VT: Ashgate, 2001.

Poland, James M. *Understanding Terrorism: Groups, Strategies, and Responses*. Second Edition. Upper Saddle River, NJ: Pearson, 2004.

Schmid, Alex P. and Jongman, Albert J. *Political*

Terrorism: A New Guide to Actors, Authors, Concepts, Data Bases, Theories, & Literature. New Brunswick, NJ: Transaction, 2005.

Steven, Graeme C. S. and Gunaratna, Rohan. *Counter-terrorism: A Reference Handbook*. Santa Barbara, CA: ABC-CLIO, 2004.

Stewart, Gail B. *Terrorists and Terrorists Groups*. Lucent Terrorism Library. Farmington Hills, MI: Thomson Learning, 2002.

Tamara, Thompson. *Emergency Response*. San Diego, CA: Lucent, 2004. Juvenile Audience.

Tan, Andrew T.H. *Politics of Terrorism: A Survey*. London: Routledge, 2006.

Thackrah, John Richard. *Encyclopedia of Terrorism and Political Violence*. New York: Routledge & Kegan Paul, 1987.

Unger, Rhoda Kesler. *Terrorism and Its Consequences*. Malden, MA: Blackwell, 2002.

Vas, E. A. *Terrorism and Insurgency: The Challenge of Modernization*. Dehra Dun: Natraj Publishers, 1984.

Wardlaw, Grant. *Political Terrorism: Theory, Tactics and Counter-Measures*. Rev. and Extended ed. Cambridge, MA: Cambridge University Press, 1989.

Watson, Francis. *Political Terrorism: The Threat and the Response*. Washington, DC: R.B. Luce Co., 1976.

Wilcox, David. *Domestic Preparedness and the WMD Paradigm*. Washington, DC: U.S. Army Command, 1998.

Wilkinson, Paul. *British Perspectives on Terrorism*. London: George Allen & Unwin, 1981.

Wilkinson, Paul. *Contemporary Research on Terrorism*. Aberdeen: Aberdeen University Press, 1987.

Young, Mitch. *The War on Terrorism*. Turning Points in World History. San Diego, CA: Greenhaven Press, 2003.

Zartman, I. William, Editor. *Negotiating With Terrorists.* Leiden, The Netherlands: Nijhoff, 2005.

Zimmerman, Ekkart. *Political Violence, Crises and Revolutions: Theories and Research.* Cambridge, MA: G.K. Hall, 1983.

Zimmermann, Doron. *The Transformation of Terrorism: The 'New Terrorism', Impact Scalability and the Dynamic of Reciprocal Threat Perception.* Zurich: ETH, 2003.

Zinn, Howard. *Terrorism and War.* New York: Seven Stories Press, 2002.

Zimmerman, Ekkart. *Political Violence, Crises and Revolutions: Theories and Research.* Cambridge, MA: G.K. Hall, 1983.

Index